# Big Data Analytics with SAS

Get actionable insights from your Big Data using the power of SAS

**David Pope**

BIRMINGHAM - MUMBAI

# Big Data Analytics with SAS

Copyright © 2017 Packt Publishing

First published: November 2017

Production reference: 1151117

Published by Packt Publishing Ltd.
Livery Place
35 Livery Street
Birmingham
B3 2PB, UK.
ISBN 978-1-78829-090-6

www.packtpub.com

# Credits

**Author**
David Pope

**Reviewers**
Ruben Oliva Ramos

**Commissioning Editor**
Amey Varangaonkar

**Acquisition Editor**
Viraj Madhav

**Content Development Editor**
Cheryl Dsa

**Technical Editor**
Suwarna Patil

**Copy Editors**
Safis Editor
Vikrant Phadkay

**Project Coordinator**
Nidhi Joshi

**Proofreader**
Safis Editing

**Indexer**
Rekha Nair

**Graphics**
Tania Dutta

**Production Coordinator**
Shraddha Falebhai

# Foreword

*"A primary lesson of history is that periodically, and often at the most inconvenient times, society needs to make a sharp break with old habits and deliberately learn new ways of behaving."*

*— Jumping the Curve, by Nicholas Imparato and Oren Harari*

For my business partner and me, lunch at iHop always heralded a serious business decision. We had lunch at iHop when we decided to incorporate our consulting firm in 1992. We had lunch there when we decided to hire a CEO. We had lunch again when we decided to fire him. We found ourselves again at iHop in 2011—me nibbling on the Breakfast Sampler, he on the steak and eggs—as we discussed whether to accept an offer to acquire our firm.

We weren't for sale. Our company, Baseline Consulting, was small by management consulting standards, but we were the leaders in the niche field of analytics and data strategy. Larger companies had begun to take notice. A few competitors had reached out by email, a large systems integrator had suggested a meeting *"in your office or ours,"* and software vendors had also come calling. We received an offer from a company that we had worked with and admired, and whose leadership we respected.

The analytics market was booming, business intelligence vendors were blowing out their numbers, and Baseline's growth promised to continue apace. The emergence of data management and curation tools, the explosion of big data, and the adoption of advanced analytics by a new crop of business users—these were just a few bellwethers of rapid industry disruption. Our engagements were getting more complicated, and our deal sizes were growing. We'd have to invest to keep up, or start taking the acquisition offers seriously.

A few short years later, big data, analytics, the cloud, IoT, and artificial intelligence are no longer the purview of tech analysts and vendors. Factories are using analytics and IoT to catch defects before products leave production. Retailers are using cloud applications to push personalized offers to your smartphone. Delivery companies are optimizing their routes, the resulting fuel savings adding double-digit percentages to their bottom lines. Physicians can now monitor a patient's vital signs in real time from their offices or golf courses. Advanced analytics is as close as an app on your tablet or the car in your garage. Your daughter is running regressions in her high school math class. Your son wants to be a data scientist.

Author David Pope, an analytics expert, has written a vital book that not only embraces the analytics industry's trends, but also proselytizes the impact of delivering newfound knowledge with the SAS® software. As the pioneer in advanced analytics and a recognized data management and analytics software leader, SAS stands out as the purveyor of leading-edge solutions in the new analytics economy.

The voice in these pages is no less authoritative than his message. David has worked for SAS for 26 years and has been on the frontlines of some of the industry's most cutting-edge use cases. In *Big Data Analytics with SAS*, he delivers a veritable toolbox of the techniques companies will be using to realize their digital futures. Users new to SAS and SAS veterans alike will recognize some of the book's themes and embrace its best practices.

I've always been a believer in a best-of-breed approach, choosing the right tool for the job. Amidst the din of vendor hype and the buzzword-du-jour, companies need to deliver insights of value—and quickly. There are more vendor choices than ever. David nimbly navigates the alleyways of software selection and usage, explaining how analytics is deployed and managed the right way. This alone is worth the price of admission.

As my partner and I tucked into our lunches, we deliberated about the future of our business and what was best for our employees. Could we grow at the rate of the industry? Could we stay ahead of it? Were there companies that could get us there faster, cultivating our talent while providing learning opportunities, and a channel for growth? We concluded that, all things considered, SAS would be the best choice.

We have no regrets choosing SAS. And neither will you. Happy reading!

**Jill Dyché**
Author of *The New IT*

# About the Author

David Pope

**David Pope** has worked for SAS for over 26 years in a variety of departments, including research and development (R&D), information technology (IT), SAS Solutions on Demand (SSOD), and sales and marketing. He graduated from North Carolina State University with a bachelor's of science in industrial engineering and a certificate in computer programming. He started his career with SAS, testing and writing code for the SAS system in R&D using C, Java, and of course SAS programming languages.

David has worked in both the United States and Europe in this capacity. Then he moved into IT within SAS to help support running it as a business, using SAS and other technologies such as JavaScript, HTML, and Unix/Linux scripting languages. He spent 4 years working as a consultant with SAS customers in SSOD prior to moving into presales support, where he worked across all industries as an analytics and SAS architecture expert. David moved into presales management to build out a team of data scientists and technical architects who support opportunities in the US energy industry, electric utilities, and oil and gas companies. He currently holds 10 patents for SAS and is an active blogger under the SASVoices corporate blog. He is a life-long learner who enjoys teaching and empowering people to solve business problems.

*I would like to recognize all the developers who have worked on SAS, without whom this book would not have been possible to write. There are too many individuals to list here whom I have learned from over the course of my career, and they have in one way or another way influenced what is in this book. However, I'd like to recognize Brian Jones for his specific help in using his graphic art skills to greatly improve the visual presentations of several of my ideas that are included in this book.*

# About the Reviewer

**Ruben Oliva Ramos** is a computer systems engineer from Tecnologico de Leon Institute, with a master's degree in computer and electronic systems engineering, teleinformatics, and networking specialization from the University of Salle Bajio in Leon, Guanajuato, Mexico. He has more than 5 years of experience in developing web applications to control and monitor devices connected with Arduino and Raspberry Pi, using web frameworks and cloud services to build Internet of Things applications.

He is a mechatronics teacher at the University of Salle Bajio and teaches students of the master's degree in design and engineering of mechatronics systems. Ruben also works at Centro de Bachillerato Tecnologico Industrial 225 in Leon, Guanajuato, Mexico, teaching subjects such as electronics, robotics and control, automation, and microcontrollers at Mechatronics Technician Career; he is a consultant and developer for projects in areas such as monitoring systems and datalogger data using technologies (such as Android, iOS, Windows Phone, HTML5, PHP, CSS, Ajax, JavaScript, Angular, and ASP.NET), databases (such as SQlite, MongoDB, and MySQL), web servers (such as Node.js and IIS), hardware programming (such as Arduino, Raspberry Pi, Ethernet Shield, GPS, and GSM/GPRS, ESP8266), and control and monitoring systems for data acquisition and programming.

He is the author of these books for Packt:

- *Internet of Things Programming with JavaScript*
- *Advanced Analytics with R and Tableau*
- *Raspberry Pi 3 Home Automation Projects*

He is also involved in monitoring, controlling, and acquiring data with Arduino and Visual Basic .NET for Alfaomega.

*I would like to thank my savior and lord, Jesus Christ, for giving me the strength and courage to pursue this project; to my dearest wife, Mayte; our two lovely sons, Ruben and Dario; my dear father, Ruben; my dearest mom Rosalia; my brother (Juan Tomas; and my sister, Rosalia, whom I love, for all their support while reviewing this book, for allowing me to pursue my dream, and tolerating me not being with them after my busy day.*
*I'm very grateful to Packt Publishing for giving the opportunity to collaborate as an author and reviewer, to belong to this honest and professional team.*

# www.PacktPub.com

For support files and downloads related to your book, please visit www.PacktPub.com.

Did you know that Packt offers eBook versions of every book published, with PDF and ePub files available? You can upgrade to the eBook version at www.PacktPub.com and as a print book customer, you are entitled to a discount on the eBook copy. Get in touch with us at service@packtpub.com for more details.

At www.PacktPub.com, you can also read a collection of free technical articles, sign up for a range of free newsletters and receive exclusive discounts and offers on Packt books and eBooks.

https://www.packtpub.com/mapt

Get the most in-demand software skills with Mapt. Mapt gives you full access to all Packt books and video courses, as well as industry-leading tools to help you plan your personal development and advance your career.

# Customer Feedback

Thanks for purchasing this Packt book. At Packt, quality is at the heart of our editorial process. To help us improve, please leave us an honest review on this book's Amazon page at https://www.amazon.com/dp/1788290909.

If you'd like to join our team of regular reviewers, you can e-mail us at customerreviews@packtpub.com. We award our regular reviewers with free eBooks and videos in exchange for their valuable feedback. Help us be relentless in improving our products!

This book is dedicated to all the employees of SAS especially those who have worked together in writing all the underlying code that makes up SAS® Software without which neither the company SAS nor this book would be possible. In addition, I'd like to dedicate this book to my wife, Jeannie, and our three children—Spencer, Rachael, and Lissa whose support and love has helped me progress in both life and in my career.

# Table of Contents

# Preface

This book will introduce the reader to how SAS can be used to perform analytics on any size of data and how it's designed to enable users to perform big data analytics. The reader will be provided an introduction to learning SAS for data management, analytics, and reporting, and get examples in each chapter to allow hands-on use of The Power to Know®, thereby teaching the reader how they can use SAS® software to further their career and improve their company's business processes.

The mission of this book is to introduce the reader to what the SAS programming language offers and how the reader can use SAS®software to further their careers and improve their company's business processes. As stated in the Money Magazine and Payscale article *The 21 Most Valuable Career Skills Now, May 16, 2016 by Kerri Anne Renzulli,Cybele Weisser, and Megan Leonhardt*, SAS® is the most valuable career skill. The study isolated *the specific skills (from about 2,300) correlated with higher pay, advancement, and career opportunities.* SAS was found to be the most valuable in terms of average increase in salary. I have programmed in a variety of computer languages, such as C, C$^{++}$, Java, and scripting languages like korn shell, and I will say that one of the reasons I enjoy using SAS is that I am confident that I can get SAS to accomplish any type of computing task or project. Don't get me wrong; this doesn't imply that SAS is the best solution/tool to use for everything, but it does mean I can use it to accomplish a task if I really want too. Like any good programmers, I chose to use applications or tools that can efficiently accomplish the task at hand. In my career, I've found SAS to be the best solution to solve complex analytics-based business problems, and it is my hope that you will find this book a great introduction to SAS that will help you advance your own career.

The reader will be provided with an introduction to learning SAS for data management, analysis, and reporting, as well as examples in each chapter, which will allow them hands-on use of The Power to Know®.

While is it impossible to become an expert on everything SAS does within one book, it is possible to start down the path to learning the fundamentals of SAS, which unpin how everything in SAS works. As such, this book is meant to be an initial primer for those who want to start the process of learning SAS and who are interested in how SAS makes it easier to solve complex business problems in a timely, efficient way.

This book will dismiss some of the misconceptions some may have heard about SAS, such as you can't learn SAS without buying a license (not true), SAS is difficult to use (not true), and so on. It should empower the reader to be better prepared to seek SAS certifications if they so choose.

 This book uses the SAS® University Edition and a combination of the SAS Studio web-based interface and an iPython Jupyter Notebook for the hands-on examples. However, all the code examples are valid when submitted to any SAS 9.4 environment for execution.

# What this book covers

Chapter 1, *Setting Up the SAS® Software Environment*, teaches how to install and use a free version of SAS that leverages both the SAS Studio and an iPython Jupyter Notebook as interfaces to work with SAS.

Chapter 2, *Working with Data Using SAS® Software*, shows how to use SAS to create data directly and how SAS can be used with external data sources. In addition, the reader will learn how data needs to be prepared differently to do analytics versus doing queries and reports.

Chapter 3, *Data Preparation Using SAS Data Step and SAS Procedures*, introduces using both SAS data step code as well as SAS procedures for preparing data for analysis and reporting. The reader will learn a couple of ways SAS can be used to transform data efficiently for doing analytics and learn about SAS macro programming.

Chapter 4, *Analysis with SAS® Software*, provides examples of performing descriptive and predictive analytics along with just one technique to improve the predictive power of a model. Furthermore, this chapter provides examples for doing forecasting as well as optimization.

Chapter 5, *Reporting with SAS® Software*, shows the reader how to use SAS Studio tasks and snippets to generate reports and graphs. In addition, it shows how to use some of the BASE SAS procedures and the ODS to deliver reports in different formats.

Chapter 6, *Other Programming Languages in BASE SAS® Software*, introduces two new languages, DS2 and FedSQL, which were developed in BASE SAS software and play important roles in performing big data analytics and moving the actual processing to where the data is stored.

Chapter 7, *SAS® Software Engineers the Processing Environment for You*, explains the importance that the SAS architecture plays in their analytics processing environment, which allows analytics to return important insights on big data in a timely manner.

Chapter 8, *Why SAS Programmers Love SAS*, wraps up the book and provides several examples of why SAS programmers love SAS and how analytics can be used across a variety of industries. It also discusses the importance of setting up an ACE and the roles and skills associated with this type of group.

# What you need for this book

The reader should be curious about how SAS can be used to analyze data of any size and have a PC or macOS that meets the requires to run the ;SAS® University Edition as a virtual application or a compatible web browser that can run the SAS® University Edition via an AWS. Chapter 1, *Setting Up the SAS® Software Environment*, provides more details on the specifics needed to run the SAS® University Edition.

# Who this book is for

SAS professionals and data analysts who wish to perform analytics on big data using SAS to gain actionable insights will find this book to be very useful. If you are a data science professional looking to perform large-scale analytics with SAS, this book will also help you. A basic understanding of SAS will be helpful but is not mandatory.

# Conventions

In this book, you will find a number of text styles that distinguish between different kinds of information. Here are some examples of these styles and an explanation of their meaning.

Code words in text, database table names, folder names, filenames, file extensions, pathnames, dummy URLs, user input, and Twitter handles are shown as follows: "We will write some SAS code that will print `Hello World`."

A block of code is set as follows:

```
/* This is one way to add comments to your code */
data _null_;
   text="Hello World";
   put text;
run;
* here is another way to add a comment or to comment out code;
```

**New terms** and **important words** are shown in bold.

Words that you see on the screen, for example, in menus or dialog boxes, appear in the text like this: "We will primarily make use of the default **SAS Programmer** view for the examples within this book."

Warnings or important notes appear in a box like this.

Tips and tricks appear like this.

# Reader feedback

Feedback from our readers is always welcome. Let us know what you think about this book-what you liked or disliked. Reader feedback is important for us as it helps us develop titles that you will really get the most out of.

To send us general feedback, simply e-mail feedback@packtpub.com, and mention the book's title in the subject of your message.

If there is a topic that you have expertise in and you are interested in either writing or contributing to a book, see our author guide at www.packtpub.com/authors.

# Customer support

Now that you are the proud owner of a Packt book, we have a number of things to help you to get the most from your purchase.

# Downloading the example code

You can download the example code files for this book from your account at `http://www.packtpub.com`. If you purchased this book elsewhere, you can visit `http://www.packtpub.com/support` and register to have the files emailed directly to you. You can download the code files by following these steps:

1. Log in or register to our website using your email address and password.
2. Hover the mouse pointer on the **SUPPORT** tab at the top.
3. Click on **Code Downloads & Errata**.
4. Enter the name of the book in the **Search** box.
5. Select the book for which you're looking to download the code files.
6. Choose from the drop-down menu where you purchased this book from.
7. Click on **Code Download**.

Once the file is downloaded, please make sure that you unzip or extract the folder using the latest version of:

- WinRAR / 7-Zip for Windows
- Zipeg / iZip / UnRarX for Mac
- 7-Zip / PeaZip for Linux

The code bundle for the book is also hosted on GitHub at `https://github.com/PacktPublishing/Big-Data-Analytics-with-SAS`. We also have other code bundles from our rich catalog of books and videos available at `https://github.com/PacktPublishing/`. Check them out!

# Downloading the color images of this book

We also provide you with a PDF file that has color images of the screenshots/diagrams used in this book. The color images will help you better understand the changes in the output. You can download this file from

`https://www.packtpub.com/sites/default/files/downloads/BigDataAnalyticswithSAS_ColorImages.pdf`

# Errata

Although we have taken every care to ensure the accuracy of our content, mistakes do happen. If you find a mistake in one of our books-maybe a mistake in the text or the code-we would be grateful if you could report this to us. By doing so, you can save other readers from frustration and help us improve subsequent versions of this book. If you find any errata, please report them by visiting http://www.packtpub.com/submit-errata, selecting your book, clicking on the **Errata Submission Form** link, and entering the details of your errata. Once your errata are verified, your submission will be accepted and the errata will be uploaded to our website or added to any list of existing errata under the Errata section of that title. To view the previously submitted errata, go to https://www.packtpub.com/books/content/support and enter the name of the book in the search field. The required information will appear under the Errata section.

# Piracy

Piracy of copyrighted material on the internet is an ongoing problem across all media. At Packt, we take the protection of our copyright and licenses very seriously. If you come across any illegal copies of our works in any form on the internet, please provide us with the location address or website name immediately so that we can pursue a remedy. Please contact us at copyright@packtpub.com with a link to the suspected pirated material. We appreciate your help in protecting our authors and our ability to bring you valuable content.

# Questions

If you have a problem with any aspect of this book, you can contact us at questions@packtpub.com, and we will do our best to address the problem.

# 1

# Setting Up the SAS® Software Environment

What is SAS? If you had never heard of SAS, most likely you would not have picked up this book. You may have thought about the airline, **Scandinavian Airline Systems (SAS)**, and wondered what an airline has to do with big data analytics. Other than the fact that airlines generate a lot of big data and they need to analyze it just like any other business, we are not talking about the airline. This book is about the SAS Institute, which is officially described like this *SAS is the world's largest privately held software company*. Third-party guide for referencing SAS trademarks, `https://www.sas.com/en_us/legal/editorial-guidelines.html`.

Privately held simply means the company is privately owned and does not sell stock. SAS, the software company that develops and sells SAS® software, has been the world's recognized leader as the best analytics platform for 41 years and counting. SAS is also the name of the fourth-generation programming language that provides the framework designed and engineered to do data management for analytics, provide advanced analytic capabilities, and provide multiple ways to deploy the results into production systems. This book will provide an introduction to this powerful solution, give you some hands-on experience, and provide you with knowledge about how SAS scales from small data to handle *Big Data Analytics with SAS*. What is really nice about SAS is that it really is much more than a programming language; it is an analytics processing environment. It is designed to scale so that you can use the existing knowledge and skills you develop using SAS on any size data to do the same type of analysis and reporting on big data. The SAS environment helps distribute where the processing of the data occurs, so you don't have to. We will get into the details of how SAS does this in Chapter 7, *SAS® Software Engineers the Processing Environment for You*, of this book.

In this chapter, we will cover the following topics:

- Acquire a free version of SAS
- Learn how to use SAS Studio, a web-based GUI for programming SAS
- An introduction to the SAS programming language
- Write and execute several SAS programs
- Understand the different levels of the SAS platform
- Learn about SAS data storage options

# What does SAS do?

The co-founder and CEO of SAS, Dr. James H. Goodnight, sums up what SAS does with this quote:

> *"SAS is the first company to call when you need to solve complex business problems."*
> 
> *-Dr. James H. Goodnight, SAS Institute Inc., CEO and co-founder*

SAS helps solve business problems by being the best at applying advanced analytics, whether it's predictive analytics (otherwise known as **data mining**), forecasting, optimization, or a combination of some or all of them, in order to improve business processes and deliver more valuable data-driven information to decision-makers so they can make the best decisions possible to help grow their organizations. The fundamental value of analytics is in being able to increase revenue and/or cut costs, and ultimately, that's what SAS provides to its clients and their organizations.

# What is your perception of SAS?

Some people will come to this book with their own perception of what SAS is, which is fine. I hope this book will serve to open their minds to a broader understanding of what SAS is beyond what they may have thought prior to reading this book. People's perceptions of SAS are typically based on either their own experience of working with SAS as a programming language, or with talking to someone else who is or was a **SAS Programmer** within their organization. Many times, people's perceptions are partially accurate, but most of the time they are basing their perception on out-dated information.

For example, many people will tell you that you have to buy a SAS license in order to learn how to use it. This was true in the past, but no longer is accurate. You will learn shortly in this chapter how to a download, install, and use a free version of SAS so that you can have hands-on experience using SAS by doing the examples provided in this book. Another perception some people have of SAS is that you must always write code, which again is based on somewhat out-dated information:

Figure 1.1: Perceptions of SAS

While it is true that you can write SAS code if you wish to, there are several ways to use SAS solutions via GUIs that provide easy-to-understand and drag and drop capabilities. Some will generate SAS code for you, while several of SAS's newer solutions are primarily driven via modern web-based interfaces that allow you to interact or integrate with other technologies via standard **application program interfaces (APIs)** such as Java, REST, Python, and even R. This book's primary focus is on teaching you some of the programming languages built into SAS; however, there will also be some overviews and references to some of the optional GUIs available within the SAS ecosystem.

# Let's get started with your free version of SAS

The free version of SAS that you should use while reading this book is known as the SAS® University Edition, and is available for download from the main SAS website: `https://www.sas.com/en_us/software/university-edition.html`.

Download and install the software yourself, or launch it in the cloud via **Amazon Web Services (AWS)**. There's no need to go through convoluted channels for software distribution. Here is the SAS® University Edition website: `https://www.sas.com/en_us/software/university-edition.html`

This free version is available for direct download for Windows, OS X, and Linux, as well as available via AWS. Please verify that for whichever version you want to use, your system meets the requirements listed here: `https://www.sas.com/en_us/software/university-edition.html#m=system-requirements`

1.  When you select **Get free software** you will activate this URL, `https://www.sas.com/en_us/software/university-edition.html#m=get-free-software`, and be presented with the following window:

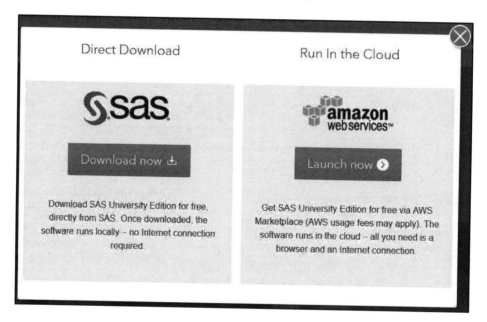

Figure 1.2: SAS® University Edition selection window

 Choose whichever option works best for you; however, for this book we will walk through and use the **Direct Download** option. On the next page, you should choose the operating system that you want to use: Windows, OS X, or Linux. For this book, we will choose Windows. It is recommended that the reader downloads the quick start guide and/or watches the video available at the given link.

2.  Now you will want to move on to the next step. Because SAS® University Edition is a **virtual application (vApp)**, you need virtualization software to run it. You can download **Oracle VirtualBox** for Windows, a free virtualization software package, using the following link: `https://www.virtualbox.org/wiki/Downloads?_sm_byp=iVVSgJ3HMfR7vg5r`.

In addition to Oracle VirtualBox, SAS® University Edition works with VMware Workstation Player virtualization software. If you prefer to use VMware Workstation Player, charges may apply. For this book, we chose to use the Oracle VirtualBox for Windows.

3.  After installing the Oracle VirtualBox, you should see the following screen when the VirtualBox application starts:

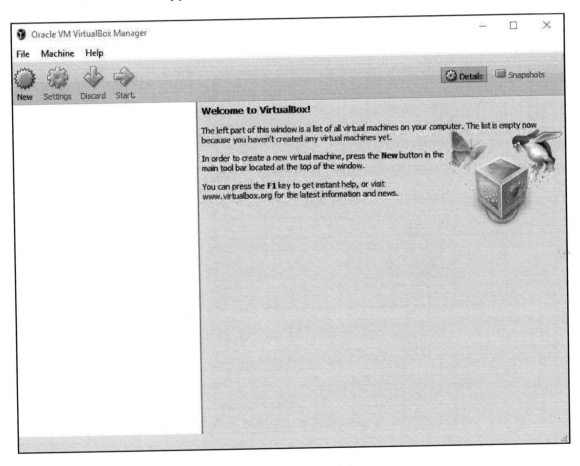

Figure 1.3: Oracle VirtualBox application

4. Leave the Oracle VirtualBox and return to the download SAS® University Edition page and perform the next step, which is to download the SAS® University Edition vApp.

 If you don't already have a profile set up on www.sas.com, you will need to create one in order to download the SAS® University Edition vApp. It is important to note that the vApp is 2.0 GB in size, and as such you should plan to connect via as large a bandwidth as you have available to complete this step.

5. After the SAS vApp downloads, you will need to import it into the Oracle VirtualBox. Once you select the SAS® University Edition from the list that pops up and select **Import**, you should see something similar to this window:

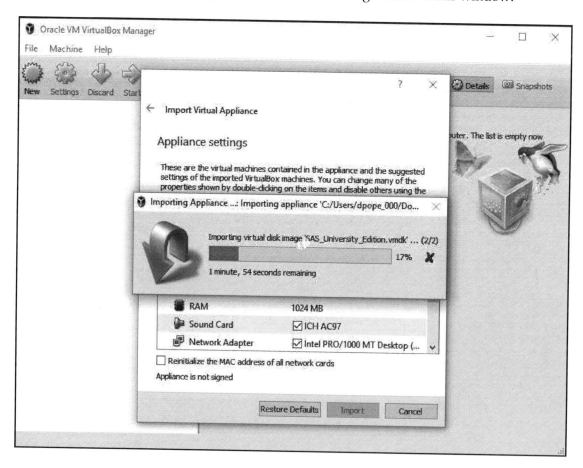

Figure 1.4: Importing the SAS® University Edition vApp into Oracle VirutalBox

6. Once you have successfully completed importing the SAS vApp, the Oracle VirtualBox application should look like this:

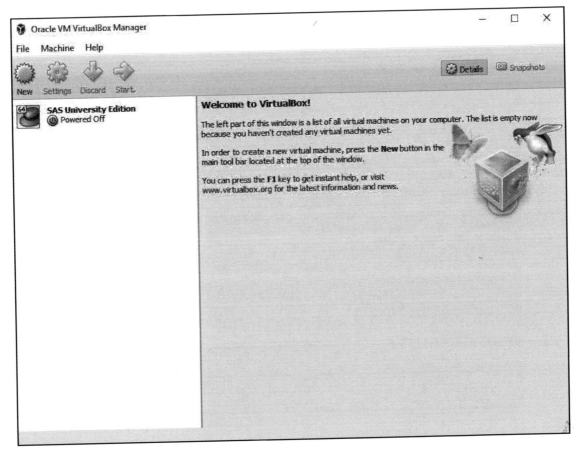

Figure 1.5: Completed import of SAS® University Edition vApp into Oracle VirtualBox

Now you will need to follow steps 3, 4, and 5 listed in the SAS® University Edition quick start guide in order to make use of your SAS® University Edition. Make sure you use the exact folder names and case as stated in the guide. For this book we used C:\SASUniversityEdition\myfolders.

7. Once you have completed step 4 in the SAS® University Edition quick start guide, you should see a window similar to this:

Figure 1.6: Successful start of the SAS® University Edition vApp

You can minimize this window; however, don't close it until you are done with your current SAS session. Once you minimize it, you can start your SAS environment via one of the supported web browsers using `http://localhost:10080`.

Your web browser should look similar to this:

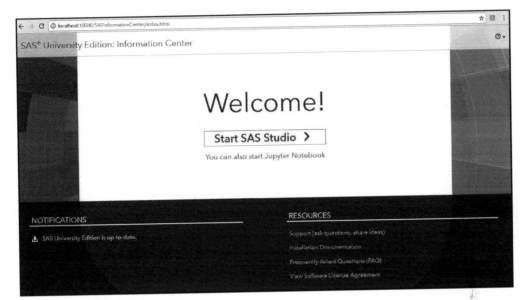

Figure 1.7: Successful start of your SAS environment from your web browser

Congratulations, you have successfully installed your free SAS® software and are now ready to begin learning your new skill, which will be your first steps in learning how to do big data analytics with SAS.

SAS Studio is the newest GUI for writing SAS code and is a web-based thin client that in this case will be communicating with SAS, running within your SAS® University Edition vApp. This is just one example of how SAS has made complex work, such as client-server setup and installation, easy for their users.

# History of SAS interfaces

Before we start getting familiar with the SAS Studio GUI, it would be best to provide the reader with a historical background of the interfaces to the SAS system. The SAS system was initially written and run on the mainframe back in the 1970s, and as such it worked with what is known as a command-line interface. This means there was no application window, but you could write one line of code and submit it, followed by your next line of code.

Interestingly enough, this command-line interface still persists today across all the operating systems that SAS runs on, which includes mainframes, Windows, and Unix/Linux. When SAS was rewritten in C in the 1980s, the original interface with SAS, which again still exists and is used today, was called the SAS **Display Management System** (**DMS**). Today, DMS is referred to as the **SAS windows environment**. This consists of three primary windows: a program editor for writing and submitting code, a log for debugging the submitted code, and an output window for displaying results. Today, you still have the capability of running SAS with DMS or with a NODMS option on several operating systems. One of the other most popular and commonly-used GUIs for SAS is known as **SAS Enterprise Guide**, which is a .NET-written Windows-only client that allows you to do quite a lot of SAS work using drag and drop functionality, and automatically generates SAS code for you for everything you do in the interface.

A more analytically advanced and data-scientist-focused interface for doing data mining within the SAS environment is known as SAS Enterprise Miner™. Once again, this type of GUI provides the user with a lot of power within a drag and drop environment, and also provides self-documentation of the process, thereby helping one data scientist become much more productive from a time perspective than always having to hand-code and then self-document their work.

Why the history on the interface to SAS? Well, first of all you should want to be seen as an experienced **SAS Programmer**, and if you don't know about the SAS DMS, SAS Enterprise Guide, and SAS Enterprise Miner™, then you will not be viewed as such. Second, as has already been stated, SAS is an analytic processing environment, and as such there is a variety of SAS solutions that provide their own business-purpose-focused GUI to interact with this single backend environment. These GUIs make it easier to perform specific tasks associated with the entire analytics lifecycle, whether it's data management and data preparation steps or data mining steps, or forecasting steps, or data visualization steps. What's nice about this is regardless of which way you interact with SAS, whether you program, interact through a GUI, or for that matter through an API or web service, from a governance and audit standpoint you are using the same set of tested and proven algorithms that provide consistent and repeatable results.

# SAS Studio web-based GUI

Once you start up SAS Studio, you'll see that the interface looks like this:

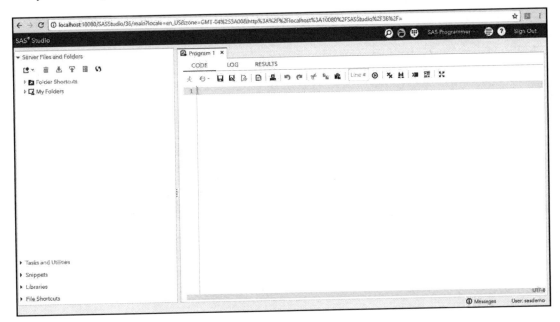

Figure 1.8: SAS Studio web based GUI

You will notice that the tabs in the right-hand window, or work area, are the tabs for **Program1** and are labeled **CODE**, **LOG**, and **RESULTS**, which basically correspond to the DMS program editor, log, and output windows. This is another example of SAS modernizing their software, but enabling their current users to still feel comfortable and to continue to leverage their existing skills in the new SAS environment, while at the same time providing new SAS users with a modern way of working with SAS. You will spend most of your time in the coding examples in this book submitting code via the **CODE** tab and reviewing its execution in the **LOG** tab.

# Describing the rest of SAS Studio

The left-hand side of SAS Studio is the navigation pane, and by default the **Servers Files and Folders** section is open. The other sections are **Tasks and Utilities**, **Snippets**, **Libraries**, and **File Shortcuts**. Across the top in the dark blue banner you will see several icons, which stand for search, open, new options, a toggle between **SAS Programmer** and **Visual Programmer** views, **More application options**, **Help**, and finally, the **Sign Out** item. We will primarily make use of the default **SAS Programmer** view for the examples within this book; however, the **Visual Programmer** view provides a process view and self-documentation of the workflow involved with your program. Feel free to explore all the help items associated with SAS Studio to learn more about this GUI for SAS coding.

## SAS Studio section – Server Files and Folders

The paper *SAS302-2014, Introduction to SAS® Studio*, Michael A. Monaco, Marie Dexter, Jennifer Tamburro, SAS Institute Inc., Cary, NC, http://support.sas.com/resources/papers/proceedings14/SAS302-2014.pdf, describes the server files and folders as follows:

*The Folders section of the navigation pane enables you to access your folders, create folder shortcuts, download and upload files, and create new SAS programs. You can expand and collapse folders, and you can open items in the folders, such as a SAS program or table, by double-clicking them or by using a drag-and-drop operation to move them to the work area.*

*The Folders section of the navigation pane references files that are stored on the same machine as the SAS server. These files can be downloaded to your workstation. Local files on your workstation must be uploaded to the server in order to be used with SAS Studio.*

## SAS Studio section – Tasks and Utilities

Similarly, the paper *SAS302-2014 Introduction to SAS® Studio*, Michael A. Monaco, Marie Dexter, Jennifer Tamburro, SAS Institute Inc., Cary, NC, http://support.sas.com/resources/papers/proceedings14/SAS302-2014.pdf describes the tasks and utilities as follows:

*The Tasks section of the navigation pane enables you to access tasks in SAS Studio. Tasks are based on SAS procedures and enable you to generate SAS code and formatted results, based on the entry of user-supplied inputs and parameter values. SAS Studio is shipped with several predefined tasks that you can run. You can also edit a copy of a predefined task, and you can create your own new tasks.*

## SAS Studio section – Snippets

As stated by the paper *SAS302-2014 Introduction to SAS® Studio*, Michael A. Monaco, Marie Dexter, Jennifer Tamburro, SAS Institute Inc., Cary, NC (`http://support.sas.com/resources/papers/proceedings14/SAS302-2014.pdf`).

*The Snippets section of the navigation pane enables you to access your code snippets, which are samples of commonly used SAS code that you can insert into your SAS program. SAS Studio is shipped with several predefined code snippets that you can use. You can also save copies of these snippets and edit them to create your own custom snippets.*

## SAS Studio section – Libraries

The paper *SAS302-2014 Introduction to SAS® Studio*, Michael A. Monaco, Marie Dexter, Jennifer Tamburro, SAS Institute Inc., Cary, NC, `http://support.sas.com/resources/papers/proceedings14/SAS302-2014.pdf` also states this:

*The Libraries section of the navigation pane enables you to access all of your SAS table libraries and their contents. You can expand a table and view the columns in that table. The icon in front of the column name indicates the data type of the column. In addition to viewing the column names, you can use a drag-and-drop operation to move the columns from the tree directly into your SAS code.*

Libraries in SAS are pointers to datasets (or tables). Within SAS, they will all look the same regardless of whether they are SAS datasets or data stored in a database or other data storage systems, such as Hadoop or SAP HANA. Datasets are referenced in SAS code by `library-name.dataset-name`. For example, open the **Libraries** section and expand **My Libraries** to see the following:

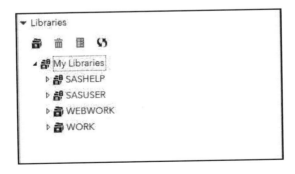

Figure 1.9: Default SAS libraries in the SAS Studio Libraries section

SAS libraries can either be permanent, which means the tables stored in them are saved as permanent tables within whatever type of data storage that library is associated with; or they can be temporary, such as **WEBWORK** and **WORK**, which means the data tables stored in these libraries will be deleted when your SAS session ends. SAS uses the **WORK** library to store intermediate tables that SAS may need to create in the process of executing SAS code. Expand **SASHELP** and you will see a lot of default data tables that are shipped with SAS. We will make use of some of these tables in the exercises associated with this book. Right-click on the **SASHELP** library and select **Properties**. In this case, you will see a list of physical path locations or directories in which all the data tables displayed under **SASHELP** are stored. In this case, **SASHELP** is a concatenated list of several physical directories. In most cases, SAS libraries either point to a single physical directory or a particular schema within a database system. The directories or database system is where the physical data tables are actually stored.

## SAS Studio section – File Shortcuts

The paper *SAS302-2014 Introduction to SAS® Studio,* Michael A. Monaco, Marie Dexter, Jennifer Tamburro, SAS Institute Inc., Cary, NC, `http://support.sas.com/resources/ papers/proceedings14/SAS302-2014.pdf` has described file shortcuts as follows:

*File shortcuts, also known as SAS File References, enable you to quickly access files. You can create a file shortcut to a file on your SAS server or via a URL.*

## SAS programming language

The core foundation of SAS technology is known as **BASE SAS**. All other modules or SAS solutions are built on top of this foundation. As mentioned previously, the SAS programming language is made up of two main parts—the SAS data step, and hundreds of SAS procedures, which are typically referred to as PROCs. **BASE SAS** also contains a SAS macro language, the new SAS FedSQL language, which is a SAS proprietary implementation of the ANSI SQL:1999 core standard, the relatively new DS2 language, which is an object-oriented multiple thread language (that we will learn more about in Chapter 6, *Other Programming Language in BASE SAS® Software* of this book), as well as the **Output Deliver System** (**ODS**), which can be used to programmically produce output in many different formats and will be discussed further in Chapter 5, *Reporting with SAS® Software,* of this book. From a historical perspective, SAS also had another language know as **Screen Control Language** (**SCL**) which was also object-oriented and was primarily used behind applications initially built with SAS/AF® software and then evolved into being able to be used behind web-based applications built in a variety of different languages, such as HTML, Java, JSP, ASP, and others.

This book will focus on providing you an introduction to the SAS data step, some SAS procedures, a little bit of SAS macro, and some DS2 and FedSQL. For more details and deeper dives into any of these individual topics, there are plenty of books and user-written papers that have been written to address these as individual topics.

# First SAS data step program

Are you ready to begin building your SAS programming skills? As has been a tradition in learning any new programming language, we will write some SAS code that will print Hello World. This is quite easy to do, and all you need to do to start is to get into your SAS Studio, and, using the right-hand pane, make sure you have the **CODE** section of your **Program1** tab highlighted and then type the following SAS data step code:

```
/* This is one way to add comments to your code */
data _null_;
   text="Hello World";
   put text;
run;
* here is another way to add a comment or to comment out code;
```

Notice that the code window automatically changes the color of various parts of the code to make it easier for you to identify specific parts. For example, both the comments are green, SAS key or reserved words are bold and dark blue, SAS statements such as the put statement are a lighter blue, variable names are black, and character values are purple. Every executable line of SAS code ends with a semi-colon and a data step starts with the keyword data and ends with the run statement. Before submitting or running this code, there a few other parts of the code that should be explained. Typically, the data keyword will be followed with the name of the data table you want the code to create, and it takes the form libraryname.tablename. For example, the statement data work.temp; will instruct SAS to create a data table in the temporary SAS library named **WORK** and name that table temp. In this case, _null_ is a special reserved word that instructs SAS to execute the data step code, but doesn't save the results into any data table.

Now, submit the code by either clicking on the running man icon on the **CODE** toolbar or by pressing the *F3* function key. You should see a window pop-up stating **Running**, and then be presented with this in SAS Studio:

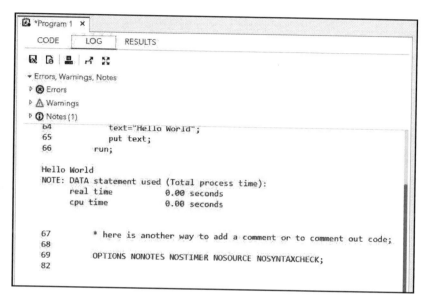

Figure 1.10: Log after submitting your Hello World data step program

As long as there was not a syntax error in your code, there should only be some blue-colored notes, the code you submitted, and the text `Hello World` printed out in the **LOG**. Congratulations on having successfully written and submitted a SAS program! Notice that similar to the color coding used in the **CODE** tab, the **LOG** tab uses color to help debug or make it easier to read how the code executed. Errors will show up in red, warnings in green, notes in blue, and code will be in black. In addition, a nice feature of the **LOG** tab in SAS Studio is that it will provide you with a linked index listing of any of the errors, warnings, or notes that occurred so a user can easily jump to that line in the log to help review and resolve them quickly. Click on the **RESULTS** tab and note that nothing showed up here. Why didn't the `Hello World` result show in the **RESULTS** tab? The **RESULTS** tab is used to show results to an end user that come from SAS PROCs, not from the `put` statement that was used in the data step program.

# First use of a SAS PROC

Move back into your **CODE** tab and use the double **Xx** in the **CODE** tool bar to clear all
code. Now type the following code:

```
proc print data=SASHELP.CARS (obs=10);
run;
```

`proc print` will print out all the rows of the data table you specify in the data part of the
statement. In this case, one of many dataset options, `obs` is being used to instruct the `proc`
to only perform its functions on the first 10 observations. Submit this code and the results
should appear in the **RESULTS** tab:

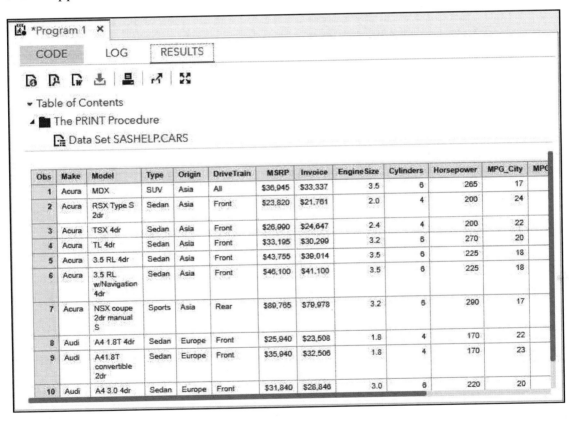

Figure 1.11: Results from proc print

Congratulations on executing a SAS PROC in a SAS program! Trust me, you will learn to appreciate and maybe even love PROCs, as they save a programmer a lot of time. Think for a moment about the small amount of code that was submitted, which printed out a subset of rows from a data table. How much code would have had to be written in any other language to achieve the same result? Yes, SQL could be used, but I doubt it could be done using less code.

Furthermore, the code window provides syntax completion for the programmer so that as you type, the programmer will be prompted for what SAS expects are valid parts of the code being written. This feature is quite useful, especially for new programmers or for experienced programmers starting to use a new PROC they may not be familiar with yet, because it gives a list of options that can be used with that particular PROC. As a programmer gains more experience, they may turn this feature off, which can easily be done by selecting the **More application options** icon to the left of the **Help** question mark icon in the top right-hand corner of SAS Studio and selecting **Preferences**:

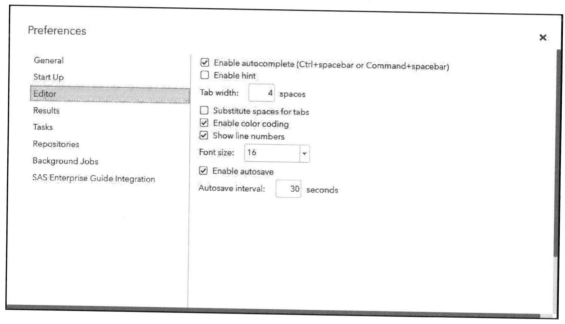

Figure 1.12: Code tab (Editor) preferences window

If the programmer wants to disable the code completion feature with the CODE tab, simply uncheck the Enable autocomplete (Ctrl+spacebar or Command+spacebar) box. To toggle this feature on and off while in the CODE tab writing code, a programmer can use either of these shortcut key combinations to accomplish this: Ctrl+spacebar or Command+spacebar.

# Saving a SAS program

Move back into the **Program1** section and the **CODE** tab. Let's verify that programs and data tables can be saved within the SAS environment. **SASUSER** is a permanent SAS library that is created automatically for each user, and in this virtual SAS server environment, this library should have been allocated to the shared folder that was set up as `C:\SASUniversityEdition\myfolders\sasuser.v94`. Select the **Save As** icon from the **CODE** toolbar, expand **My Folders**, select `sasuser.v94`, and change the program name to `Proc_print`:

Figure 1.13: Save as window

Select **Save** and then verify that it automatically showed up under the **Server Files and Folders** section of the left-hand pane of SAS Studio and as a physical file in the `C:\SASUniversityEdition\myfolders\sasuser.v94` directory:

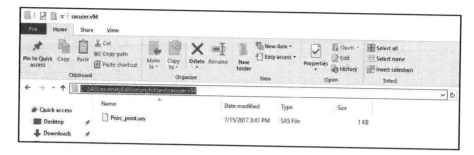

Figure 1.14: Proc_print.sas stored as a physical file on a PC

# Creating a new SAS program

Move back into SAS Studio, and on the left-hand pane under the **Server Files and Folders** select the **New** icon and then select **SAS Program(F4)**. SAS Studio allows a user to have multiple programs open at the same time and each program will have their own **CODE**, **LOG**, and **RESULTS** tabs:

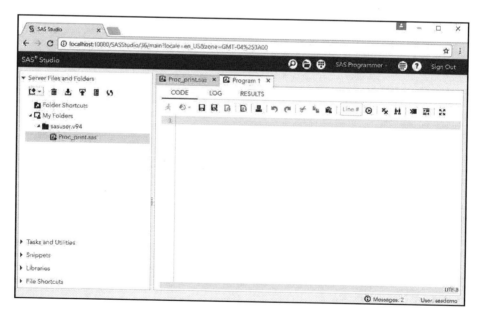

Figure 1.15: SAS Studio showing two program sections

Now, copy some data from the **SASHELP** library into the **WORK** library using both data step code and a PROC. Type in the following code into the **CODE** tab of the new **Program 1** section:

```
/* Data set code to copy a data table */
data WORK.MYCARS;
    set SASHELP.MYCARS;
run;

/* PROC code to copy a data table */
proc copy out=WORK in=SASHELP;
    SELECT CLASS;
run;
```

The more a programmer learns about the SAS language, they will discover that typically there is more than one way to accomplish a task or solve a problem using SAS. This shows the great flexibility a programmer is offered within SAS; however, there are some who may get frustrated trying to figure out which way is the best. This as a strength because not everyone thinks the same, and as a result SAS, provides different users different avenues that ultimately lead them to solve the issue at hand using the methods that make sense to them. After the problem is solved and if the programmer has the time, they can always go back and refine the code.

Submit this code and notice that SAS Studio adds an additional tab to your **Program 1** section labeled **OUTPUT DATA**:

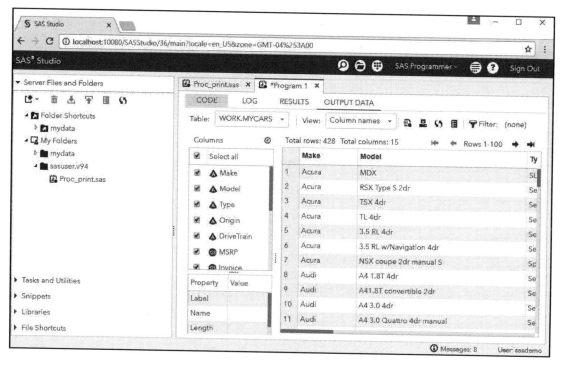

Figure 1.16: SAS Studio OUTPUT DATA tab

The SAS Studio user can toggle between both of the datasets created by this code with the Table drop-down list. This tab also shows the columns or variables within the tables and shows the user what the rows look like within the datasets.

# The AUTOEXEC file

There is a special SAS program file called `autoexec.sas`. This file allows an individual user or a server administrator to put any type of SAS executable statement in it, and whenever the individual starts a SAS session or, for a server, whenever the server is started, then the code in this file executes automatically. On a server, this makes it easy to set up consistent libraries that are named the same for multiple users, which saves time and resources because there is only one connection/pointer needed for a particular data source, instead of multiple libraries from multiple users making multiple connections to a single data source.

Likewise, at the individual user level, this empowers the user to set up libraries, create data, create user-defined formats, and/or create SAS macros that they themselves use all the time. SAS Studio provides the user with access to their own `autoexec` file through the **More application options** icon located in the top right-hand corner to the left of the **Help** question mark icon. Select the icon for **More application options** and select **Edit Autoexec File**:

Figure 1.17: SAS Studio autoexec

There are two tabs **Autoexec.sas** and **Log**. The **Autoexec.sas** tab is simply a special code pane, and the **Log** allows you to debug any code that is put in the **Autoexec.sas** pane and **Run**.

# Visual Programmer versus SAS Programmer

In this book, the reader will primarily use the **SAS Programmer** perspective; however, SAS Studio also provides a **Visual Programmer** perspective, which is designed for users who would prefer to work with process flows in a project-based environment. In the upper right-hand corner of SAS Studio, right-click on **SAS Programmer** and then switch to the **Visual Programmer** perspective:

Figure 1.18: Switching between SAS and Visual Programmer persceptives

Notice how the right-hand side of SAS Studio changes from a **Program 1** section with **CODE, LOG,** and **RESULTS** tabs to a **Process Flow 1** section with **FLOW, RESULTS,** and **PROPERTIES** tabs:

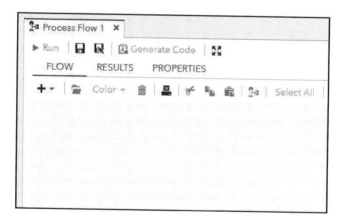

Figure 1.19: SAS Studio process flow section

The reader can now build a process flow using drag and drop functionality. On the left-hand side of SAS Studio, select/expand **Libraries** and select/expand **SASHELP**, which will provide the user with a list of default datasets that come with SAS:

Figure 1.20: SASHELP library

Left-click and hold down on the **AIR** dataset and drag this over to the **Process Flow 1** section and drop it:

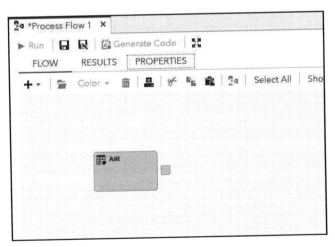

Figure 1.21: The AIR dataset graphically represented within a process flow

Notice a block representing the **AIR** dataset is created on the process flow. This is not a copy of the **AIR** dataset, but simply a graphical representation of the table within the process flow that the reader is building.

To continue building a simple process flow, the user should now select/expand **Tasks and Utilities** on the left-hand side of SAS Studio and select/expand **Tasks**. As the user did for dragging and dropping the **SASHELP. AIR** dataset onto the process flow, drag and drop the **List Table Attributes** task to the right of the **AIR** table and then connect the two icons by left-clicking and holding on the control point, the little square, on the right side of the **AIR** icon, and drag the arrow over to connect it to the control point on the left side of the **List Table Attributes** icon:

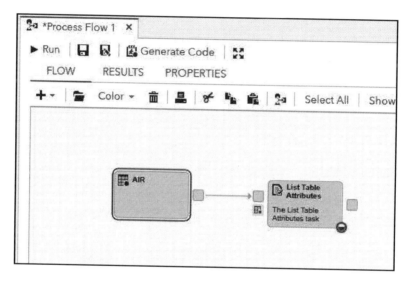

Figure 1.22: Process flow with two icons connected

The **Run** icon of the **Process Flow 1** section should have ungrayed now that a table has been connected to a task; however, you will notice the task has a red half-filled circle icon in the lower right-hand corner. The red circle means that the task's properties have not yet been generated or manually added. Select the **Run** icon and the user should see the following popup window:

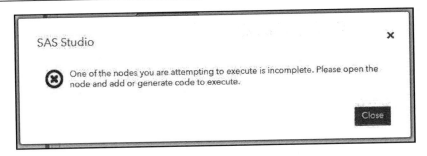

Figure 1.23: Process flow popup information window

To resolve this situation, select **Close** and then right-click the **List Table Attributes** icon and select **Open**. Once the user does this, SAS Studio generates the necessary code for this task and the reader should see the following window:

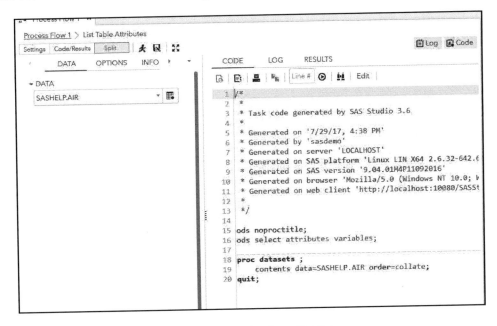

Figure 1.24: SAS Studio Auto-Generated Task Code

Select **Process Flow 1** in the upper left-corner to return to the process flow and now select **Run**. A popup window that says **Running** will appear while the process flow executes. Select the **RESULTS** tab, and it will provide the status and time of each executable step in the flow:

| FLOW | RESULTS | PROPERTIES | | |
|---|---|---|---|---|
| **Name** | | **Status** | **Elapsed** | **Output** |
| List Table Attributes | | Success | 0:0:0:0.785 | |

Figure 1.25: Process Flow Results

Click back on the **Process** tab and right-click on the **List Table Attributes** icon and select **Open**:

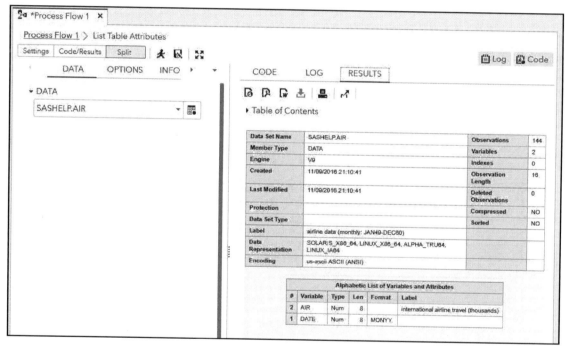

Figure 1.26: List Task Attributes results

When the **List Table Attributes** task opens this time, instead of the **CODE** tab being active and seeing the SAS Studio auto-generated code, the **RESULTS** tab is active and displays the output from the code that ran successfully when the user ran the process flow. Switch SAS Studio back to the **SAS Programmer** perspective using the drop down list in the upper right-hand corner.

# What's in the SAS® University Edition?

Since SAS is an analytic platform with many modules and solutions, let's see which pieces of the SAS environment are included in the SAS® University Edition. Return to the **Program 1** section and clear all the code using the **Xx** icon on the **CODE** tab toolbar. Type the following code in the **CODE** tab:

```
/* This lists the SAS foundation products that are installed on your system
*/
/* along with their version numbers.
*/
proc product_status;
run;

/* This lists the SAS products that have been licensed and the date through
*/
/* which the licensed software is valid.
*/
proc setinit;
run;
```

Click and highlight only the `proc product_status; run;` part of the code and submit this by selecting the running man icon from the **CODE** tab toolbar.

A programmer can submit specific lines of code by simply highlighting the pieces of code they would like to execute and then selecting the running man icon.

1.27: PROC product_status results for SAS® University Edition

As the results show, the SAS® University Edition contains custom versions of BASE SAS, SAS/STAT® software, SAS/ETS® software, SAS/IML® software, High Performance Suite, and SAS/ACCESS® Interface to PC files based on the SAS 9.4 M4 (Maintenance 4) release. Feel free to submit the older version `proc setinit;` in order to compare the output from the two different PROCs.

Please take some time to review the SAS product documentation by selecting the question mark icon in the upper right-hand corner of SAS Studio. This will take the user to an index listing of documentation for all SAS products and will help the user to understand the broad and deep power that the SAS language brings to solving business issues. Simply by looking at the listing of all the PROCs included in BASE SAS, a programmer should understand why this particular book will not be providing you a complete understanding of all the PROCs in any one of the included SAS products.

However, this book will provide the reader with a thorough understanding of SAS, and how once a programmer learns some of the SAS language, how easy it is to leverage the knowledge gained here in order to continue to learn other parts of the SAS system over a programmer's entire career.

At a high level, here are what the different pieces of the SAS® University Edition do—BASE SAS provides the bulk of data access, management, and preparation capabilities; SAS/STAT adds powerful descriptive and predictive analytics; SAS/ETS adds powerful forecasting capabilities; and SAS/IML adds matrix algebra and some optimization capabilities.

# Different levels of the SAS analytic platform

The SAS language originally started out as a bunch of tools, such as BASE, SAS/STAT, SAS/GRAPH, and SAS/ETS. These tools are what many today refer to as foundation (SAS) tools. Today, the simplest bundle of SAS® software is known as **SAS Analytics Pro** and contains BASE, SAS/STAT, and SAS/GRAPH. In the mid-1990s, SAS developed a metadata-based platform, at the heart of which lies what is called **SAS Integration Technologies**, which evolved into the **SAS Intelligence Platform**. It was on top of this metadata layer and foundation tools that several horizontal SAS solutions were developed. Chief among these horizontal solutions are SAS Enterprise Miner™, the gold standard in providing an easy-to-use intuitive descriptive and predictive analytics GUI, and **SAS Forecast Server**, which provides an easy-to-use intuitive GUI for forecasting.

The reason these are described these as horizontal solutions is because they are used to solve their respective types of business issues across all industries. Around the year 2000, SAS started bringing to the market, at their customer's requests, what are referred to as vertical solutions. These solutions are built from a combination of the horizontal metadata-based solutions and the foundation tools. They are designed purposefully to address a specific business issue either in a certain department, such as marketing, or for a specific industry problem. Some examples of these types of vertical solutions are load forecasting in utilities and anti-money laundering in financial services. Typically, these solutions also contain intellectual property in the form of a data model that aligns well with the data needed to solve the business issue at hand.

As the age-old saying goes, a picture is worth a thousand words, so here is an image of the three levels that were just described:

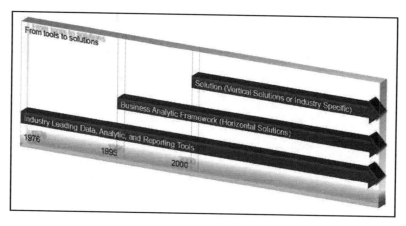

Figure 1.28: Evolution from tools to solutions

# SAS data storage

There are several aspects of data storage within the SAS environment and how the data storage helps to optimize how the overall system processes the data.

### The SAS dataset

The simplest storage is a SAS dataset, and it is made up of observations (rows) and variables (columns).

A SAS variable can be either numeric or character, and the number of bytes required to store variables can be set or controlled by the LENGTH statement.

The DS2 language was developed to allow the processing of a more extensive variable and natively supports ANSI SQL data types for precise data manipulation.

Numeric variables in SAS are stored in default lengths of 8 bytes, while character variables are stored 1 byte per character for a single byte character set and, two bytes per character for double byte character sets. SAS stores numeric data using floating point notation. By reducing the length of variables, one can help reduce both the amount of physical data storage needed as well as reduce the **Input/Output (I/O)** operations needed to read and write the data. While working with small datasets, this may not seem that important, but as you move into working with larger and larger sized data, or big data, the ability to be as efficient as possible with both reading/writing and storing the data becomes extremely important. The more efficient you are able to be with data, the faster your programs will execute, which results in delivering important and valuable information to decision-makers so they can make use of it in making better, more informed decisions. SAS datasets also have a COMPRESS option, which can be used to save storage space. Compression reduces the number of bytes needed to represent each observation.

A compressed dataset may require less storage space and fewer I/O operations to do reads/writes during processing; however, additional CPU resources may be required to access compressed files compared to uncompressed files.

If a file has very short records or there are no character variables with blank spaces to be compressed, then compressing the SAS dataset may result in a larger file.

## The SAS® Scalable Performance Data Engine

Another option to store SAS datasets is to use the **Scalable Performance Data (SPD) Engine**. The **Resources / Focus Areas / Scalability & Performance** section on support.sas.com, http://support.sas.com/rnd/scalability/spde/index.html describes SPD Engine as follows:

*The purpose of this engine is to speed the processing of large data sets by accessing data that has been partitioned into multiple physical files called partitions. The SPD Engine initiates multiple threads with each thread having a direct path to a partition of the data set. Each partition can then be accessed in parallel (by a separate processor) which allows the application to analyze data in parallel, as fast as the data is read from disk. This can effectively reduce any I/O bottlenecks and substantially decrease the elapsed time to process data.*

If you don't have multiple CPUs or cores the SPD Engine will not provide you any benefit. It was initially developed to help PC users take advantage of the multiple CPUs within their individual PCs.

*The SPD Engine evolved from the SPD Server product; therefore, many of its feature are derived from SPD Server. SPD Server supports a client/server environment requiring multiple SAS sessions. It also provides more functionality than the SPD Engine. However, the need to bring support of partitioned data into Base SAS resulted in the creation of the SPD Engine. Unlike SPD Server, the engine runs entirely in the same SAS process or session as the rest of your SAS job.*

## The Scalable Performance Data Server

The **Resources / Focus Areas / Scalability & Performance**, section on `support.sas.com` `http://support.sas.com/rnd/scalability/spds/index.html` describes the SPD Server as follows:

*SPD Server provides a high performance data store of very large SAS data sets. The Scalable Performance Data Server (SPD Server) is a client/server, multi-user data server designed to optimize storage and to speed the processing of large SAS data sets. SPD Server does this by parallelizing many of the SAS I/O functions. SPD Server requires an SMP machine and is designed to use all resources available on the machine to achieve maximum scalability.*

 SPD Server and SPD Engine predated open source solutions like Hadoop by many years. This SAS technology has been evolved to integrate and work within the Hadoop ecosystem. This is just one way SAS technology has proven itself to be flexible and agile in its ability to work with new technology as it becomes adopted as part of an organization's IT infrastructure.

As a matter of fact, as stated in *The SAS® Scalable Performance Data Engine: Moving Your Data to Hadoop without Giving Up the SAS Features You Depend On*, by Lisa Brown, SAS Institute `https://support.sas.com/resources/papers/proceedings15/SAS1956-2015.pdf`, *if you currently use the Base SAS® engine or the SAS® SPD Engine, then using the SPD Engine with Hadoop will enable you to continue accessing your data with as little change to your existing SAS programs as possible.*

## SAS HDAT

Another example of SAS' commitment to innovation and continuous development of new technology was the introduction of a its own special data storage format for Hadoop, called **SAS HDAT**. As described in *What's New in SAS® Data Management*, by Nancy Rausch, SAS Institute Inc., Cary, NC; Malcolm Alexander, SAS Institute Inc., `https://support.sas.com/resources/papers/proceedings13/070-2013.pdf` *SAS HDAT is highly optimized for fast load of data into SAS in-memory based analytic solutions built on either the SAS LASR server in SAS 9 or the new SAS Viya **Cloud Analytic Server (CAS)**. SAS can write data in this format from any SAS system.*

# SAS formats and informats

One very important feature of the SAS language and its data storage is the concept of the format and informat. Formats tell you how to display stored data, and informats tell you how to read them. While some programming languages provide limited formatting capabilities, SAS provides a robust and user-expandable system of formats. As a result, formats and informats play a far more valuable role within SAS than they do in other languages.

Within SAS, there are two types of formats/informats: those that are supplied by SAS called system formats, and those that allow a **SAS Programmer** to extend the system called user-defined formats. Because formats provide another method for storing and using information, they are important to understand and use as a **SAS Programmer**. When we start discussing SAS in-database technology in Chapter 7, *SAS® Software Engineers the Processing Environment for You* of this book, formats are a piece of SAS that you can push down into a **massively parallel processing (MPP)** data storage system such as an MPP database or Hadoop, and use them to extend the functionality of those systems just like they do within the SAS environment.

# Date and time data

SAS date and time variables are stored in SAS as numeric data. Storing dates and times in this numeric form makes it easier to deal with interval calculations, but can present a problem when using the raw data in a report or when printing it out. Dates are expressed as integers and indicate the number of days since January 1, 1960. Time variables are represented as the number of seconds since midnight. Variables that contain both date and time parts and are referred to as datetime variables. Datetime variables indicate the number of seconds since midnight on January 1, 1960. This is why it is important to understand and use the date and time related formats and informats so the data is represented in a familiar looking format that is easy for users to understand. Once a programmer understands how dates and times are stored in SAS and how to make use of all the date- and time-related formats/informats and functions, they usually appreciate the power and ease with which one can use SAS to read in dates and times from any source system, and write them out in any format required by a target system or end user report.

A programmer can use this knowledge to save physical storage space by storing a date, time, or datetime variable in one variable instead of storing the same date in multiple variables, simply to represent different ways to display that date. With one variable and formats, the programmer will be able to render reports on the fly for end users around the globe, who are used to seeing dates in the format most used in their countries.

# Summary

The reader has been introduced to SAS and now understands how SAS® software has evolved over the years, from supplying analytic tools to building an analytic platform on which not just the tools run, but horizontal and vertical solutions as well.

The reader has been made aware of several ways to access the SAS programming language, which includes command-line input, GUIs such as SAS Enterprise Guide and SAS Studio, and purpose-built GUIs for specific horizontal and vertical solutions.

The reader has been given step-by-step instructions on how to set up their own SAS® University Edition of SAS and has been lead through a few simple examples of submitting both data step code and a SAS PROC.

The reader has been shown the difference between the SAS Studio **SAS Programmer** perspective and the SAS Studio **Visual Programmer** perspective and was lead through an example of running a process flow in the **Visual Programmer** perspective.

The reader has been made aware of the different SAS data storage capabilities as well as some of the internal workings of SAS, such as how SAS stores data as either numeric or character, and the importance of FORMATS/INFORMATS, and in particular how these work hand-in-hand with how SAS stores date- and time-related data.

In Chapter 2, *Working with Data Using SAS® Software* of this book, the reader will learn how to make data within SAS, bring data in from external data sources as well as continuing to write and execute SAS programs!

# 2

# Working with Data Using SAS®
# Software

Data can be stored in many forms and in many systems. In Chapter 1, *Setting Up the SAS®
Software Environment*, the topic of SAS data storage was covered from a SAS-centric view,
meaning the options available to a user in storing data in SAS datasets. However, SAS can
work and store data in a variety of other forms and formats. One of the most powerful
features of SAS lies within the data management capabilities designed to read and, more
importantly, write data efficiently from all sorts of storage, including database systems, flat
files, spreadsheets, mainframe-based formats, and big data storage platforms such as
Hadoop and SAP HANA. SAS developers work in partnership with many other vendors in
co-developing SAS ACCESS engines, specifically designed to make reading and writing
data from their systems as fast and seamless as possible. As a result, SAS data management
solutions are used by many customers as a bridge to consolidate and/or share data across all
these other systems.

In addition to the co-developed SAS ACCESS engines for specific other systems, SAS also
develops engines that work with the libname statement and other file access methods
available with the fileref statement that allow SAS to read and write files using many
other data standards (XML, HTTP, and FTP, just to name a few). For more details and
information on both the libname engines and fileref data access methods, see *SAS
Engines and External Files* under *Part 5: SAS Files Concepts of the SAS documentation: SAS 9.4*
and *SAS Viya 3.2 Programming Documentation / SAS Language Reference: Concepts - SAS® 9.4
Language Reference: Concepts, Sixth Edition.*

Since SAS is a programming language, it is possible for users to write their own custom
import code for specific file formats that may not follow a well-known standard, thereby
extending the usefulness of SAS specifically for their own users and organization.

Many people have stated the big data is the new oil; however, having worked in the energy industry, I prefer to use these two analogies instead—big data is like an oil or gas reservoir and analytics helps you to identify and extract the valuable hydrocarbons, or in this case, valuable information from the rest of the field or data. Analytics is a truly renewable resource, because once you have the proper analytic environment set up to work within an organization, you can solve complex business issues and improve processes across all the different departments that make up your enterprise.

 The algorithms or math doesn't change, but the data and the questions vary from department to department and over time.

This is why analytics differs from typical business intelligent reports, which only focus on what has happened in the past or what may be happening right now.

 Business intelligent reports are important in helping to keep an organization running today, or as some may say, keeping the lights on a day-to-day basis. Business analytics provides guidance as to the root cause analysis and what will happen tomorrow or next week or sometime in the future. It can prescribe how best resources can be used to obtain a goal.

Business analytics provides insights that give decision-makers a competitive advantage in order to ensure the long-term success of their organizations.

This chapter will focus primarily on using the data step part of SAS, as well as the some of the SAS PROCs that are designed for working with data within the SAS platform.

In this chapter, we will:

- Learn that there is a difference between storing data for querying versus for preparing data for analytics
- Use the SAS programming language to make data
- See how to work with external data sources with SAS
- Write and execute several SAS programs

# Preparing data for analytics

It is important to understand that preparing data for analytics is different than storing data efficiently in a data warehouse, which focuses on normal reporting / business intelligent type and/or ad hoc queries. Regular **database administrators (DBAs)** will need to be educated and/or convinced that analytics requires the data to be in a different form in order for the algorithms to process the data. It is especially important for the data to be prepared for analytic processing in order for the actual processing to run in a timely manner. **Information Technology (IT)** employees play an increasingly important role in helping organizations leverage data and analytics. While it isn't necessary for someone in IT to understand statistics or analytics, it is important for them to support the data scientist in acquiring the proper hardware and software to build an analytics platform that runs efficiently so that the business can best leverage the information locked in their data, regardless of the size of the data.

SAS identified the need for what some may call an **analytic DBA**, or what others may call a **data steward** who should be paired to work with data scientists since at least 2013. More recently, SAS launched a SAS academy for data science to provide two underlying certifications, **SAS Certified Big Data Professional** and **SAS Certified Advanced Analytics Professional**. The reader will learn skills that will start to prepare them to earn other SAS certifications, such as **SAS Certified Programmer for SAS 9** and **SAS Certified Advanced Programmer for SAS 9**. These will provide them with a great foundation that can be leveraged in doing big data analytics with SAS.

There are other books on the topic of preparing data for analytics and several on how to prepare data for analytics with SAS, so we will not go deeper into this particular topic, but here is some interesting information I'd like to share with you.

 The typical database storage format like a star schema that contains fact tables in **Third Normal Form (3NF)**, and dimension tables that are denormalized, is not the form needed to facilitate efficient and fast analytic processing.

Typically, data needs to be prepared into an **Analytic Base Table (ABT)**, which typically contains one row of data or record corresponding to one entity (which might be a customer, product, and so on), and many variables or columns associated with that entity in some way. Depending on the department and the industry, it is common to have 100s, 1000s, and even 10,000s of columns that are attributes associated with that entity.

This form allows analytic processing to take place as efficiently as possible, given that the proper hardware is provisioned and configured optimally for analytics, instead of data being stored and systems being tuned to return queries or to process transactions very fast. Data storage tuned for transactions will not be configured to process analytics efficiently, especially at the scale associated with big data analytics.

Even big data platforms that are designed to handle big data are not necessarily good at processing analytics efficiently, especially if the system isn't dedicated for analytics. When you try to co-locate both transaction and query workloads, along with analytics workloads in the same environment, one type of workload will suffer and it tends to be the analytics, since the transactions are used to run the enterprise's daily business processes. This topic will be addressed in more detail in Chapter 4, *Analysis with SAS® Software*.

# Making data in SAS

A SAS programmer can make SAS datasets using data step code or with some specific PROCs such as PROC IMPORT, which is designed to import data from external sources.

## Data step code to make data

Bring up a new program in SAS Studio and type the following code:

```
data work.data1;
   name="Mary";
   x=1;
   output;
   name="Steve";
   x=2;
run;
```

Submit this code by using *F3* or selecting the running man icon and you will see this in the **OUTPUT DATA** tab:

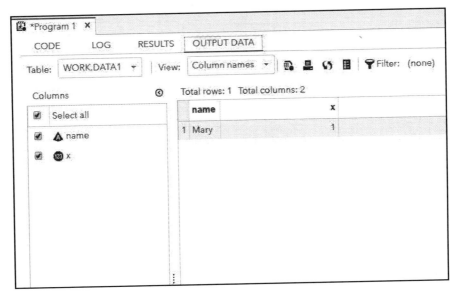

Figure 2.1: Output result from data step code making a dataset first submit

Was the result what you expected? Are you wondering why there is only one row of data? In this case, this temporary SAS dataset (temporary because we stored it in the **WORK** library), contains two variables: name, which is a character, and x, which is numeric.

Notice that you did not have to explicitly declare these variables nor their types. SAS implicitly does these types of declarations (so that a programmer does not need to) based on the first instance of the variable it encounters.

The reason there is only one row of data instead of two rows is that the code did not explicitly output; the second set of variables; so they were not written out and saved into the dataset.

Add the second `output;` statement before the `run;` statement and submit the code again:

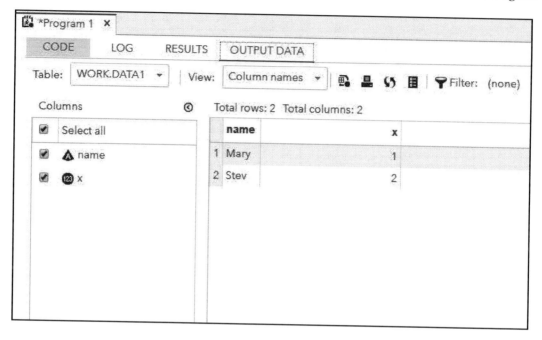

Figure 2.2: Output result from the data step code making a dataset second submit

The result now has two rows of data, which is more likely what the user expected; however, there is still something not quite right. Why is the second value for the `name` variable truncated? The answer is that, even though SAS implicitly declared name to be a character based on the first instance, it also implicitly declared the length of the character variable based on the only value it had information on, which was `Mary`. So, the length was implicitly set to 4. As a result, the second value of `name`, which should have been `Steve`, gets truncated to `Stev`. To fix this, all the user has to do is use the `length` data step statement. The code should now look like the following:

```
data work.data1;
    length name $5;
    name="Mary";
    x=1;
    output;
    name="Steve";
    x=2;
    output;
run;
```

Now, submitting this code will produce the following in the **OUTPUT DATA** tab:

| | name | x |
|---|---|---|
| 1 | Mary | 1 |
| 2 | Steve | 2 |

Total rows: 2  Total columns: 2

Figure 2.3: Output from the data step code making a dataset third submit

Recall from Chapter 1, *Setting Up the SAS® Software Environment*, the reason one does not have to explicitly use a length statement to define numeric variables in SAS, by default, all numbers in SAS use eight bytes to store their values.

Fortunately, this is not the only way to make data within SAS; otherwise, it would be very time consuming and inefficient. Another way is the input and cards data step statements which read in multiple rows of data all at once in combination with the necessary length statements to explicitly declare the types and lengths of variables that will make up the dataset. There is an alias for the cards statement, the alias is datalines. Clear your **CODE** window and type the following code:

```
data work.data2;
  input name $ x y;
  length name $5, x y 8;
  cards;
  Mary 1 2
  Steve 3 4
  ;
run;
```

Submit this code to see what happens. If the **LOG** tab is not immediately active, click on the **LOG** tab and then scroll to the top to see the following debug information:

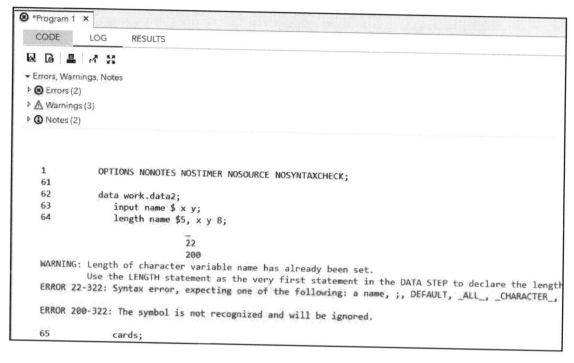

Figure 2.4: Log of code submitted with errors

This is how a SAS programmer uses a combination of submitting and viewing the **LOG** in order to debug the code until it runs without errors. Remove the comma after the $5, which is the cause of the error and resubmit the code:

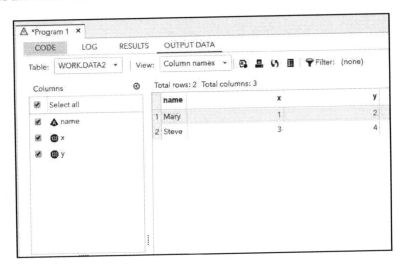

Figure 2.5: Output data tab of code submitted that generated a warning

Even though this produced the output dataset that was expected, notice the yellow triangle next to **Program 1** in the top-left part of the window. This means that even though there were no errors that prevented the code from executing, there was a warning. This should be checked to see whether it can be resolved. Some warnings may not need to be fixed; however, it is best practice to resolve them so that they don't cause unexpected results sometime in the future. Going to the **LOG**, the following warning was generated:

**WARNING: Length of character variable name has already been set.**

Use the `length` statement as the very first statement in the data step to declare the length of a character variable. Change the code as suggested by the warning by putting the `length` statement as the very first statement:

```
data work.data2;
    length name $5 x y 8;
    input name $ x y;
    cards;
    Mary 1 2
    Steve 3 4
    ;
run;
```

Submit this code and notice that there are no errors or warnings. The resulting dataset has three variables: one character, `name`, and two numerics, `x` and `y`. Although this is an improvement over having to explicitly use the `output;` statement after manually setting values for every variable, there are much more efficient ways to make datasets based on external files and data from other data storage systems, such as databases and Hadoop. In addition, for those who are already familiar with **Structured Query Language (SQL)**, SAS has implemented PROC `SQL`, which can also be used to make datasets using SQL type statements. Furthermore, `FEDSQL` is a new part of SAS that allows queries to be distributed in order to enhance performance when dealing with big data.

## PROC SQL to make data

Type the following code to see how a programmer can use PROC `SQL` to make data within SAS:

```
proc sql;
   create table work.sqlex1
         (name char(5),
          x num,
          y num );
quit;
```

This will make a new dataset in work named `sqlex1` with three variables and no observations or rows. Return to the **CODE** section and clear the existing code. Type the following code and submit it:

```
proc sql;
   describe table work.sqlex1;
quit;
```

The following **LOG** should be produced from executing the preceding code:

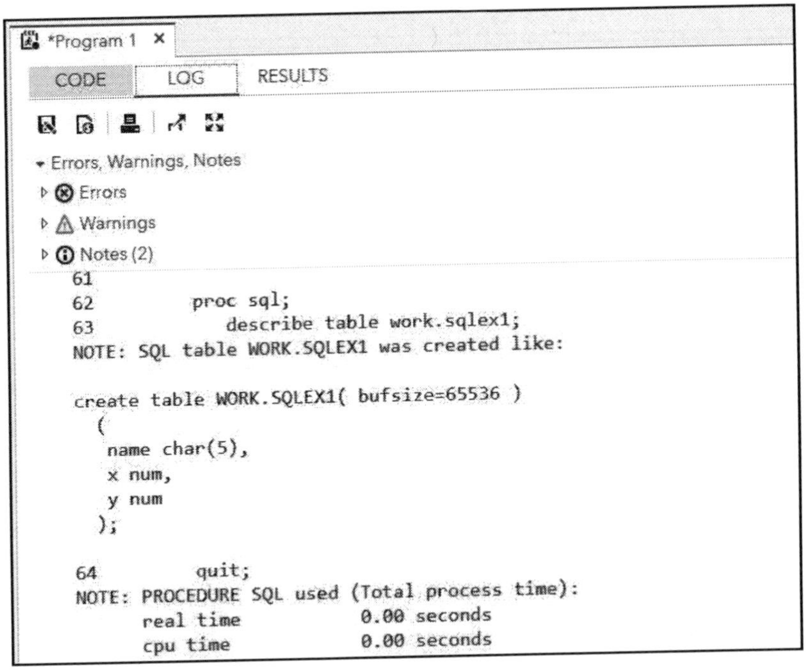

Figure 2.6: PROC SQL describe results

One nice thing about the describe statement is that a programmer can use it against any SAS library.tablename regardless of whether that table was made with SQL or not and get the necessary create statements to make another table that contains the exact same type of variables.

Typically, you will use PROC SQL to create new datasets as a result of a query of a table that already exists within an existing SAS library. Return to the **CODE** section and clear the existing code using the **X**x icon. Type the following code and submit it:

```
/* The outobs option limits the new table to the first 15 rows returned
from the query */
proc sql outobs=15;
    create table work.sqlex2 as
    select * from sashelp.cars;
/* The new work.sqlex2 is made with the above code */
/* However, it will not display any output unless you query the new table
*/
    select * from work.sqlex2;
quit;
```

The following **RESULTS** should be produced from executing the preceding code:

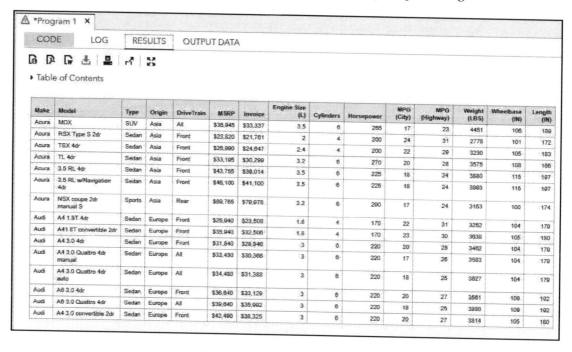

| Make | Model | Type | Origin | DriveTrain | MSRP | Invoice | Engine Size (L) | Cylinders | Horsepower | MPG (City) | MPG (Highway) | Weight (LBS) | Wheelbase (IN) | Length (IN) |
|---|---|---|---|---|---|---|---|---|---|---|---|---|---|---|
| Acura | MDX | SUV | Asia | All | $36,945 | $33,337 | 3.5 | 6 | 265 | 17 | 23 | 4451 | 106 | 189 |
| Acura | RSX Type S 2dr | Sedan | Asia | Front | $23,820 | $21,761 | 2 | 4 | 200 | 24 | 31 | 2778 | 101 | 172 |
| Acura | TSX 4dr | Sedan | Asia | Front | $26,990 | $24,647 | 2.4 | 4 | 200 | 22 | 29 | 3230 | 105 | 183 |
| Acura | TL 4dr | Sedan | Asia | Front | $33,195 | $30,299 | 3.2 | 6 | 270 | 20 | 28 | 3575 | 108 | 186 |
| Acura | 3.5 RL 4dr | Sedan | Asia | Front | $43,755 | $39,014 | 3.5 | 6 | 225 | 18 | 24 | 3880 | 115 | 197 |
| Acura | 3.5 RL w/Navigation 4dr | Sedan | Asia | Front | $46,100 | $41,100 | 3.5 | 6 | 225 | 18 | 24 | 3893 | 115 | 197 |
| Acura | NSX coupe 2dr manual S | Sports | Asia | Rear | $89,765 | $79,978 | 3.2 | 6 | 290 | 17 | 24 | 3153 | 100 | 174 |
| Audi | A4 1.8T 4dr | Sedan | Europe | Front | $25,940 | $23,508 | 1.8 | 4 | 170 | 22 | 31 | 3252 | 104 | 179 |
| Audi | A41.8T convertible 2dr | Sedan | Europe | Front | $35,940 | $32,506 | 1.8 | 4 | 170 | 23 | 30 | 3638 | 105 | 180 |
| Audi | A4 3.0 4dr | Sedan | Europe | Front | $31,840 | $28,846 | 3 | 6 | 220 | 20 | 28 | 3462 | 104 | 179 |
| Audi | A4 3.0 Quattro 4dr manual | Sedan | Europe | All | $33,430 | $30,366 | 3 | 6 | 220 | 17 | 26 | 3583 | 104 | 179 |
| Audi | A4 3.0 Quattro 4dr auto | Sedan | Europe | All | $34,480 | $31,388 | 3 | 6 | 220 | 18 | 25 | 3627 | 104 | 179 |
| Audi | A6 3.0 4dr | Sedan | Europe | Front | $36,640 | $33,129 | 3 | 6 | 220 | 20 | 27 | 3561 | 109 | 192 |
| Audi | A6 3.0 Quattro 4dr | Sedan | Europe | All | $39,640 | $35,992 | 3 | 6 | 220 | 18 | 25 | 3880 | 109 | 192 |
| Audi | A4 3.0 convertible 2dr | Sedan | Europe | Front | $42,490 | $38,325 | 3 | 6 | 220 | 20 | 27 | 3814 | 105 | 180 |

Figure 2.7: Output from querying a table via PROC SQL

The use of ⋆ in the code is treated as a wildcard alias, meaning all variables without the programmer having to worry about typing out each individual column. Instead of using ⋆, a programmer can list out individual columns if they only want a few from the table being queried.

If a programmer wants to make a duplicate table with no rows from an existing table, they can make use of the `like` statement. Type the following code and submit:

```
proc sql;
   create table work.sqlex3
   like sashelp.cars;
quit;
```

Figure 2.8: New table resulting from the like PROC SQL statement

One unique aspect of PROC SQL compared to implementations of SQL used with other databases is that, within SAS, you can make use of other SAS language elements along with PROC SQL. For example, a programmer can use SAS dataset options on the create statement within PROC SQL. In addition, a SAS programmer can make use of global statements, dataset functions, formats, and informats. PROC SQL can be used for more than just making tables. It can also be used to generate reports, make summary statistics, retrieve data from tables or views, combine data from tables and views, make views, create indexes on tables, and update or modify values within tables.

# Working with external data

In order to work with external data and reduce the amount of manual effort involved in data entry to make data, there are data step statements. They make it very easy to import data from external raw files or data storage systems.

# Data step code for importing external data

When dealing with raw files, files that only contain data with no data dictionary, the `infile` and `file` statements serve as the interfaces to external files that work in combination with the `input` and `put` statements to read and write data from and to those external files. Furthermore, these statements work together with the `filename` and `cards` statements in such a way that the `infile` and `file` statements provide a programmer with a great deal of power and flexibility to work with external files, regardless of the format and structure used by those files. If the reader has to work with a lot of raw files, it is strongly recommended to study the documentation on these statements as well as other SAS-user-written papers on these topics.

# PROC IMPORT

Instead of manually writing the data step code to work with external files, SAS has provided the programmer with PROC `IMPORT`, which is designed to automate the process of converting external files into SAS datasets and generates the necessary data step code for the user. This can then be recalled and customized if necessary. PROC `IMPORT` comes with BASE SAS, with the functionality to import JMP files and delimited files. A delimited file is one that uses a delimiter such as a comma, space, or tab to separate columns' data values. For example, one of the most common delimited file types is known as **Comma Separated Variable (CSV)**. The types of external files that PROC `IMPORT` works with is extensible by licensing the SAS/ACCESS interface to PC files, which adds the addition types of MS ACCESS database files, Microsoft Excel files, and Lotus spreadsheets. SAS provides PROC EXPORT to take any table SAS references within the SAS platform and export it into those external file formats. Type this code and submit it:

```
proc export data=sashelp.cars
file="/folders/myfolders/sasuser.v94/cars.csv"; run;
```

The following information should now be in your **LOG**:

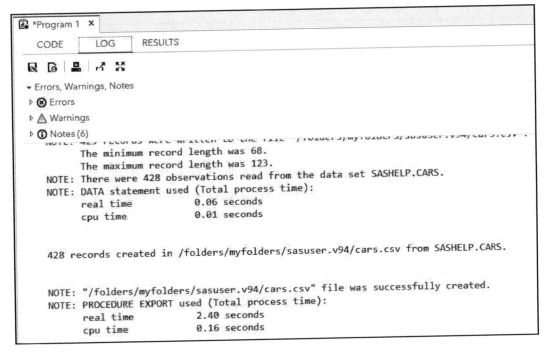

Figure 2.6A: PROC EXPORT log

As mentioned for PROC IMPORT, PROC EXPORT generates the necessary data step code behind the scenes for the programmer; so if you scroll up in the **LOG**, you will ses the data _null_; block that executed in order to write the dataset into the .csv file:

```
Program 1  x

 CODE       LOG      RESULTS

▼ Errors, Warnings, Notes
  ▷ ⊗ Errors
  ▷ ⚠ Warnings
  ▷ ① Notes (6)

  1          OPTIONS NONOTES NOSTIMER NOSOURCE NOSYNTAXCHECK;
  61
  62         proc export data=sashelp.cars file="/folders/myfolders/sasuser.v94/cars.csv";
  62       !
                                                                                  run;

NOTE: Unable to open parameter catalog: SASUSER.PARMS.PARMS.SLIST in update mode. Temporary paramete
WORK.PARMS.PARMS.SLIST.
  63         /*********************************************************************
  64         *    PRODUCT:    SAS
  65         *    VERSION:    9.4
  66         *    CREATOR:    External File Interface
  67         *    DATE:       12AUG17
  68         *    DESC:       Generated SAS Datastep Code
  69         *    TEMPLATE SOURCE:  (None Specified.)
  70         *********************************************************************/
  71         data _null_;
  72         %let _EFIERR_ = 0; /* set the ERROR detection macro variable */
  73         %let _EFIREC_ = 0;    /* clear export record count macro variable */
  74         file '/folders/myfolders/sasuser.v94/cars.csv' delimiter=',' DSD DROPOVER lrecl=32767
```

Figure 2.7A: PROC EXPORT generates a data _null_ block

Rather than write the PROC IMPORT code to make another SAS dataset from the cars.csv file, let's make use of the SAS Studio import data feature. On the left-hand side of SAS Studio, select **Servers Files and Folders**. Now, select the first icon under the header label and select **Import Data**:

Figure 2.8A: SAS Studio Import Data

A new program section will pop up, with a top section that allows the user to either drag and drop the external file, or select a file to import. Choose **Select a file to import** and then select the `cars.csv` file from under your `sasuser.v94` folder:

Figure 2.9: SAS Studio Import Data file selection

When the programmer selects **Open**, the new program section will display the settings for the file import in the top section and the code generated in the bottom part.

 The programmer, by default, is in the **Split** display view; however, there are two other displays views that can easily be toggled: **Settings** and **Code/Results** listed in the top-left corner of the top section.

Look at the **Settings** section. You'll see that the programmer can change **Library** and **Data set name** of the file to be imported, which in this case will (by default) store the data in a new dataset named IMPORT in the WORK library, or work.import. Run the code by selecting the running man icon in the top section. In the bottom section, the **RESULTS** tab should display the top of PROC CONTENTS, which was run as part of the generated code for the import of data:

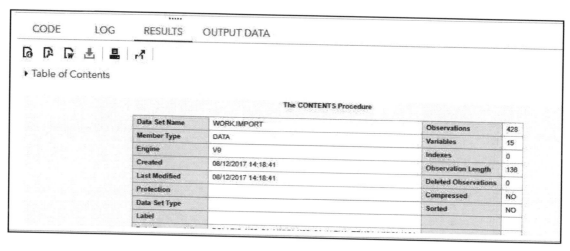

Figure 2.10: PROC CONTENTS results

PROC CONTENTS provides the programmer with quite a lot of information about the data and as such is quite useful when a programmer is given new data to process, regardless of where that data is stored. Instead of working with raw external files, the majority of the time, a user will be working with data stored in a structured format such as Excel, a comma delimiter file, a database, or Hadoop. In this case, the SAS programmer will make use of the power of a variety of SAS ACCESS engines and libname statements, which serves as pointers within the SAS environment to the external database or file. Once a libname statement has been executed to an external source like a database with the proper userid and password granted by the sources administrator, then the tables stored in those systems will appear within the SAS environment to the SAS user like a SAS dataset. For example, if you have an Oracle database with a schema in it that contains tables that need to be analyzed rather than within a SAS program or the SAS autoexec, the following type of libname can be assigned:

```
libname ora_sch1 oracle user=<username> password=<password> (other
options);
```

Once the library is assigned, then all the tables with the Oracle DBA-granted access to that user are now available to the SAS programmer via simple data step statements such as set, which the reader has already used in the examples from Chapter 1, *Setting Up the SAS Environment*:

```
/* This pseudo code shows an example of making a SAS dataset stored in the
work library from */
/* an oracle data table stored in the oracle database associated with the
ora_sch1 library   */
data work.<tablename>;
    set ora_sch1.<oracle tablename>;
run;
```

Regardless of whether that data resides in Oracle, Teradata, MySQL, Microsoft SQL, Greenplum (or for that matter any ODBC or JDBC compliant data store), Hadoop, SAP, or any other systems when a SAS library is assigned, the SAS code a programmer writes is the same in order to interact and process that data.

A SAS library typically allows not only data to be read from the source system but also SAS to write data back into that system. This provides SAS with a very powerful capability within the data management/data integration part of the analytics life cycle. This is leveraged by many organizations to use SAS to standardize and cleanse data from a variety of different data systems, so that the data can be viewed as an enterprise-wide asset, regardless of which system they choose to land that consolidated view of all their other data storage systems. Typically, this enterprise system may be referred to as a data lake or their big data platform, which usually means the use of Hadoop and/or SAP HANA.

Combining data from one SAS library with data from any other SAS library is very easy, whether you choose to use dataset statements or PROC SQL. Here is a simple example of using one dataset within the **SASHELP** library to make a duplicate **WORK** version of the data twice the size of the original, simply by using the set statement. Type the following code in a program in SAS Studio and then submit it:

```
data work.cartemp;
  set sashelp.cars sashelp.cars;
  run;
```

Select the **LOG** section and notice the **Notes** written in the **LOG**:

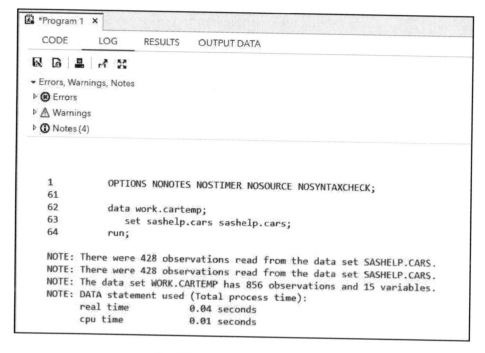

Figure 2.11: Log notes from the set statement example

As noted in the **LOG**, SAS informs the programmer how many observations or rows were read in from both input datasets specified in the `set` statement. In this case, we read the same dataset twice in order to make a work version double in size. A programmer can easily set up libraries pointing to different databases or data storage systems. See how easy it is to combine these different sources into a new dataset, which could be saved as a SAS dataset, or for that matter, written as a table within one of the source libraries! The reader will now learn to use PROC SORT with one of its options to eliminate duplicates within the dataset `work.cartemp`. Clear the program section using the $X_x$ icon, type the following code, and submit it:

```
proc sort data=work.cartemp nodupkey;
   by _ALL_;
run;
```

The use of the special keywork _ALL_ informed SAS that the programmer wanted to eliminate duplicates based on rows that matched across all of its columns. _ALL_ saved the programmer's time by not having to know and then type out each column name within PROC SORT.

Select the **LOG** section after submitting this code and notice that the **Notes** written out into the **LOG** inform the user of the number of records read, as well as the number of duplicate records that were eliminated from the input dataset specified in the `data=` option of the PROC statement. In addition, the reader should note that SAS implicitly sorted this dataset in place and saved the results in the same dataset that was provided as input to the PROC. If the programmer does not want to lose the original input dataset, then the `out=` option can be used to specify a new target dataset that would contain the results from processing the source dataset specified in the `data=` option. Type the following code and submit:

```
data work.cartemp;
    set sashelp.cars sashelp.cars;
run;

proc sort data=work.cartemp out=work.nodup nodupkey;
    by _ALL_;
run;
```

In the **OUTPUT DATA** section, the reader will see the `work.cartemp` preview with 856 observations:

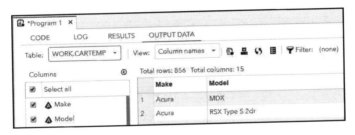

Figure 2.12: Output data results for work.cartemp

Select the **Table:** drop-down in the upper-left corner of the **OUTPUT DATA** section and choose the `work.nodup` table. See the preview of this table with 428 observations:

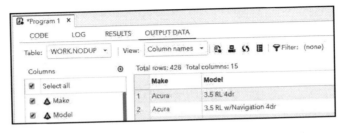

Figure 2.13: Output data results for work.nodup

There are several dataset utility type of PROCs, which makes it easier to get information about a dataset and/or perform administrative tasks at a dataset level. PROC CONTENTS, which has been used in the examples, is for displaying information about a particular dataset, while PROC DATASETS is a utility PROC that is used to assist a programmer in managing all their SAS files within a library. SAS files are not only datasets, but also data views or catalogs (SAS catalogs store other elements or objects associated with the SAS language; for example, formats and informats are stored in catalog entries). PROC CATALOG is a utility PROC that operates at the catalog level.

# Referencing external files

While a SAS library is a pointer to a data storage location that has data stored in tables, SAS programmers can also use statements and data step options to work directly with raw external files. SAS provides programmers with the flexibility of referencing files either directly or indirectly.

## Directly referencing external files

Data step code has two statements for working with external files. The infile statement uses the external file for reading or for input, and the file statement is used to write information into an external file for storage. Both the infile and file statements refer directly to the external file using the directory location and name of the file. For example, here is some pseudo-SAS code for using an external file named raw.txt as input in a data step:

```
data work.raw;
    infile "c:<somepath>\raw.txt";
    input <define variables to read from infile>;
    /* more data step logic */
run;
```

The file data step statement works similarly. In SAS Studio, bring up a new program and type the following code:

```
data _null_;
    file "/folders/myfolders/sasuser.v94/rawfile.txt";
    set sashelp.class;
    put Name Sex Age Height Weight;
run;
```

Submit the code by selecting the running man icon:

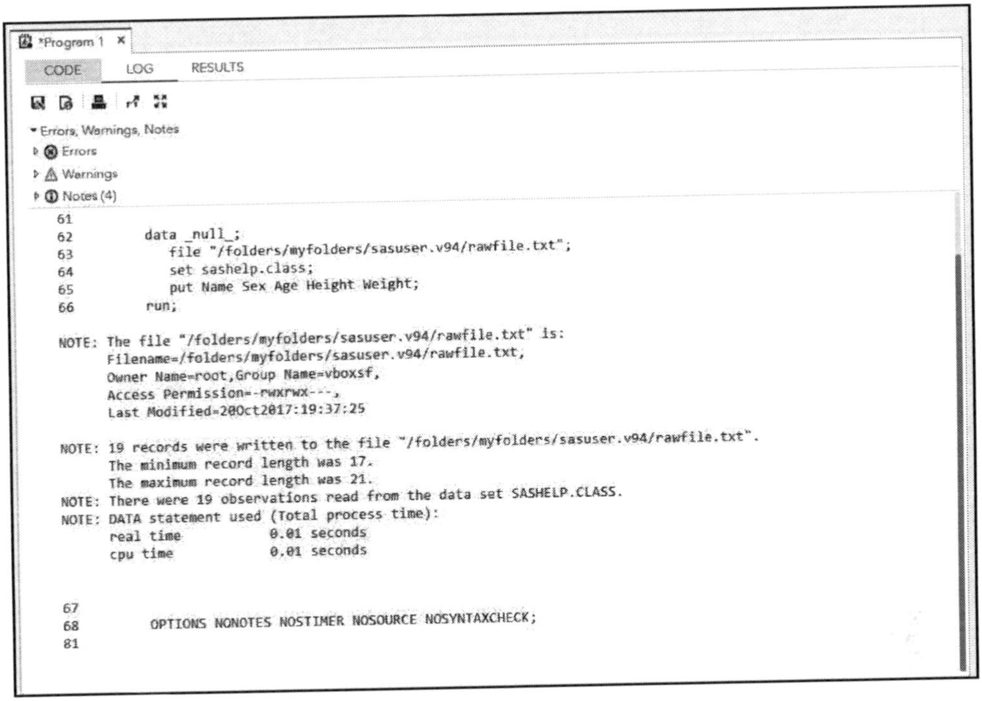

Figure 2.14: Log from using file statement

Not only will you see this information in the **LOG**, but also the `raw.txt` file will be seen. Select **Server Files and Folders** in the left of SAS Studio and expand **My Folders** and then `sasuser.v94`.

## Indirectly referencing external files

SAS also provides a `filename` statement that works similarly to the `libname` statement. While the `libname` statement creates a pointer or `libref` to a location that stores data in tables, the `filename` statement assigns a pointer or `fileref` to an external file. This indirect reference is convenient to make one reference to a file within a program, which may be used multiple times and therefore can easily be updated in the future by changing one line instead of multiple direct references. Here is what a `filename` statement looks like in code:

```
filename myfile "/folders/myfolders/sasuser.v94/rawfile.txt";
```

Now, a programmer can use this `fileref` in combination with the direct `infile` and `file` statements. Type the following code in a new SAS Studio program section:

```
filename myfile "/folders/myfolders/sasuser.v94/rawfile.txt";
data work.myraw;
   infile myfile;
   input Name $ Sex $ Age Height Weight;
run;
```

Submit this code by selecting the running man icon:

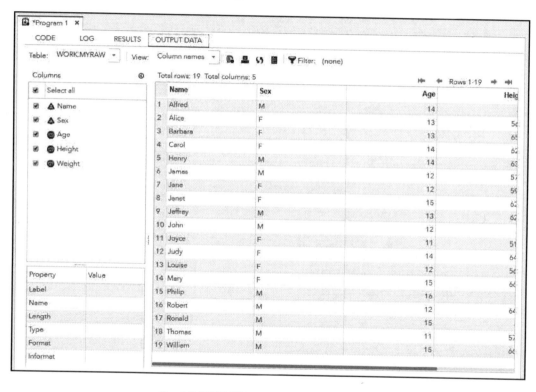

Figure 2.15: WORK.MYRAW dataset made using filename and infile

# Specialty PROCs for working with external data

SAS developers continuously work to make new procedures that make it easier for programmers to work with new data sources and/or new hardware improvements. As such, new PROCs that help programmers work with big data have been added to BASE SAS.

# PROC HADOOP and PROC HDMD

*PROC HADOOP and PROC HDMD were developed to make it easier for SAS programmers to interact and work with data stored in Hadoop. Apache Hadoop is an open source framework written in Java that provides distributed data storage and processing of large amounts of data. PROC HADOOP interfaces with the Hadoop JobTracker. This is the service within Hadoop that controls tasks to specific nodes in the cluster. PROC HADOOP enables you to submit the following:*

- **Hadoop Distributed File System (HDFS)** *commands*
- *MapReduce programs*
- *Pig language code*

*Base SAS® 9.4 Procedures Guide, Seventh Edition Overview: HADOOP Procedure* (http://documentation.sas.com/?cdcId=pgmmvacdccdcVersion=9.4docsetId=procdocsetTarget=n0c02ws1auznusn1mq4t4ixjvyud.htmlocale=en).

*PROC HDMD generates XML-based metadata that describes the contents of files that are stored in HDFS. This metadata enables the SAS/ACCESS interface for Hadoop and SAS high-performance procedures to read Hadoop data directly, without an intermediate metadata repository such as Hive. You can use PROC HDMD to describe tabular HDFS files for these formats:*

- *Fixed-record-length (binary) data*
- *Delimited text*
- *XML-encoded text*

*Base SAS® 9.4 Procedures Guide, Seventh Edition Overview:*
*HDMD Procedure* (http://documentation.sas.com/?cdcId=pgmmvacdc&cdcVersion=9.4&docsetId=proc&docsetTarget=p1uabrk4v1u7xbn1mn5oiqdluzjk.htm&locale=en).

# PROC JSON

**Java Script Object Notation (JSON)** *is a text-based, open standard data format that is designed for human-readable data interchange. JSON is based on a subset of the JavaScript programming language and uses JavaScript syntax for describing data objects. The JSON procedure reads data from a SAS dataset and writes it to an external file in JSON representation. You can control the exported data with several options that remove content and affect the format.*

In addition to exporting data from a SAS dataset, PROC JSON provides statements that enable you to write additional data to the external file and control JSON containers. *Base SAS® 9.4 Procedures Guide, Seventh Edition Overview: JSON Procedure* (http://documentation.sas.com/?cdcId=pgmmvacdccdcVersion=9.4docsetId=procdocsetTarget=p06hstivs0b3hsn1cb4zclxukkut.htmlocale=en).

# Specialty PROCs for working with computer languages

In the same way that SAS adds PROCs to help with working with specific data sources, SAS develops PROCs that make it easier for a programmer to interact with other programming languages. PROC HADOOP, mentioned in the previous section, allows working with data in Hadoop as well as executing HDFS commands, MapReduce programs, and Pig language code.

## PROC GROOVY

Groovy is a dynamic language that runs on a **Java Virtual Machine (JVM)** so SAS developed a PROC **GROOVY** which enables SAS code to execute Groovy code in a JVM. *Base SAS® 9.4 Procedures Guide, Seventh Edition Overview: Groovy Procedure* (http://documentation.sas.com/cdcId=pgmmvacdccdcVersion=9.4docsetId=procdocsetTarget=p1x8agymll9gten1ocziihptcjzj.htmlocale=en).

## PROC LUA

*The Lua programming language is an embeddable scripting language that runs on any platform that has a standard C compiler. This includes all versions of UNIX, Windows, and mobile operating systems, including Android, iOS, and others. Lua uses simple syntax, runs fast computations, and automatically manages memory allocation. The LUA PROC enables you to run statements from the Lua programming language within SAS code. You can submit Lua statements from an external Lua script, or enter Lua statements directly in the SAS code.*

*PROC* LUA *enables you to perform these tasks:*

- *run Lua code within a SAS session*
- *call most SAS functions within Lua statements*
- *call PROC* FCMP *functions within Lua statements*
- *submit SAS code from Lua*

*Base SAS® 9.4 Procedures Guide, Seventh Edition Overview: Lua Proceduce* (http://
documentation.sas.com/?cdcId=pgmmvacdccdcVersion=9.4docsetId=procdocsetTarget=
n1csk38ocks0rgn1rr8d302ofqgs.htmlocale=en).

# Summary

The reader learned that data must be stored in a different format in order for analytics to efficiently run, and that this format differs from how data is typically stored in a database. In addition, the reader learned how to make data using SAS statements, as well as how to bring external data into the SAS environment.

The reader should now understand that a SAS library is a pointer to where data is stored, whether the data is stored as a SAS dataset or in some other data storage format such as a database. The reader wrote and executed their first SAS programs, making use of both data step statements and a few BASE SAS procedures. At this point, the reader should be comfortable with working with the **CODE, LOG, RESULTS,** and other sections that make up a program section within SAS Studio.

In addition, you were introduced to several specialty SAS procedures or PROCs, which enable a programmer to more easily work with specific external data sources or other computer languages.

In Chapter 3, *Data preparation Using SAS Data Step and SAS Procedures,* the reader will learn how to use SAS to prepare data for analysis and reporting.

# 3

# Data Preparation Using SAS Data Step and SAS Procedures

As was discussed in Chapter 2, *Working with Data Using SAS® Software*, data needs to be prepared in a format that allows certain analytics to actually be able to run and process efficiently.

In this chapter, we will cover the following topics:

- Creating indicators for the first and last observation in a by group
- Transposing the rows and columns in a table
- Statistical and mathematical data transformations
- SAS macro facility

## Data preparation for analytics

SAS has been dealing with data for over 41 years and specifically preparing data to be analyzed using analytics. There are certain features of the data step language, as well as certain PROCs, that save a programmer's time and effort in preparing data for analytics.

Analytical data management and analytics is an iterative process done many times. During analysis, the two phases are iterated over and over until the final results are available:

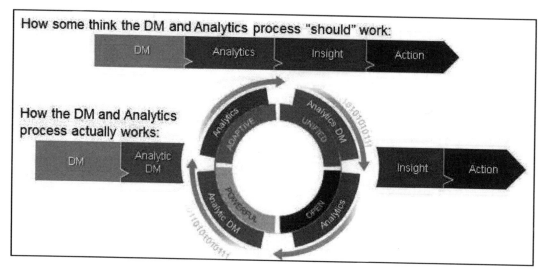

Figure 3.1: Data management for analytics

It is indispensable for an analytic environment for data management features and analytics capabilities to be seamlessly integrated and available in one platform. One of the most powerful aspects of using SAS for analytics is the fact that SAS has always offered powerful data management capabilities along with a comprehensive set of analytics, all within on environment or platform. In this chapter, we will be looking at some of the unique features within SAS that either take much more code and effort to obtain the same result, or just don't exist in other languages. For example, SAS provides data management that exceeds the functionality of SQL or procedural extensions of SQL.

# Creating indicators for the first and last observation in a by group

It is very convenient to be able to easily identify the first and last observation with a group of observations. For example, if you need to identify a sequence of events that some entity performs, but the data you receive from various sources doesn't happen to provide you with the data in this type of format, it can be difficult and time-consuming to rearrange this data into the proper sequence.

When the SAS data step executes, several temporary special variables are created, and they can be used to help control the program logic; for example, _N_ is a special variable that corresponds to the current row of data being processed. One simple way to use this automatic variable is to add a row number variable to a table that doesn't already have one. Type the following code in a program section in SAS Studio and submit it:

```
data work.cars;
    set sashelp.cars;
    row_num=_N_;
run;
```

In the **OUTPUT DATA** table preview window, scroll all the way to the right within the window and you will see the new column named run_num. It contains the value that corresponds to the row number within the new work.cars table (1 through 428):

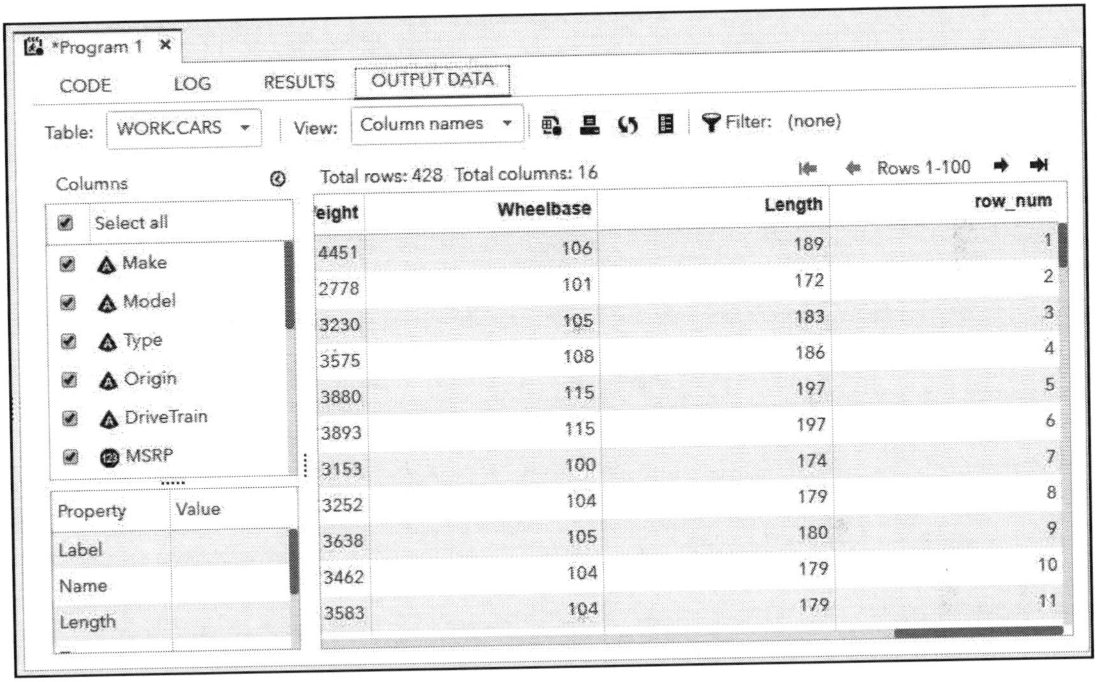

Figure 3.2: Example of using _N_ to set a row number variable within a dataset

Likewise, the SAS data step identifies the first observation and last observation of a by group by creating temporary variables for each variable listed in the by statement. These temporary variables are named FIRST.variablename and LAST.variablename. Similar to _N_, these temporary variables can be used to control program logic within the execution of the data step.

These temporary variables are not added as output variables to the dataset unless the programmer wants to capture their values for some reason that would require them to explicitly add new variables, and assign them the values of these temporary variables in the same way as we just did for the last example using _N_.

*The values of* FIRST.variablename *and* LAST.variablename *indicates whether an observation with that* by *group is one of the following positions:*

- *The first one in a* by *group*

- *The last one in a* by *group*

- *Neither the first nor the last one in a* by *group*

- *Both first and last, as is the case when there is only one observation in a* by *group*

*As a result users can take actions conditionally, based on whether they are processing the first or the last observation in a by group.* You can learn more about this under *SAS® 9.4 Programming Documentation / SAS Language.Concepts - Processing Observations in a BY Group* at (http://documentation.sas.com/?cdcId=pgmmvacdccdcVersion=9.4docsetId=lrcondocsetTarget=n01a08zkzy5igbn173zjz82zsi1s.htmlocale=en#n0oteuuy1erlmvn1l9valku9ihmi).

The value of FIRST.variablename = 1 for the first row associated with the BY variable; otherwise it has a value of 0. Likewise, the value of LAST.variablename = 1 for the last row associated with the by variable; otherwise it has a value of 0. Type the following code in a program section in SAS Studio and submit it:

```
proc sort data=sashelp.cars out=work.cars2;
   by Make Type;
quit;

data work.cars3;
   set work.cars2;
   by Make Type;
   if FIRST.Make and FIRST.Type then output;
   if NOT FIRST.Make and FIRST.Type then output;
run;
```

This code will result in a dataset, `work.cars3`, which is a single type of car from each make (or manufacture) instead of multiple types from the same make. The first `if` statement outputs the row corresponding to the car associated with a specific make and the first type from that make, while the second `if` is responsible for outputting the first type of each other type associated with that particular make. To further illustrate the usefulness of these temporary variables, let's add a fake sequence number associated with each make from `work.cars2`:

```
data work.cars4;
    set work.cars2;
    by Make;
    if FIRST.Make then sequence=1;
    else sequence=sequence+1;
    retain sequence;
    if LAST.Make then put "There are " sequence "of " make;
run;
```

Notice the use of the `retain` statement in order to make sure your `sequence` variable is assigned the proper value for each iteration through the dataset. The `retain` variable is a statement that informs the data step to keep the value of the specific variable or variables identified in the statement within the next iteration through the data step execution.

This code also introduced the `put` statement, which is a simple way to write messages or variable values out in the **LOG**. In this case, the `put` statement writes out to the **LOG** how make types of each make happen to exist in the original `work.cars2 dataset`.

A SAS programmer can make use of the `put` statement as a simple way to help them debug the data step code while in the process of writing it:

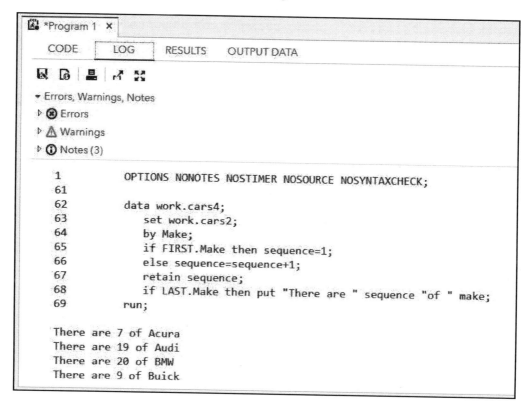

Now go to the **OUTPUT DATA** tab and once again scroll the table preview all the way to the right so that you can see the `sequence` variable added. See that it has been added correctly by restarting at 1 for each new make the program encounters in reading the `work.cars2` dataset:

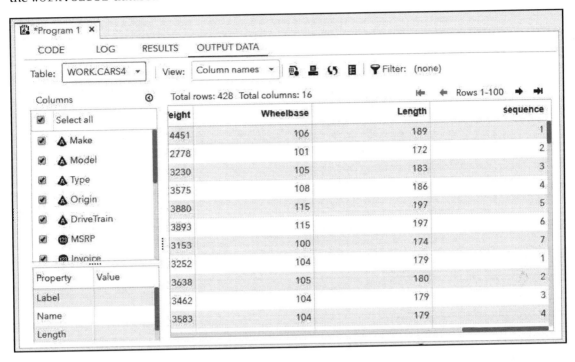

Figure 3.4: Adding a sequence to existing data

In this particular example, the value of the `sequence` variable was seen in the `put` statement to **LOG**, informing the programmer how many types there were for each make. However it should be easy to think of how useful this would be in sequencing other information, such as the paths associated with visitors to a website.

# Transposing

Transposing variables (columns) into observations (rows) is a common task when preparing data for analytics. In data step or other languages, it can take quite a lot of code as well as processing time to get the results a data scientist wants before they can start their analysis. For those who either program in SAS or use other languages to call SAS APIs, there is PROC TRANSPOSE, which provides an easy way to accomplish this task:

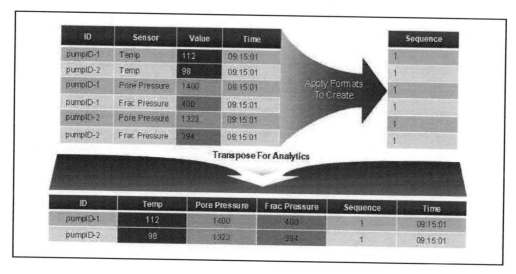

Figure 3.5: An example of transposing data to prepare for analytics

The example provided in *Figure 3.5* actually combines the power of using formats along with transposition in order to get the data in the proper format for analytics to be applied. In this case, a custom format based on the time stamp associated with the various pumps would be created in order to align the data up in the sequence of events that are being captured at different times throughout the day. Notice how the resulting table at the bottom lines up the entity, in this case pumps, in such a way that all the data or attributes associated with individual pumps are in one row per pump per sequence number.

One of the major advantages of using PROC TRANSPOSE is that a programmer can learn to use it on small data and the same syntax can be used on any size of data. Furthermore, PROC TRANSPOSE has been re-engineered over the years to take advantage of the hardware and memory of the environment it is running on, whether it is a **Symmetrical Multiprocessing (SMP)** based server or newer hardware, such as the **Massively Parallel Processing (MPP)** based database or Hadoop data storage platform.

PROC TRANSPOSE can also be run in-database within the data storage system that houses the data, thereby reducing the overall time necessary to accomplish its task. In-database and in-memory processing capabilities of the SAS platform will be discussed further in Chapter 7, *SAS® Software Engineers the Processing Environment for You.*

# PROC TRANSPOSE

PROC TRANSPOSE restructures the values of an input data table into an output data table by transposing selected columns (or variables) into rows (or observations). PROC TRANSPOSE can perform both simple transpositions of columns into rows or complex transpositions that involve transposing with by groups and/or renaming transposed columns.

Type the following code in a program section of SAS Studio and submit it:

```
proc transpose data=sashelp.failure
               out=work.failure_transposed(drop=_NAME_);
          id cause;
          by process day;
quit;
```

Total rows: 70  Total columns: 4 — Rows 1-70

|  | Cause | Process | Count | Day |
|---|---|---|---|---|
| 1 | Contamination | Process A | 15 | Monday |
| 2 | Corrosion | Process A | 2 | Monday |
| 3 | Doping | Process A | 1 | Monday |
| 4 | Metallization | Process A | 2 | Monday |
| 5 | Miscellaneous | Process A | 3 | Monday |
| 6 | Oxide Defect | Process A | 8 | Monday |
| 7 | Silicon Defect | Process A | 1 | Monday |
| 8 | Contamination | Process A | 16 | Tuesday |
| 9 | Corrosion | Process A | 3 | Tuesday |
| 10 | Doping | Process A | 1 | Tuesday |
| 11 | Metallization | Process A | 3 | Tuesday |
| 12 | Miscellaneous | Process A | 1 | Tuesday |

Figure 3.6: SASHELP.FAILURE dataset

As shown in the following screenshot, look how little code is needed to be written using PROC TRANSPOSE to easily rearrange the data within a table in order to view information much more clearly:

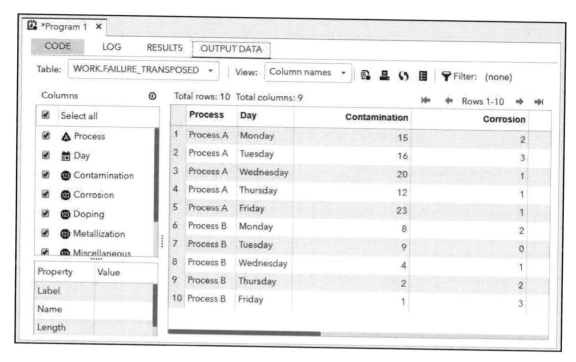

Figure 3.7: SASHELP.FAILURE transposed into work.failure_transposed

# SAS Studio Transpose Data task

SAS Studio also provides a data task that generates the necessary code, including PROC TRANSPOSE. In the left of SAS Studio, expand **Tasks and Utilities**; then expand **Tasks** and **Data** so that you can see the list of **Data** tasks:

Figure 3.8: List of SAS Studio Data Tasks

Now double-click on the **Transpose Data** task, which will open up a program section on the right-hand side of SAS Studio. In the **Data** drop-down box, select SASHELP.FAILURE. Under **ROLES**, assign the **Count** column; then expand **ADDITIONAL ROLES** and add **Process** and **Day**:

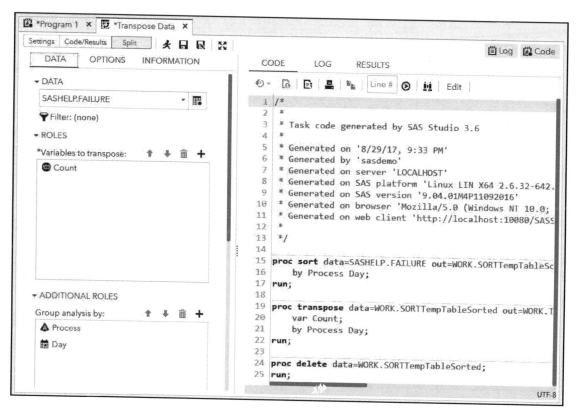

Figure 3.9: Transpose Data task

Now select the **OPTIONS** tab in the left-hand-side section and uncheck the **Use prefix** checkbox. Check the **Select a variable that contains the names of the new variables** box and add **Cause**:

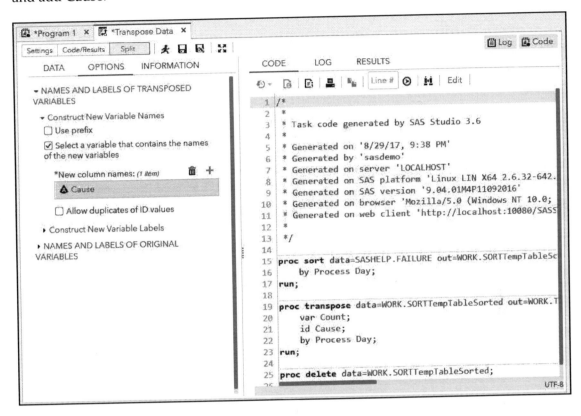

Figure 3.10: Transpose Data task options

Return to the **DATA** tab in the left-hand-side section and scroll all the way to the bottom. Check the **Show output data** box. Now submit the code by selecting the running man icon. Since we checked **Show output data**, a PROC PRINT was added to the generated code and shows this in the **RESULTS** tab.

The following **Transpose Data** task example provides the exact same transposed results as the previous example using PROC TRANSPOSE code:

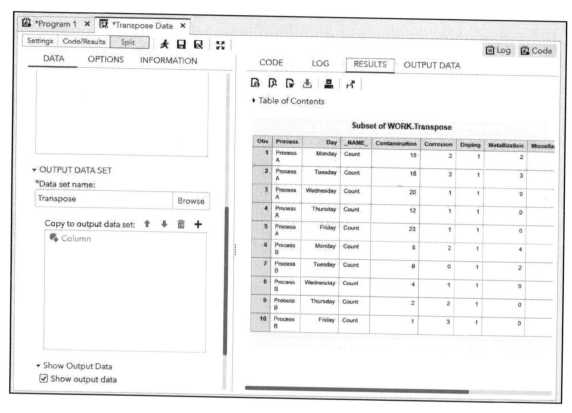

Figure 3.11: Transpose Data task results

# Statistical and mathematical data transformations

Data scientists and analysts not only want to transpose data within tables, but also tend to enrich the data with statistics related to the existing numeric data within the table. SAS once again makes this enrichment easy with procedures, for example, PROC MEANS.

## PROC MEANS

*The MEANS procedure provides data summarization tools to compute descriptive statistics for variables across all observations and within groups of observations. For example, PROC MEANS does the following:*

- *Calculates descriptive statistics based on moments*
- *Estimates quantiles, which includes the median*
- *Calculates confidence limits for the mean*
- *Identifies extreme values*
- *Performs a t test*

*SAS® 9.4 Programming Documentation / BASE SAS Procedures Guide: Overview: MEANS Procedure* (http://documentation.sas.com/?cdcId=pgmmvacdccdcVersion=9.4docsetId= procdocsetTarget=n0k7qr5c2ah3stn10g1lr5oytz57.htmlocale=en).
The following example of PROC MEANS will continue to use the work.failure_transposed dataset that was produced using the prior PROC TRANSPOSE example:

```
proc transpose data=sashelp.failure
               out=work.failure_transposed(drop=_NAME_);
          id cause;
          by process day;
quit;

proc means data=work.failure_transposed n mean max min Q1 median Q3 std;
     class Process;
quit;
```

Submitting the above code will produce the following RESULTS.

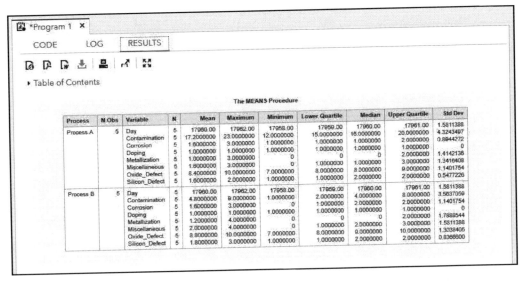

The MEANS Procedure

| Process | N Obs | Variable | N | Mean | Maximum | Minimum | Lower Quartile | Median | Upper Quartile | Std Dev |
|---|---|---|---|---|---|---|---|---|---|---|
| Process A | 5 | Day | 5 | 17960.00 | 17962.00 | 17958.00 | 17959.00 | 17960.00 | 17961.00 | 1.5811388 |
| | | Contamination | 5 | 17.2000000 | 23.0000000 | 12.0000000 | 15.0000000 | 18.0000000 | 20.0000000 | 4.3243497 |
| | | Corrosion | 5 | 1.6000000 | 3.0000000 | 1.0000000 | 1.0000000 | 1.0000000 | 2.0000000 | 0.8944272 |
| | | Doping | 5 | 1.0000000 | 1.0000000 | 1.0000000 | 1.0000000 | 1.0000000 | 1.0000000 | 0 |
| | | Metallization | 5 | 1.0000000 | 3.0000000 | 0 | 0 | 0 | 2.0000000 | 1.4142136 |
| | | Miscellaneous | 5 | 1.6000000 | 3.0000000 | 0 | 1.0000000 | 1.0000000 | 3.0000000 | 1.3416408 |
| | | Oxide_Defect | 5 | 8.4000000 | 10.0000000 | 7.0000000 | 8.0000000 | 8.0000000 | 9.0000000 | 1.1401754 |
| | | Silicon_Defect | 5 | 1.6000000 | 2.0000000 | 1.0000000 | 1.0000000 | 2.0000000 | 2.0000000 | 0.5477226 |
| Process B | 5 | Day | 5 | 17960.00 | 17962.00 | 17958.00 | 17959.00 | 17960.00 | 17961.00 | 1.5811388 |
| | | Contamination | 5 | 4.8000000 | 8.0000000 | 1.0000000 | 2.0000000 | 4.0000000 | 8.0000000 | 3.5637059 |
| | | Corrosion | 5 | 1.6000000 | 3.0000000 | 0 | 1.0000000 | 2.0000000 | 2.0000000 | 1.1401754 |
| | | Doping | 5 | 1.0000000 | 1.0000000 | 1.0000000 | 1.0000000 | 1.0000000 | 1.0000000 | 0 |
| | | Metallization | 5 | 1.2000000 | 4.0000000 | 0 | 0 | 0 | 2.0000000 | 1.7888544 |
| | | Miscellaneous | 5 | 2.0000000 | 4.0000000 | 0 | 1.0000000 | 2.0000000 | 3.0000000 | 1.5811388 |
| | | Oxide_Defect | 5 | 8.8000000 | 10.0000000 | 7.0000000 | 8.0000000 | 9.0000000 | 10.0000000 | 1.3038405 |
| | | Silicon_Defect | 5 | 1.8000000 | 3.0000000 | 1.0000000 | 1.0000000 | 2.0000000 | 2.0000000 | 0.8366600 |

Figure 3.12: PROC MEANS results

This type of information is useful in helping to identify unusual patterns and/or outliers. As can be seen from this example, an analyst can easily pick out days that contain specific types of failure that fall outside the upper and lower quartiles for those types of failure. They can also identify the failures that have the highest standard deviation, which indicates that those types of failures tend to have a wider range of values at which failure can occur.

Similar to PROC TRANSPOSE, PROC MEANS has been re-engineered over the years to allow it to process in-database across a variety of different databases and data storage systems: **Aster, DB2, Greenplum, HADOOP, Impala, Netezza, Oracle, SAP HANA**, and **Teradata**.

While PROC MEANS is an easy way to provide more insights into the data and can add this type of information as additional columns to a dataset, imputing missing values is another way to increase the value of certain types of analysis. Missing values are an issue that can negatively impact the results associated with quite a lot of statistical analyses. For example, if a row of data has 100 columns associated with some entity and any one of those is missing, then regression analysis throws out the entire row from the analysis. This is why imputing missing values is important since it brings more of the data back into play, especially in the case of regression analysis, which is very useful in many problems across a wide variety of industries and use cases.

# Imputation

Imputation is a common technique in which missing values for a particular column are replaced by a value derived from all the rest of the values for that column that are not missing. A typical example of a basic type of imputation is to calculate a single statistical value such as the average or mean and replace all missing values for that column with a single value. This type of strategy is referred to as **single imputation**.

> *"Single imputation does not reflect the uncertainty about the predictions of the unknown missing values, and the resulting estimated variances of the parameter estimates are biased toward zero"*
> *– Rubin, D. B. (1987 p 13), Multiple Imputation for Nonresponse in Surveys, New York: John Wiley & Sons*

*Multiple imputation does not attempt to estimate each missing value through simulated values, but rather to represent a random sample of the missing values. This process results in valid statistical inferences that properly reflect the uncertainty due to missing values; for example, valid confidence intervals for parameters.*

*SAS/STAT® 14.2 / SAS/STAT User's Guide - Overview: MI Procedure* (https://support.sas.com/documentation/cdl/en/statug/63962/HTML/default/viewer.htm#statug_mi_sect001.htm).

SAS provides programmers and analysts different ways to perform imputation; for example, the SAS/STAT procedure MI allows a programmer to perform imputation ahead of doing further analysis. Another way is through PROCs that have implemented IMPUTE statements; they allow a programmer to impute values on-the-fly while executing that specific PROC.

# Identifying missing values

While imputation helps resolve the problems that missing values present to some types of analysis, how are you to find out that you have missing values in your data? SAS Studio provides a very easy way using one of the built-in tasks under **Tasks and Utilities**. In the left side of SAS Studio, expand **Tasks and Utilities**, then expand **Tasks**, and then **Data** so that you can see the list of **Data** tasks. Now double-click on the **Describe Missing Data** task, which will open up a program section on the right-hand side of SAS Studio. In the **DATA** drop-down box, select SASHELP.ZIPCODE:

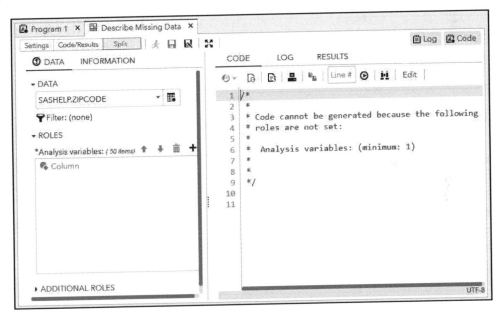

Figure 3.13: Describe Missing Data task

Under the **ROLES** section, select the + icon next to the trash can icon so that you can then select all the variables from the list. Scroll down to the bottom and select **OK**. This will return you to the previous window, but now the list of **Analysis variables:** should be filled in and you will notice the code that has been generated for you in the **CODE** section:

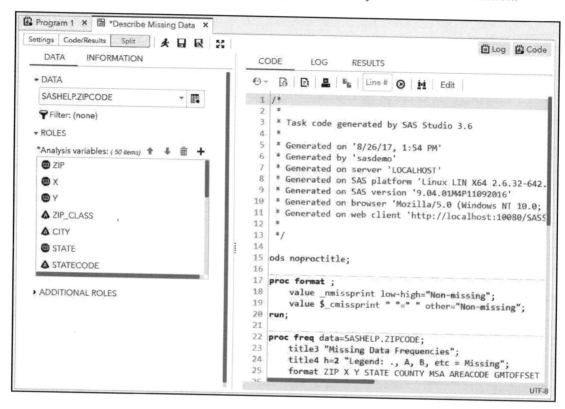

Figure 3.14: Describe Missing Data task with SASHELP.ZIPCODE

Now, submit or run this code by selecting the running man icon and see the nice report that is generated. It presents the programmer with all information regarding the extent of missing data within all the variables in the SASHELP.ZIPCODE dataset:

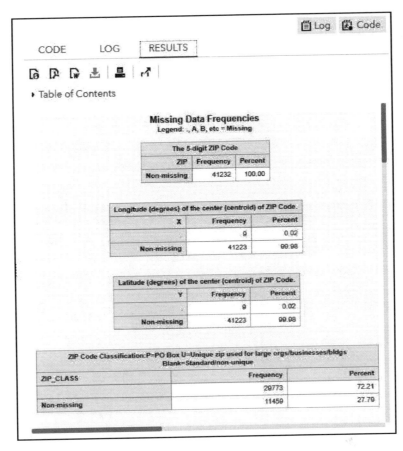

Figure 3.15: Results from the Describe Missing Data task

Be sure to return to the **CODE** window and review the code that this task generated for you. This is one way to learn more about coding in SAS. You will see that a user-written format is created using PROC FORMAT, which is then followed by two PROC FREQ procedures that apply the newly created formats. Finally, we have PROC PRINT, which is what generates the previous report in *Figure 3.15*. The final bit of generated code shows a good practice using PROC DELETE to delete the temporary work dataset, Work._MissingData_. This was generated during the task and used to build the report.

# Characterizing data

Prior to applying analytics, a programmer will want to find out as much as possible about the data itself since that will help an analyst determine which types of analyses they will use to answer questions related to the data. SAS Studio provides an easy way to describe the characteristics of any data through the use of the **Data** task **Characterize Data**:

 Whenever a programmer is given new data to work with, they should run this **Characterize Data** task in order to familiarize themselves with the initial state of the data for their new project.

Within SAS Studio, on the left, expand the **Tasks and Utilities** section, then expand **Tasks** and then **Data**. Double-click on the **Characterize Data** task:

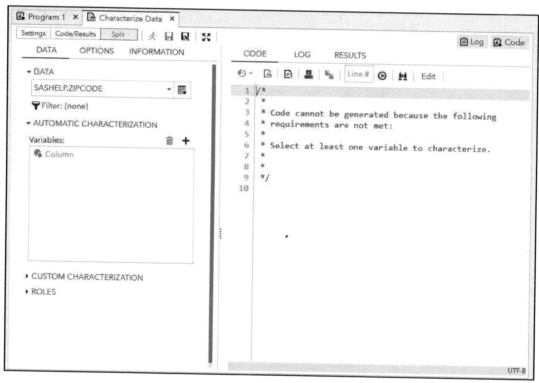

Figure 3.16: Characterize Data task

In the **DATA** drop-down box, select SASHELP.CARS. Then, under the **AUTOMATIC CHARACTERIZATION** section, select the + icon and add all the variables. Select **OK**:

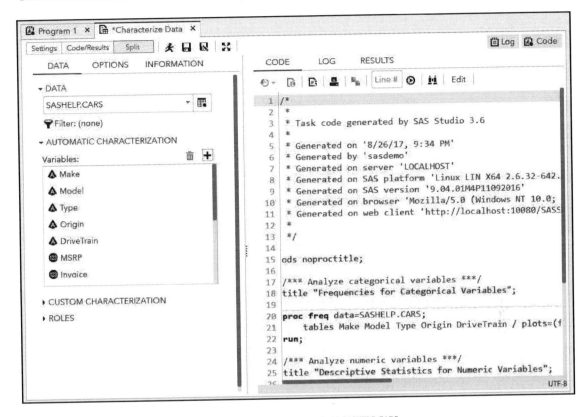

Figure 3.17: The Characterize Data task with SASHELP.CARS

Now submit or run this code by selecting the running man icon and see the nice report that is generated. It presents the programmer with quite a detailed report on the data within the SASHELP.CARS dataset. The report contains not only descriptive statistics of all the variables but also graphs that show the distribution shapes for all the of data. It shouldn't be a surprise that many of the numeric variables distribution graphs are normally distributed; however, MSRP and invoice both seem to be skewed distributions:

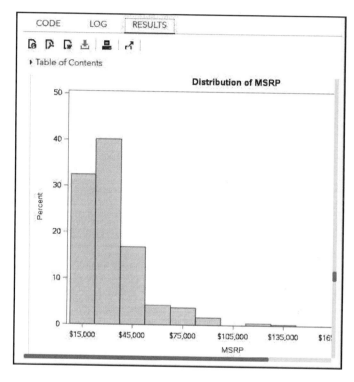

Figure 3.18: Skewed MSRP distribution

Return to the **CODE** section of the task and review the generated code for the **Characterize Data** task. Notice that this task generates PROC FREQ, PROC MEANS, as well as PROC UNIVARIATE, which is responsible for generating the histograms within the outputted report.

All three of these PROCs used by this **Characterize Data** task are included in BASE SAS.

# List Table Attributes

If you want to see the attributes of a table instead of the data within the table, SAS Studio provides the **List Table Attributes** task for you. Within SAS Studio, on the left, expand the **Tasks and Utilities** section. Then expand **Tasks** and **Data**. Double-click on the **List Table Attributes** task:

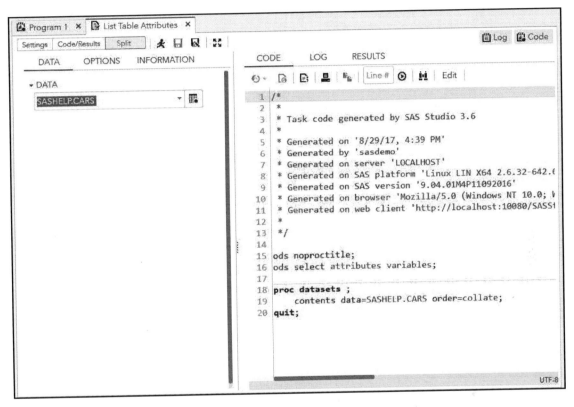

Figure 3.19: List Table Attributes with SASHELP.CARS

Run this code by selecting the running man icon:

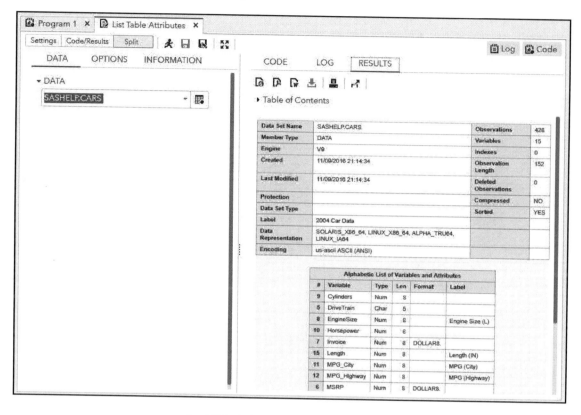

Figure 3.20: Results of List Table Attributes with SASHELP.CARS

This provides information on the table such as when it was created, when it was last modified, the encoding, number of rows (observations), number of columns (variables), a list of variable names, the types of variables, the length of the variables, variable formats, and labels associated with the variables. Return to the **CODE** section and review the automatically generated code for the **List Table Attributes** task. This task makes use of the DATASETS procedure, as shown in the following screenshot:

SAS Studio makes it easy for a programmer to see the procedure, or procedures, that a particular task will automatically generate for the users. Simply right-click on any task, such as the **List Table Attributes** task, and then select the **Properties** icon under the **Tasks and Utilities** section, which is the second-to-the last icon to the left of the refresh icon.

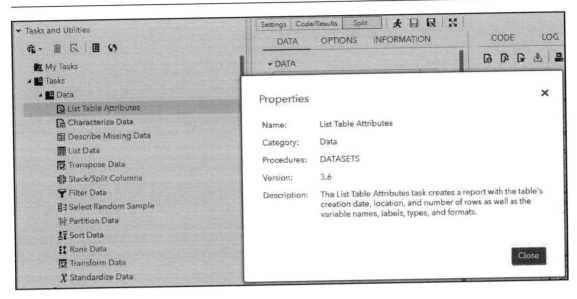

Figure 3.21: Tasks and Utilities Properties for List Table Attributes

SAS Studio provides not only the procedure or procedures used with the task, but also an expanded description of the result the task delivers to the user.

# SAS macro facility

The macro facility is part of BASE SAS and allows a programmer to extend and customize SAS programs. Programmers in general look for ways to reduce the amount of code they need to write to accomplish a task, and the macro facility does exactly that; it reduces the amount of code that needs to be written to perform common tasks. The macro facility is made up of two components: the macro processor, which does the work, and the macro language, which a programmer uses to communicate with the macro processor. The following two delimiters within a SAS program trigger the macro processor:

- Macro variables, which allow a programmer to replace text strings within SAS programs
- Macros, which are sets of instructions callable from within other SAS programs

# Macro variables

The simplest way to define a macro variable is with the `%let` statement. Type the following code in a SAS program **CODE** section, and submit it:

```
%let name=MyName;

data _null_;
    put "&name";
run;

%put "Hello the my name is &name..";
```

The following output will show up in the **LOG**.

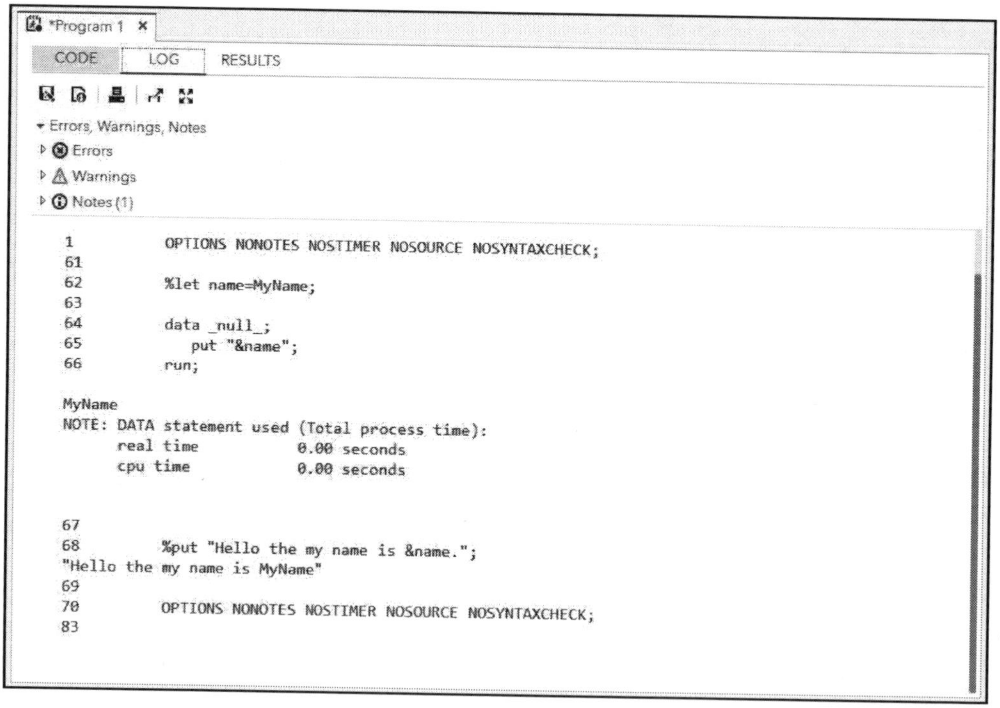

Figure 3.22: Example of defining and using a macro variable

In this case, we defined the macro variable name and assigned it the value of the text MyName. As can be seen when the code was submitted, the put statement within the data step references the macro variable using the ampersand (&) with no space and then the name of the macro variable. When the code compiles, the &name is replaced with the text stored within it as if the programmer had written that text instead. %put is a macro statement that writes whatever follows it to the **LOG**, and in this case, it's text that also contains the same reference to &name. Notice that the two periods . . in the previous code snippet immediately following the macro reference results in only one period written to **LOG**. The reason is that the first . is considered an explicit end to the macro variable and whatever text follows the first . is appended to the value of the macro variable. If the programmer actually wants a period as part of the output to **LOG**, it must be doubled-up in this case. The reason for the explicit period to end the reference to a macro variable is for cases when the programmer may want to reference two macro variables together. Here is code you can submit in order to see the different results.

```
%let fname=firstname;
%let lname=lastname,;

%put &lname&fname;
%put &lname.&fname;
%put &lname. &fname;
```

Submitting the previous code will provide this output in the **LOG**:

```
1              OPTIONS NONOTES NOSTIMER NOSOURCE NOSYNTAXCHECK;
61
62            %let fname=firstname;
63            %let lname=lastname,;
64
65            %put &lname&fname;
lastname,firstname
66            %put &lname. &fname;
lastname, firstname
67            %put &lname.x&fname;
lastname,xfirstname
68
69            OPTIONS NONOTES NOSTIMER NOSOURCE NOSYNTAXCHECK;
82
```

Figure 3.23: Macro variable reference results

There is no way for the last version to be written out without the . being interpreted this way, because submitting this `%put &lnamex&fname;` results in **WARNING: Apparent symbolic reference LNAMEX not resolved** being written to **LOG**. In addition to allowing programmers to define user-written macro variables, the SAS system comes with a set of system or automatic macro variables that a programmer can reference within their programs. For example, submit the following code:

```
%put &sysvlong;
```

This will write out to the **LOG** the release number and maintenance level with a 2-year SAS date value.

For a list of all automatic macro variables, see *SAS® 9.4 Programming Documentation / Macro Language Reference: Macro Variables Defined by the Macro Processor* (`http://documentation.sas.com/?cdcId=pgmmvacdc&cdcVersion=9.4&docsetId=mcrolref &docsetTarget=p0zngb6kwmbgywn1qvnsge9td43x.htm&locale=en`).

# Macros

*A SAS program can contain any number of macros and a single program can invoke any particular macro any number of times. Similar to macro variables, macros can be used to generate text.*

*However, macros provide additional capabilities:*

- *Macros can contain programming statements that enable you to control how and when text is generated.*
- *Macros can accept parameters. You can write generic macros that can serve a number of uses.*

*SAS® 9.4 Programming Documentation / Macro Language Reference: Defining and Calling Macros* (`http://documentation.sas.com/?cdcId=pgmmvacdccdcVersion=9.4docsetId=mcrolref docsetTarget=p1gjh9paxeeq2hn17l8f0irr6d8i.htmlocale=en`).

Like macro variables, macros can be user written or SAS provided. The SAS system comes with sets of libraries that contain autocall macros depending on the products you have licensed. Unlike user-written macros, which need to be compiled before they are called (or used), autocall macros come pre-compiled and therefore can simply be called by a programmer. User-written macros can also be promoted or added to a SAS environment's autocall macro libraries so that programmers can share their macros with one another:

| Selected Autocall Macros | |
|---|---|
| **Macro** | **Description** |
| CMPRES and QCMPRES | Compresses multiple blanks and removes leading and trailing blanks. QCMPRES masks the result so that special characters and mnemonic operators are treated as text instead of being interpreted by the macro facility. |
| COMPSTOR | Compiles macros and stores them in a catalog in a permanent SAS library. |
| DATATYP | Returns the data type of a value. |
| LEFT and QLEFT | Left-aligns an argument by removing leading blanks. QLEFT masks the result so that special characters and mnemonic operators are treated as text instead of being interpreted by the macro facility. |
| SYSRC | Returns a value corresponding to an error condition. |
| TRIM and QTRIM | Trims trailing blanks. QTRIM masks the result so that special characters and mnemonic operators are treated as text instead of being interpreted by the macro facility. |
| VERIFY | Returns the position of the first character unique to an expression. |

Figure 3.24: Subset of SAS supplied Autocall Macros[23] SAS® 9.4 Programming Documentation / Macro Language Reference

A SAS programmer who wants to write their own macros can use macro statements, macro functions, and automatic macro variables. The basic form of a macro is as follows:

```
%macro <macro name> (optional parameters);
    /* put code here */
%mend (optional macro name);
/* If you chose to use the optional macro name on the %mend statement it
must */
/* match exactly the macro name the programmer uses in the %macro statement
*/
```

Macro programming in SAS can be a very powerful part of a SAS programmer's skill set, especially in preparing data for analysis since many of the steps to prepare data for different types of analysis typically share quite a lot of repeated steps, which can be generalized into autocall macros. For a simple example, write the following code and submit it:

```
/* Simple example of a user written macro with two optional parameters with
*/
/* default values provided.
*/
%macro myfirstmacro(libn=sashelp,tablen=cars);
    proc datasets;
        contents data=&libn..&tablen order=collate;
    quit;
%mend myfirstmacro;

%myfirstmacro;

%myfirstmacro(libn=sashelp,tablen=zipcode);
```

Once the macro is compiled, the first call to it not using parameters which causes the DATASET procedure code to run with `sashelp.cars`, the default values for the macro. The second call to the macro uses the parameters, and so the same `proc datasets` code is run on `sashelp.zipcode`.

# Summary

We learned that analytic data management and analysis is not a linear sequence but an highly iterative step within the analytical life cycle.

We also learned how to make use of the data step `FIRST.` and `LAST.` functionality, PROC TRANSPOSE, and the SAS Studio **Data** task **Transpose Data** to rearrange data to prepare it for further analysis by PROC MEANS.

We learned about the importance of imputation, the difference between single imputation and multiple imputation, as well as how to use the SAS Studio **Data** task **Describe Missing Data**. The reader also learned how to review autogenerated code as another way to learn more about SAS coding.

We then saw how to use the SAS Studio **Data** task **Characterize Data** in order to learn more about the data prior to doing further analyses and how to use the SAS Studio **Data** task **List Table Attributes**. In addition, the reader learned how the Tasks and Utilities properties provide a list of procedures that the task uses as well as a description of the results to be delivered.

Finally, we saw a brief introduction to the SAS macro facility, macro variables, and macro programming.

In the next chapter, we will learn how to perform some predictive analysis, some forecasting analysis, and some optimization analysis.

# 4

# Analysis with SAS® Software

In this chapter, we will cover the following topics:

- Descriptive and predictive analysis
- Some techniques for improving the predictive power of a model
- Forecasting
- Optimization

## Analytics

Analytics starts from simply understanding more about the data you are going to work with, such as how many variables are character versus numeric, and attributes related to the variables such as length, number of missing values, and number of unique values for any given column. Advanced analytics includes data mining, forecasting, and/or optimization. Data mining involves both descriptive analytics and predictive analytics, which can be used to segment entities into like groups, describing characteristics of groups and providing likelihood scores from 0 to 100% of an event or type of behavior for individual entities being analyzed. Forecasting tends to use a different set of mathematical algorithms to help determine the number of entities that will be needed within some future time range and/or when an event may occur in the future with a confidence rating between 0 to 100% on the results.

Optimization provides algorithms that help determine the maximum or minimum values of complex situations, taking into account limited resources and the business and feasibility constraints associated with the particular problem. At a high level, these three areas of analysis provide descriptive, predictive, and prescriptive information to help us make better decisions based on data-driven information.

It is very important to clarify the meanings of words when working with different organizations, departments, and customers, because people sometimes use one word that means something specific to their business but it differs slightly from the meaning in the analytics or data science domain. A simple example of this is when people interchange or swap the words **predictive analytics** and **forecasting**. This is very common since it is easy to understand how forecasting a future value or event could be seen as providing a prediction. However, with analytics, the data, the type of data needed, and the form in which it needs to be stored are slightly different between data mining and forecasting. Learning how to listen and ask questions is very important in becoming an effective data scientist. Running analytics is sometimes the easiest part of the overall project because defining the problem correctly and getting the necessary data in the right form typically takes up to 80% of the overall work on any project, especially any analytics-based project.

The SAS® University Edition provides a programmer with capabilities that fall into all three of these advanced analytic areas. BASE and SAS/STAT provides data mining capabilities, SAS/ETS provides forecasting capabilities, and SAS/IML through the use of PROC IML offers some optimization capabilities. These are powerful analytic tools in their own right and serve as fundamental underlying pieces of several other SAS solutions built on top of these, such as **SAS Enterprise Miner**, **SAS Forecast Server**, and **SAS Factory Miner**.

# Descriptive and predictive analysis

The majority of the PROCs the reader has used in the previous chapters were BASE SAS procedures. BASE SAS provides capabilities within the descriptive analytics area, as can be seen using PROC MEANS or SUMMARY, in addition BASE SAS includes these three statistical focused procedures:

- *PROC FREQ: This produces one-way to n-way frequency and contingency (crosstabulation) tables*
- *PROC CORR: This computes Pearson correlation coefficients, three non-parametric measures of association, polyserial correlation coefficients, and the probabilities associated with these statistics*
- *PROC UNIVARIATE: Descriptive statistics based on moments (including skewness and kurtosis), quantiles or percentiles (such as median), frequency tables, and extreme values*

*SAS® 9.4 Programming Documentation / Base SAS Procedures Guide: Statistical Procedures*
(`http://documentation.sas.com/?cdcId=pgmsascdccdcVersion=9.4_3.2docsetId=`
`procstatdocs`).

To start predictive analysis, SAS/STAT, which is part of the SAS® University Edition, is needed. SAS/STAT is just the tip of the iceberg for performing predictive analysis with SAS.

# Descriptive analysis

The following are some examples of descriptive analysis. Let us take a look at each one in detail.

### PROC FREQ

How many males versus females are in a particular table, say SASHELP.CLASS? PROC FREQ can be used to easily find the answer to this type of question. Type the following code in a SAS Studio program section and submit it:

```
proc freq data=sashelp.class;
    tables sex;
quit;
```

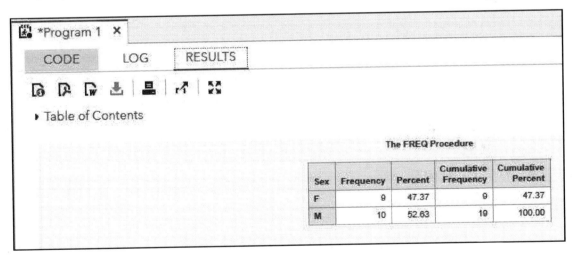

Figure 4.1: PROC FREQ example output

If you remove the tables statement, then, by default, PROC FREQ produces a one-frequency table for all the variables within the dataset.

## PROC CORR

Are the height and weight of a fish related to each other, and do their lengths have any impact on this relationship if it exists? PROC CORR can be used to determine this. In these examples, the plots option will be used to provide more insights by producing an additional graphic plot output along with the statistical results. Type the following code in a SAS Studio program section and submit it:

```
proc corr data=sashelp.fish plots=matrix(histogram);
    var height weight length1 length2 length3;
quit;
```

The CORR Procedure

| 5 Variables: | Height Weight Length1 Length2 Length3 |
|---|---|

### Simple Statistics

| Variable | N | Mean | Std Dev | Sum | Minimum | Maximum |
|---|---|---|---|---|---|---|
| Height | 159 | 8.97099 | 4.28621 | 1426 | 1.72840 | 18.95700 |
| Weight | 158 | 398.69557 | 359.08620 | 62994 | 0 | 1650 |
| Length1 | 159 | 26.24717 | 9.99644 | 4173 | 7.50000 | 59.00000 |
| Length2 | 159 | 28.41572 | 10.71633 | 4518 | 8.40000 | 63.40000 |
| Length3 | 159 | 31.22704 | 11.61025 | 4965 | 8.80000 | 68.00000 |

### Pearson Correlation Coefficients
### Prob > |r| under H0: Rho=0
### Number of Observations

| | Height | Weight | Length1 | Length2 | Length3 |
|---|---|---|---|---|---|
| **Height** | 1.00000 | 0.72869 | 0.62538 | 0.64044 | 0.70341 |
| | | <.0001 | <.0001 | <.0001 | <.0001 |
| | 159 | 158 | 159 | 159 | 159 |
| **Weight** | 0.72869 | 1.00000 | 0.91644 | 0.91937 | 0.92447 |
| | <.0001 | | <.0001 | <.0001 | <.0001 |
| | 158 | 158 | 158 | 158 | 158 |
| **Length1** | 0.62538 | 0.91644 | 1.00000 | 0.99952 | 0.99203 |
| | <.0001 | <.0001 | | <.0001 | <.0001 |
| | 159 | 158 | 159 | 159 | 159 |
| **Length2** | 0.64044 | 0.91937 | 0.99952 | 1.00000 | 0.99410 |
| | <.0001 | <.0001 | <.0001 | | <.0001 |
| | 159 | 158 | 159 | 159 | 159 |
| **Length3** | 0.70341 | 0.92447 | 0.99203 | 0.99410 | 1.00000 |
| | <.0001 | <.0001 | <.0001 | <.0001 | |
| | 159 | 158 | 159 | 159 | 159 |

Figure 4.2: PROC CORR statistics table output

The simple statistics table provides the descriptive univariate statistics for all five variables listed in the `var` statement. An insight regarding a very minor data quality issue can be seen in this table—one of the `159` observations in this dataset is missing a value for `weight`. The higher the Pearson correlation coefficient for a pair of variables (which means closer to `1.0`), the stronger the relationship between the variables. While `height` and `weight` do have a strong relationship, it is interesting to note that the relationships of `weight` to all three length variables are stronger than the relationships of `height` to all three length variables:

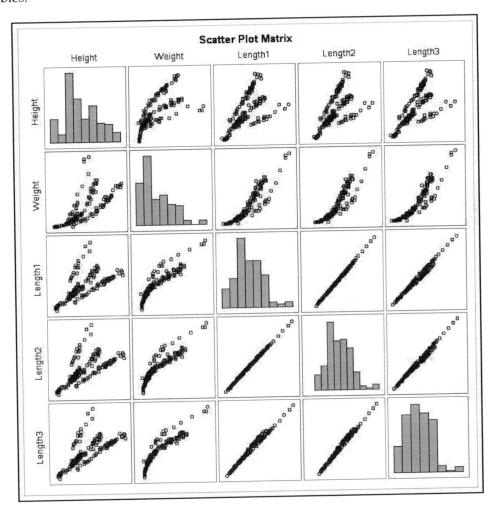

Figure 4.3: PROC CORR matrix plot output

In this next example, the code is still searching for a relationship between `height` and `weight`. However, now the relationship is being adjusted for the effect of the partial variables for which the three length variables have been assigned. Instead of requesting a `matrix` plot, the code requests a `scatter` plot with three different prediction ellipses. Type the following code in a SAS Studio program section and submit it:

```
proc corr data=sashelp.fish plots=scatter(alpha=.15 .25 .35);
    var height weight;
    partial length1 length2 length3;
quit;
```

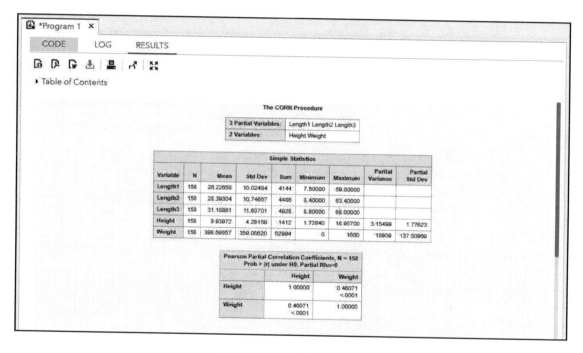

Figure 4.4: PROC CORR statistics table output

The results indicate that the partial relationship between `height` and `weight` is weaker than the unpartialled one; $0.46071$ is less than $0.72869$. However, both relationships are statistically relevant since both have p-values of $<.0001$. The smaller the p-value becomes, the more statistically relevant the variable is to what is being analyzed:

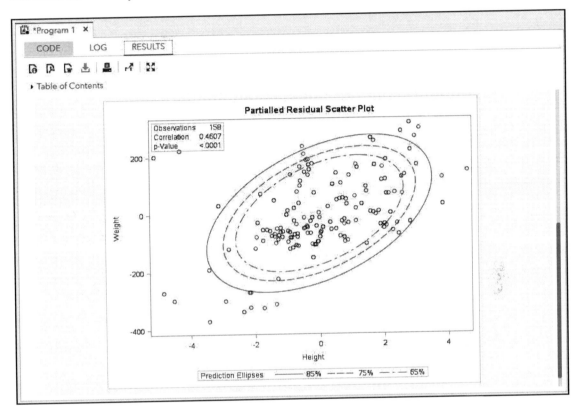

Figure 4.5: PROC CORR scatter plots with prediction ellipses

 Prediction ellipses are regions used to predict an observation based on values of the associated population. This particular code requests three prediction ellipses, each of which contains a specified percentage of the population, in this case, 85%, 75%, and 65%.

Change the `plots` option to the following, and submit the code:

```
proc corr data=sashelp.fish plots=scatter(ellipse=confidence alpha=.10
.05);
   var height weight;
   partial length1 length2 length3;
quit;
```

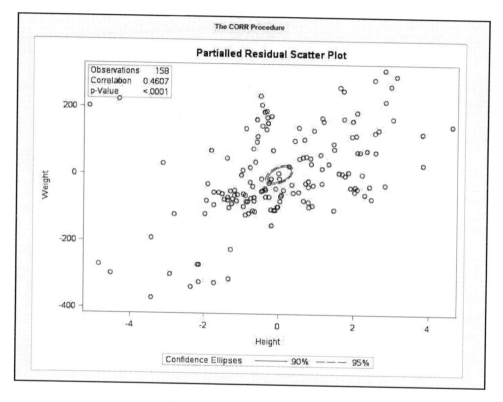

Figure 4.6: PROC CORR confidence ellipses output

A confidence ellipse provides an estimate range for the population's mean associated with a level of confidence in that range. In this example, there are two ellipse ranges, one at a 90% confidence level and one at a 95% confidence level.

If the relationships between variables are not linear, or there are a lot of outliers in the data being analyzed, the correlation coefficient might incorrectly estimate the strength of the relationship. Therefore, visualizing the data through these types of plots enables an analyst to verify the linear relationship and spot potential outliers.

# PROC UNIVARIATE

Some of the output associated with PROC UNIVARIATE was seen in the simple statistics table in the output associated with the PROC CORR examples in the previous section.

Type the following code in a SAS Studio program section and submit it:

```
proc univariate data=sashelp.fish;
quit;
```

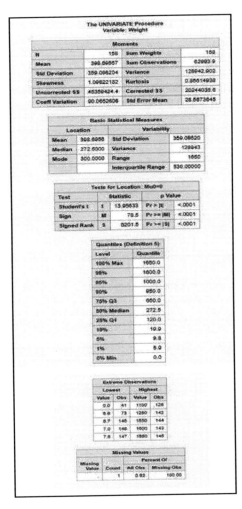

Figure 4.7: PROC UNIVARIATE output

By running PROC UNIVARIATE on an entire table, the applicable variable within that data will have the descriptive statistics seen in *Figure 4.7.*

An analyst can control which tables show up in the results by using certain **Output Delivery System (ODS)** statements along with procedures. ODS is another part of BASE SAS that helps produce output and graphics in a variety of different formats. The reader will learn more about ODS in Chapter 5, *Reporting with SAS® Software*.

For example, if an analyst is only interested in the extreme observations of all the variables within a table, they can limit the PROC UNIVARIATE output to only the extreme observations table. Type this code in a SAS Studio program section and submit it:

```
title "Extreme Observations in SASHELP.FISH";
ods select ExtremeObs;
proc univariate data=sashelp.fish;
quit;
```

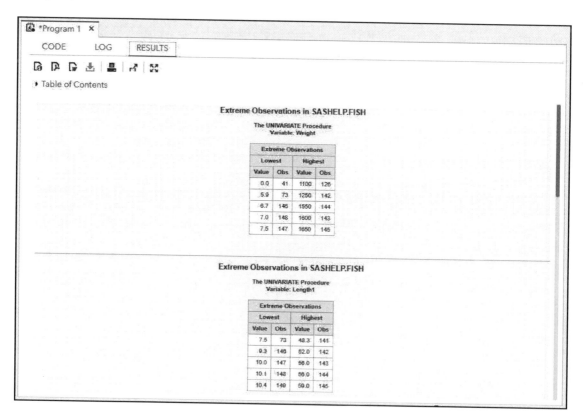

Figure 4.8: PROC UNIVARIATE with ODS output

# Predictive analysis

*SAS/STAT provides more than 90 procedures for performing statistical analyses and is constantly being updated with the newest proven methods and techniques. Some of the analyses that SAS/STAT provides include variance, categorical data analysis, cluster analysis, multiple imputation, multivariate analysis, non-parametric analysis, power and sample size computations, psychometric analysis, regression, survey data analysis, and survival analysis, SAS/STAT® 14.2 / SAS/STAT User's Guide - Introduction* (`http://documentation.sas.com/?cdcId=statcdccdcVersion=14.2docsetId=statugdocsetTarget=statug_intro_toc.htmlocale=enshowBanner=yes`).

It is outside the scope of this book to attempt to teach statistical analysis in depth; nor is it our intent to provide examples for every type of analysis capable within SAS or even within the SAS® University Edition. However, the reader will learn some analysis and become aware of the depth and breadth of learning that SAS offers them for their career. For more in-depth examples associated with SAS/STAT procedures, a sample library is available within SAS help or at this location on SAS's `http://support.sas.com` website `http://support.sas.com/documentation/onlinedoc/stat/ex_code/index.html`.

## Regression analysis

Regression analysis is one of the earliest predictive techniques most people learn because it can be applied across a wide variety of problems dealing with data that is related in linear and non-linear ways. Linear data is one of the easier use cases, and as such PROC REG is a well-known and often-used procedure to help predict likely outcomes before they happen.

*The* REG *procedure provides extensive capabilities for fitting linear regression models that involve individual numeric independent variables. Many other procedures can also fit regression models, but they focus on more specialized forms of regression, such as robust regression, generalized linear regression, nonlinear regression, non-parametric regression, quantile regression, regression modeling of survey data, regression modeling of survival data, and regression modeling of transformed variables. The SAS/STAT procedures that can fit regression models include the* ADAPTIVEREG, CATMOD, GAM, GENMOD, GLIMMIX, GLM, GLMSELECT, LIFEREG, LOESS, LOGISTIC, MIXED, NLIN, NLMIXED, ORTHOREG, PHREG, PLS, PROBIT, QUANTREG, QUANTSELECT, REG, ROBUSTREG, RSREG, SURVEYLOGISTIC, SURVEYPHREG, SURVEYREG, TPSPLINE, *and* TRANSREG *procedures. Several procedures in SAS/ETS software also fit regression models.*

*SAS/STAT® 14.2 / SAS/STAT User's Guide - Introduction to Regression Procedures - Overview: Regression Procedures* (http://documentation.sas.com/?cdcId=statcdccdcVersion=14.2 docsetId=statugdocsetTarget=statug_introreg_sect001.htmlocale=enshowBanner=yes).

Regression analysis attempts to model the relationship between a response or output variable and a set of input variables. The response is considered the target variable or the variable that one is trying to predict, while the rest of the input variables make up parameters used as input into the algorithm. They are used to derive the predicted value for the response variable.

## PROC REG

One of the easiest ways to determine if regression analysis is applicable to helping you answer a question is if the type of question being asked has only two answers. For example, should a bank lend an applicant money? Yes or no? This is known as a **binary response**, and as such, regression analysis can be applied to help determine the answer. In the following example, the reader will use the SASHELP.BASEBALL dataset to create a regression model to predict the value of a baseball player's salary.

*The SASHELP.BASEBALL dataset contains salary and performance information for Major League Baseball players who played at least one game in both the 1986 and 1987 seasons, excluding pitchers. The salaries (Sports Illustrated, April 20, 1987) are for the 1987 season and the performance measures are from 1986 (Collier Books, The 1987 Baseball Encyclopedia Update). SAS/STAT® 14.2 / SAS/STAT User's Guide - Example 99: Modeling Salaries of Major League Baseball Players* (http://documentation.sas.com/?cdcId=statcdccdcVersion=14.2docsetId=statug docsetTarget=statug_reg_examples01.htmlocale=enshowBanner=yes).

Let's first use PROC UNIVARIATE to learn something about this baseball data by submitting the following code:

```
proc univariate data=sashelp.baseball;
quit;
```

While reviewing the results of the output, the reader will notice that the variance associated with logSalary, 0.79066, is much less than the variance associated with the actual target variable Salary, 203508. In this case, it makes better sense to attempt to predict the logSalary value of a player instead of Salary.

Write the following code in a SAS Studio program section and submit it:

```
proc reg data=sashelp.baseball;
   id name team league;
   model logSalary = nAtBat nHits nHome nRuns nRBI YrMajor CrAtBat
                     CrHits CrHome CrRuns CrRbi;
quit;
```

The REG Procedure
Model: MODEL1
Dependent Variable: logSalary Log Salary

| Number of Observations Read | 322 |
|---|---|
| Number of Observations Used | 263 |
| Number of Observations with Missing Values | 59 |

### Analysis of Variance

| Source | DF | Sum of Squares | Mean Square | F Value | Pr > F |
|---|---|---|---|---|---|
| Model | 11 | 119.48586 | 10.86235 | 31.10 | <.0001 |
| Error | 251 | 87.66787 | 0.34927 | | |
| Corrected Total | 262 | 207.15373 | | | |

| Root MSE | 0.59099 | R-Square | 0.5768 |
|---|---|---|---|
| Dependent Mean | 5.92722 | Adj R-Sq | 0.5583 |
| Coeff Var | 9.97085 | | |

### Parameter Estimates

| Variable | Label | DF | Parameter Estimate | Standard Error | t Value | Pr > \|t\| |
|---|---|---|---|---|---|---|
| Intercept | Intercept | 1 | 4.29479 | 0.15701 | 27.35 | <.0001 |
| nAtBat | Times at Bat in 1986 | 1 | -0.00107 | 0.00108 | -1.00 | 0.3193 |
| nHits | Hits in 1986 | 1 | 0.00866 | 0.00410 | 2.11 | 0.0355 |
| nHome | Home Runs in 1986 | 1 | -0.00116 | 0.01093 | -0.11 | 0.9156 |
| nRuns | Runs in 1986 | 1 | 0.00538 | 0.00487 | 1.10 | 0.2704 |
| nRBI | RBIs in 1986 | 1 | 0.00228 | 0.00471 | 0.48 | 0.6292 |
| YrMajor | Years in the Major Leagues | 1 | 0.07297 | 0.02295 | 3.18 | 0.0017 |
| CrAtBat | Career Times at Bat | 1 | -0.00005186 | 0.00022077 | -0.23 | 0.8145 |
| CrHits | Career Hits | 1 | 0.00029704 | 0.00101 | 0.29 | 0.7687 |
| CrHome | Career Home Runs | 1 | 0.00033922 | 0.00287 | 0.12 | 0.9060 |
| CrRuns | Career Runs | 1 | 0.00025429 | 0.00105 | 0.24 | 0.8086 |
| CrRbi | Career RBIs | 1 | -0.00003844 | 0.00122 | -0.03 | 0.9750 |

Figure 4.9: PROC REG output

Notice that there are 59 observations as specified in the first output table with at least one of the input variables with missing values; as such those are not used in the development of the regression model. The **Root Mean Squared Error (RMSE)** and R-square are statistics that typically inform the analyst how good the model is in predicting the target. These range from *0* to *1.0* with higher values typically indicating a better model. The higher the R-squared values typically indicate a better performing model but sometimes conditions or the data used to train the model over-fit and don't represent the true value of the prediction power of that particular model.

Over-fitting can happen when an analyst doesn't have enough real-life data and chooses data or a sample of data that over-presents the target event, and therefore it will produce a poor performing model when using real-world data as input.

Since several of the input values appear to have little predictive power on the target, an analyst may decide to drop these variables, thereby reducing the need for that information to make a decent prediction. In this case, it appears we only need to use four input variables YrMajor, nHits, nRuns, and nAtBat. Modify the code as follows and submit it again:

```
proc reg data=sashelp.baseball;
    id name team league;
    model logSalary = YrMajor nHits nRuns nAtBat;
quit;
```

The p-value associated with each of the input variables provides the analyst with an insight into which variables have the biggest impact on helping to predict the target variable. In this case, the smaller the value, the higher the predictive value of the input variable.

Both the RMSE and R-square values for this second model are slightly lower than the original. However, the adjusted R-square value is slightly higher. In this case, an analyst may chose to use the second model since it requires much less data and provides basically the same predictive power. Prior to accepting any model, an analyst should determine whether there are a few observations that may be over-influencing the results by investigating the influence and fit diagnostics. The default output from PROC REG provides this type of visual insight:

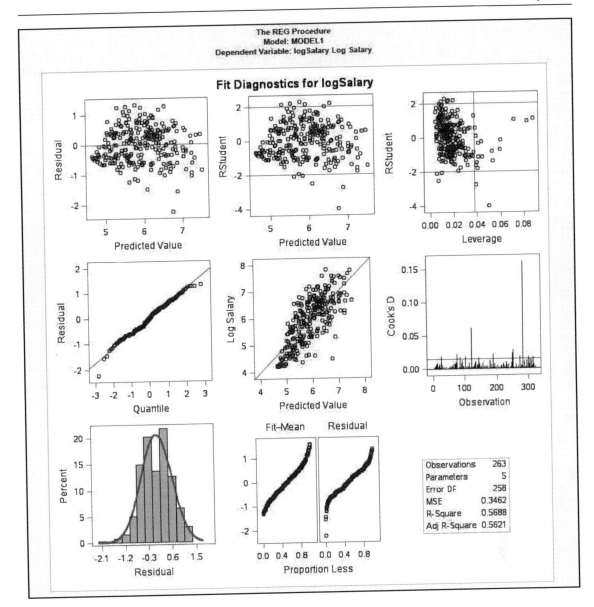

Figure 4.10: PROC REQ fit diagnostics

The top-right corner plot, showing the externally studentized residuals (RStudent) by leverage values, shows that there are a few observations with high leverage that may be overly influencing the fit produced. In order to investigate this further, we will add a `plots` statement to our PROC REG to produce a labeled version of this plot.

Type the following code in a SAS Studio program section and submit:

```
proc reg data=sashelp.baseball
    plots(only label)=(RStudentByLeverage);
    id name team league;
    model logSalary = YrMajor nHits nRuns nAtBat;
quit;
```

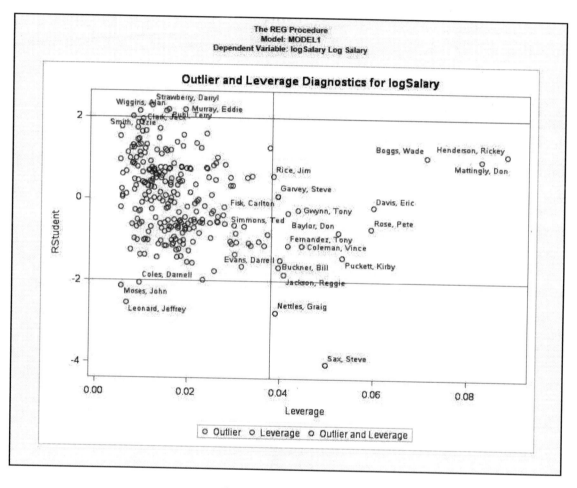

Figure 4.11: PROC REG labeled output

Sure enough, there are three to five individuals whose input variables may have excessive influence on fitting this model. Let's remove those points and see if the model improves. Type this code in a SAS Studio program section and submit it:

```
proc reg data=sashelp.baseball plots=(residuals(smooth));
    where name NOT IN ("Mattingly, Don", "Henderson, Rickey",
                        "Boggs, Wade", "Davis, Eric", "Rose, Pete");
    id name team league;
    model logSalary = YrMajor nHits nRuns nAtBat;
quit;
```

This change, in itself, has not improved the model but actually made the model worse as can be seen by the R-square, `0.5592`. However, the plots `residuals(smooth)` option gives some insights as it pertains to `YrMajor`; players at the beginning and the end of their careers tend to be paid less compared to others, as can be seen in *Figure 4.12*:

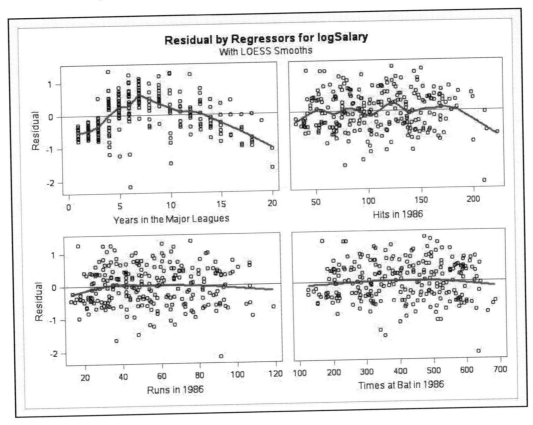

Figure 4.12: PROC REG smoothed residual plots

In order to address this lack of fit, an analyst can use polynomials of degree two for this variable, `YrMajor`. Type the following code in a SAS Studio program section and submit it:

```
data work.baseball;
   set sashelp.baseball;
   where name NOT IN ("Mattingly, Don", "Henderson, Rickey",
                      "Boggs, Wade", "Davis, Eric", "Rose, Pete");
   YrMajor2 = YrMajor*YrMajor;
run;

proc reg data=work.baseball;
   id name team league;
   model logSalary = YrMajor YrMajor2 nHits nRuns nAtBat;
quit;
```

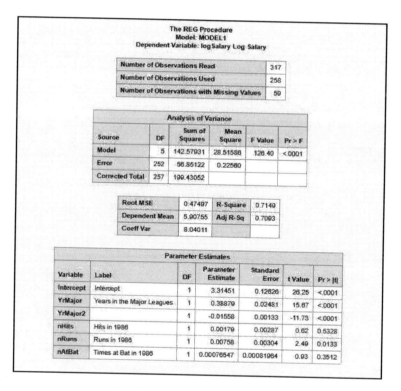

Figure 4.13: PROC REG output showing improvement

After removing some outliers and adjusting for the `YrMajor` variable, the model's predictive power has improved significantly as can be seen in the much improved R-square value of 0.7149.

# Forecasting analysis

Forecasting always involves the use of time series data. SAS/ETS is the foundation tool within the SAS system that focuses on this type of analysis.

*Major uses of SAS/ETS procedures are economic analysis, forecasting, economic and financial modeling, time series analysis, financial reporting, and manipulation of time series data. Although SAS/ETS software is most closely associated with business, finance, and economics, time series data also arise in many other fields. SAS/ETS software is useful whenever time dependencies, simultaneous relationships, or dynamic processes complicate data analysis. SAS/ETS® 14.2 / SAS/ETS User's Guide - Introduction: Uses of SAS/ETS Software* (`http://documentation.sas.com/?cdcId=etscdccdcVersion=14.2docsetId=etsugdocsetTarget=etsug_intro_sect002.htmlocale=enshowBanner=yes`).

For example, in the medical field, forecasting can be used to help improve medicine compliance with patients, or provide load forecasting for utilities.

Sometimes, the times series data that an analyst has access to may be in a time interval that isn't necessarily the most useful interval from a business perspective. One of the unique features of SAS/ETS is PROC EXPAND, which enables an analyst to change the time interval on a series of data to a different interval that can provide more valuable information to decision makers. It can also be used to interpret missing values without changing the time interval. Unfortunately, the limited version of SAS/ETS in the SAS® University Edition does not contain PROC EXPAND. However, it does contain PROC TIMEDATA, which will be used in the next exercise.

## PROC TIMEDATA

*The TIMEDATA procedure analyzes time-stamped transactional data with respect to time and accumulates the data into a time series format. SAS/ETS® 14.2 / SAS/ETS User's Guide - Overview: The TIMEDATA Procedure* (`http://documentation.sas.com/?cdcId=etscdccdcVersion=14.2docsetId=etsugdocsetTarget=etsug_timedata_overview.htmlocale=en`).

It would be great if all the data you wanted to analyze were in the format you needed it to be. However, as we all know, that is not the case, especially for data on which you want to run analytics. Even if an analyst has one set of data in the time interval they want to work in, there will most likely be other data sources the analyst will want to combine with the original data. More than likely the other data will not be in the same time series as the original data; as such, PROC TIMEDATA can be used to convert data to a specific time series interval.

In the following example, the datasets SASHELP.CITIDAY and SASHELP.CITIWK will be used along with PROC TIMEDATA to easily convert a subset of the daily data to weekly data for some stock market data from 1988 and 1989. Type the following code into a SAS Studio program section and submit it:

```
data work.weekly;
   set sashelp.citiwk;
   where year(date) > year('31dec1987'd) and
         year(date) < year('01jan1990'd);
   keep date wspca;
run;

data work.daily;
   set sashelp.citiday;
   where year(date) > year('31dec1987'd) and
         year(date) < year('01jan1990'd);
   keep date snydjcm;
run;

proc print data=work.daily;
quit;

proc timedata data=work.daily out=tempwk;
   id date interval=week
           accumulate=median
           setmiss=0;
   var snydjcm;
quit;

proc print data=work.tempwk;
quit;
```

Submitting the above code will produce the following outputs.

| Obs | DATE | SNYDJCM |
|-----|-----------|---------|
| 1 | 01JAN1988 | . |
| 2 | 04JAN1988 | 740.20 |
| 3 | 05JAN1988 | 747.38 |
| 4 | 06JAN1988 | 750.40 |
| 5 | 07JAN1988 | 757.04 |
| 6 | 08JAN1988 | 711.36 |
| 7 | 11JAN1988 | 721.92 |
| 8 | 12JAN1988 | 715.20 |
| 9 | 13JAN1988 | 713.59 |
| 10 | 14JAN1988 | 708.35 |
| 11 | 15JAN1988 | 721.81 |
| 12 | 18JAN1988 | 724.43 |
| 13 | 19JAN1988 | 718.29 |
| 14 | 20JAN1988 | 701.59 |
| 15 | 21JAN1988 | 700.70 |
| 16 | 22JAN1988 | 709.46 |
| 17 | 25JAN1988 | 721.52 |
| 18 | 26JAN1988 | 714.05 |
| 19 | 27JAN1988 | 712.94 |
| 20 | 28JAN1988 | 722.49 |
| 21 | 29JAN1988 | 731.40 |
| 22 | 01FEB1988 | 731.40 |
| 23 | 02FEB1988 | 727.66 |
| 24 | 03FEB1988 | 731.22 |

Figure 4.14: Daily data prior to using PROC TIMEDATA

| Obs | DATE | SNYDJCM |
|---|---|---|
| 1 | Sun, 27 Dec 1987 | 0.00 |
| 2 | Sun, 3 Jan 1988 | 747.38 |
| 3 | Sun, 10 Jan 1988 | 715.20 |
| 4 | Sun, 17 Jan 1988 | 709.46 |
| 5 | Sun, 24 Jan 1988 | 721.52 |
| 6 | Sun, 31 Jan 1988 | 727.66 |
| 7 | Sun, 7 Feb 1988 | 731.15 |
| 8 | Sun, 14 Feb 1988 | 744.71 |
| 9 | Sun, 21 Feb 1988 | 759.10 |
| 10 | Sun, 28 Feb 1988 | 769.76 |
| 11 | Sun, 6 Mar 1988 | 767.96 |
| 12 | Sun, 13 Mar 1988 | 774.96 |
| 13 | Sun, 20 Mar 1988 | 776.45 |
| 14 | Sun, 27 Mar 1988 | 749.43 |
| 15 | Sun, 3 Apr 1988 | 771.62 |
| 16 | Sun, 10 Apr 1988 | 780.96 |
| 17 | Sun, 17 Apr 1988 | 745.24 |
| 18 | Sun, 24 Apr 1988 | 758.21 |
| 19 | Sun, 1 May 1988 | 758.28 |
| 20 | Sun, 8 May 1988 | 739.64 |
| 21 | Sun, 15 May 1988 | 725.74 |
| 22 | Sun, 22 May 1988 | 727.29 |
| 23 | Sun, 29 May 1988 | 765.67 |
| 24 | Sun, 5 Jun 1988 | 780.88 |

Figure 4.15: Result of converting daily data to weekly using PROC TIMEDATA

Now that the subset of data that was in a daily time series has been converted to weekly, it can easily be combined with the `work.weekly` dataset in order to do a further time series analysis. Type this code in a SAS Studio program window and submit it:

```
data work.wkcombined;
   merge work.weekly work.tempwk;
   by date;
run;

proc print data=work.wkcombined;
quit;
```

Submitting the above code will produce this output.

| Obs | DATE | WSPCA | SNYDJCM |
|---|---|---|---|
| 1 | Sun, 27 Dec 87 | . | 0.00 |
| 2 | Sun, 3 Jan 88 | 10.5000 | 747.38 |
| 3 | Sun, 10 Jan 88 | 10.1000 | 715.20 |
| 4 | Sun, 17 Jan 88 | 9.9000 | 709.46 |
| 5 | Sun, 24 Jan 88 | 9.7100 | 721.52 |
| 6 | Sun, 31 Jan 88 | 9.8500 | 727.66 |
| 7 | Sun, 7 Feb 88 | 10.0000 | 731.15 |
| 8 | Sun, 14 Feb 88 | 9.8600 | 744.71 |
| 9 | Sun, 21 Feb 88 | 9.8500 | 759.10 |
| 10 | Sun, 28 Feb 88 | 10.0300 | 769.76 |
| 11 | Sun, 6 Mar 88 | 10.0500 | 767.95 |
| 12 | Sun, 13 Mar 88 | 10.2400 | 774.96 |
| 13 | Sun, 20 Mar 88 | 10.1900 | 776.45 |
| 14 | Sun, 27 Mar 88 | 10.2200 | 749.43 |
| 15 | Sun, 3 Apr 88 | 10.1100 | 771.62 |
| 16 | Sun, 10 Apr 88 | 10.4000 | 780.96 |
| 17 | Sun, 17 Apr 88 | 10.4000 | 745.24 |
| 18 | Sun, 24 Apr 88 | 10.4600 | 758.21 |
| 19 | Sun, 1 May 88 | 10.5000 | 758.28 |
| 20 | Sun, 8 May 88 | 10.6100 | 739.64 |
| 21 | Sun, 15 May 88 | 10.6100 | 725.74 |
| 22 | Sun, 22 May 88 | 10.5100 | 727.29 |
| 23 | Sun, 29 May 88 | 10.4300 | 765.67 |
| 24 | Sun, 5 Jun 88 | 10.2000 | 780.88 |

Figure 4.16: Resulting WORK.WKCOMIBINED

Now we have both of these variables (WSPCA, which is the standard and poor's weekly bond yield, and SNYDJCM, which is the New York Dow Jones Composite) in one table with a weekly time series interval; whereas previously, the data was stored in two tables and the SNYDJCM had been stored with a daily time series interval. Now, the reader will use PROC ARIMA to do a basic forecast using WORK.WKCOMBINED.

## PROC ARIMA

*The ARIMA procedure analyzes and forecasts equally spaced univariate time series data, transfer function data, and intervention data by using the autoregressive integrated moving-average (ARIMA) or autoregressive moving-average (ARMA) model. An ARIMA model predicts a value in a response time series as a linear combination of its own past values, past errors (also called shocks or innovations), and current and past values of other time series. SAS/ETS® 14.2 / SAS/ETS User's Guide - Overview: The ARIMA Procedure* (http://documentation.sas.com/?cdcId=etscdc cdcVersion=14.2docsetId=etsugdocsetTarget=etsug_arima_overview.htmlocale=en showBanner=yes).

Type the following code in a SAS Studio program section and submit it:

```
proc arima data=work.wkcombined;
   identify var=wspca(1,12);
   estimate q=(1)(12) noint method=ml;
   forecast id=date interval=week;
quit;
```

This will produce the following outputs:

| Obs | Forecast | Std Error | 95% Confidence Limits | |
|---|---|---|---|---|
| | | | **Forecasts for variable WSPCA** | |
| 107 | 9.5456 | 0.1230 | 9.3045 | 9.7868 |
| 108 | 9.4744 | 0.1854 | 9.1111 | 9.8377 |
| 109 | 9.4406 | 0.2315 | 8.9870 | 9.8943 |
| 110 | 9.4345 | 0.2698 | 8.9056 | 9.9633 |
| 111 | 9.3689 | 0.3034 | 8.7744 | 9.9635 |
| 112 | 9.3878 | 0.3335 | 8.7341 | 10.0415 |
| 113 | 9.3945 | 0.3612 | 8.6865 | 10.1024 |
| 114 | 9.3722 | 0.3869 | 8.6140 | 10.1305 |
| 115 | 9.3922 | 0.4110 | 8.5867 | 10.1978 |
| 116 | 9.3645 | 0.4337 | 8.5144 | 10.2146 |
| 117 | 9.3822 | 0.4554 | 8.4898 | 10.2747 |
| 118 | 9.4111 | 0.4760 | 8.4782 | 10.3441 |
| 119 | 9.4229 | 0.4958 | 8.4511 | 10.3946 |
| 120 | 9.3516 | 0.5148 | 8.3426 | 10.3607 |
| 121 | 9.3179 | 0.5332 | 8.2728 | 10.3629 |
| 122 | 9.3117 | 0.5509 | 8.2319 | 10.3915 |
| 123 | 9.2462 | 0.5681 | 8.1326 | 10.3597 |
| 124 | 9.2650 | 0.5848 | 8.1188 | 10.4113 |
| 125 | 9.2717 | 0.6011 | 8.0937 | 10.4498 |
| 126 | 9.2495 | 0.6169 | 8.0405 | 10.4585 |
| 127 | 9.2695 | 0.6323 | 8.0303 | 10.5087 |
| 128 | 9.2417 | 0.6473 | 7.9730 | 10.5104 |
| 129 | 9.2595 | 0.6620 | 7.9620 | 10.5570 |
| 130 | 9.2884 | 0.6764 | 7.9627 | 10.6141 |

Figure 4.17A: Forecast results in table form

In addition to the table the code will also produce this graph:

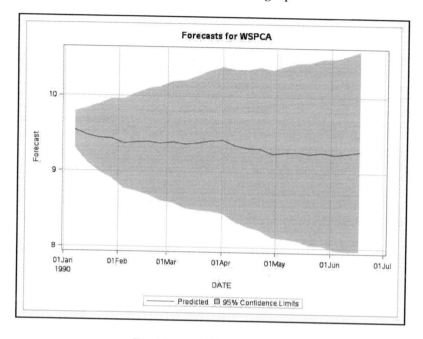

Figure 4.17: Forecast with 95% confidence limits

# Optimization analysis

While predictive analytics and forecasting deal with providing insights as to what will most likely happen in some time frame in the future, optimization provides guidance as to what outcomes are feasible given the resources available along, with rules or constraints that define the business process or situation. Optimization helps solve issues such as staffing requirements, resource allocation, most efficient routing/delivery, and the best mix of ingredients or sub-components to maximize the output of a particular product. While all analyses tend to be used for increase revenue or reduce costs, optimization in particular is used to maximize or minimize a target and show decision makers what is feasible given known inputs associated with a situation or process. A classic example of an optimization problem is determining the maximum number of parking spaces that can fit in a specific-sized space. At first, this may sound simple.

However, even this can get complex when taking into account the rules about the number of spaces desired for compact cars and regular cars, as well as any spaces for handicap and/or electrical cars. Although the algorithms behind optimization problems remain the same, the difficulty with optimization problems is that each one of them is unique because the rules or constraints differ from one problem to the next. The two main offerings of optimization capabilities within the SAS environment are SAS/OR, **Operations Research (OR)**, and SAS/IML, **Iteractive Matrix Language (IML)**. SAS/IML is available within the SAS® University Edition and will be used in the following hands-on exercise.

## SAS/IML

While the rest of the SAS system and most other programming languages or platforms work on tables of data, the fundamental object in SAS/IML is a data matrix. A matrix is a two-dimensional array of numeric or character values. SAS/IML makes it easier for an analyst to solve problems that require matrices such as linear algebra because it automatically takes care of the activities of memory allocation and dimensioning of matrices, which are necessary and would typically have to be done manually prior to the analysis part of the problem solving process. Once again, showing another way, the SAS platform allows an analyst to focus more of their time on doing the analysis than prepping the data or environment for the analysis.

## Interacting with the R programming language

R is a freely available open source language for performing statistical computing and graphics, and like SAS/IML, it provides a programmer with the ability to manipulate matrices and vectors. There are also a large number of user-contributed packages in R that implement specialized computations that may not be available in SAS so in 2009 SAS/IML introduced a feature to call R functions, and as of SAS/IML 9.22 this functionality was available in PROC IML. This book will briefly discuss this topic because the SAS® University Edition runs within a virtual machine and as such does not allow the user the access/permission required to install R on the server, which is necessary in order to make use of this feature. In addition, this is only one way SAS allows integration or use with other programming languages such as R. Since 2009, other ways of working with R and other open source languages like Python and Lua have been added to the SAS platform. The latest ways SAS integrates with other programming languges includes providing APIs for R, Python, and Lua.

The RLANG SAS system option can be checked to determine whether your SAS environment has been configured properly to interact with the R programming. It will return to the log a value of either NORLANG or RLANG. Type the following code in a SAS Studio program section and submit it:

```
proc options option=RLANG;
run;
```

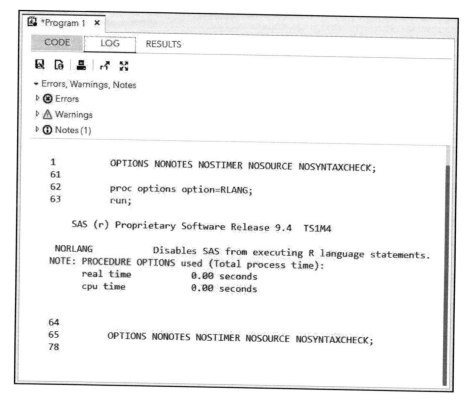

Figure 4.18: The value of the RLANG SAS system option in the SAS® University Edition

# PROC IML

Since the fundamental object in SAS/IML is a matrix, SAS/IML provides its own language designed to interact and process data within matrices, and as such it is out of scope for this book to do a deep dive into this particular part of the SAS platform. However, the following example will use PROC IML to solve the following manufacturing product mix type of problem. There are three machines: m1, m2, and m3. They are used to produce four products: p1, p2, p3, p4. The following table shows how many hours each machine must be used to produce one of each product:

| Product | m1 | m2 | m3 |
|---------|-----|-----|----|
| p1 | 2 | 1.5 | 3 |
| p2 | 1 | 2 | 1 |
| p3 | 2.5 | 1 | 2 |
| p4 | 3 | 2 | 1 |

Table 4.1: Hours necessary on each machine to produce 1 unit of each product

The weekly time in hours available for each machine is 3000, 2500, and 1500. Finally, the profit that each product produces is 4.25, 2.50, 3.00, and 4.00. Type the following code in a SAS Studio program section and submit it to find out the mix of these four products that will maximize the profit:

```
proc iml;
    names={'p1' 'p2' 'p3' 'p4'};
/* coefficients of the linear objective function: profits */
c = {4.25 2.50 3.00 4.00};
/* coefficients of the constraint equation: hours on machines */
A = { 2.0 1.0 2.5 3.0,
      1.5 2.0 1.0 2.0,
      3.0 1.0 2.0 1.0 };

/* right-hand side of constraint equation: hours on machines */
b = { 3000, 2500, 1500 };
/* operators: 'L' for <=, 'G' for >=, 'E' for = */
ops = { 'L', 'L', 'L' };

n=ncol(A); /* number of variables */
cntl = j(1,7,.); /* control vector */
cntl[1] = -1; /* 1 for minimum; -1 for maximum */
call lpsolve(rc, value, x, dual, redcost,
             c, A, b, cntl, ops);
```

```
print x[r=names L='Optimal Product Mix'];
print value[L='Maximum Profit'];
lhs = A*x;
Constraints = lhs || b;
print Constraints[r={"m1" "m2" "m3"}
                  c={"Actual" "Upper Bound"}
                  L="Time Constraints"];
```

Submitting the previous code will produce this result:

**Optimal Product Mix**

| p1 | 111.11111 |
|----|-----------|
| p2 | 361.11111 |
| p3 | 0 |
| p4 | 805.55556 |

**Maximum Profit**

| 4597.2222 |
|-----------|

**Time Constraints**

|    | Actual | Upper Bound |
|----|--------|-------------|
| m1 | 3000 | 3000 |
| m2 | 2500 | 2500 |
| m3 | 1500 | 1500 |

Figure 4.19: PROC IML optimization results

The optimal product mix, given the profit and machine constraints, is to produce 111 units of p1, 361 units of p2, no units of p3, and 805 units of p4. This will produce a profit of 4597.2222 and make maximum utilization of all three machines.

# Summary

You learned how to perform some descriptive analysis using the following BASE SAS statistical procedures: FREQ, CORR, and UNIVARIATE. You were also introduced to performing predictive analysis using PROC REG and learned some techniques used by data scientists to improve the predictive power of a model.

You learned how to prepare time series data for further analysis using PROC TIMEDATA and how to do a basic forecast using PROC ARIMA. You also learned a way in which SAS can work with the R programming language and how to check if their SAS environment is configured properly to allow this interaction to occur. Finally, you learned about optimization and performed an optimization analysis using PROC IML.

In the next chapter, you will be introduced to some of the capabilities within SAS to produce reports.

# 5

# Reporting with SAS® Software

In this chapter, we will cover the following topics:

- SAS Studio tasks and snippets that generate reports and graphs
- BASE procedures designed for reporting
- The **Output Display System (ODS)**
- How to make a user-defined snippet

## Reporting

Reporting is just one way to deploy the results of analytics. Other ways involve publishing scoring models into operational systems or enabling other systems to make API calls to make use of the analytics. This chapter will discuss the use of some BASE procedures used for reporting, and the use of the ODS, which is a part of BASE that produces output in a variety of different formats.

 SAS Studio provides default tasks for making basic graphs and will generate the code necessary to produce these graphs. By default, the output in SAS Studio will produce results in HTML5, PDF, and RTF. A user can change the default styles or output results in the preferences window for SAS Studio.

In the upper-right-hand corner of SAS Studio, left click the **More applications options** icon and select **Preferences** as follows:

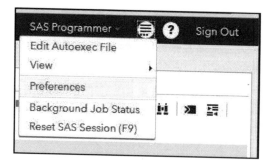

Figure 5.1: SAS Studio Preferences

Then, select **Results** to see the different options and styles associated with the three default outputs, **HTML5**, **PDF**, and **RTF**:

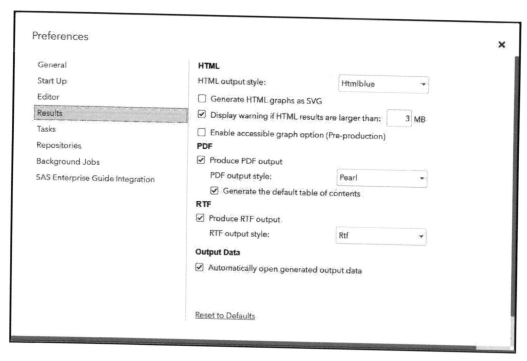

Figure 5.2: SAS Studio preferences results

# SAS Studio tasks and snippets that generate reports and graphs

One of the most basic reports any system can generate is a table that prints the columns and rows of a data table. SAS Studio provides the user with a task called the **List Data** task that prints this type of report. Expand the **Tasks and Utilities** section on the left-hand section of SAS Studio, then expand **Tasks** and **DATA** and double-click on the **List Data** task. When the program section on the right-hand side pops up, select SASHELP.FAILURE from the **DATA** drop-down list:

Figure 5.3: SAS Studio List Data task with SASHELP.FAILURE

Even for this basic type of report, SAS Studio brings up options that the user can change to impact the look of the report. Next to the **DATA** tab on the left-hand side of the **List Data** section, select the **OPTIONS** tab:

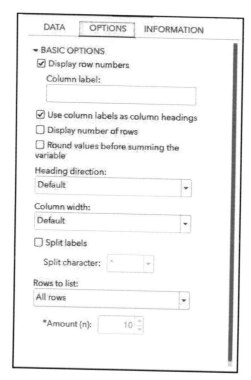

Figure 5.4: SAS Studio List Data task options

Check the box next to **Display row numbers** then change the value of the **Rows to list:** drop-down list from **All rows** to **First n rows**, leave the default **Amount(n):** as **10**, and submit this code to view the results:

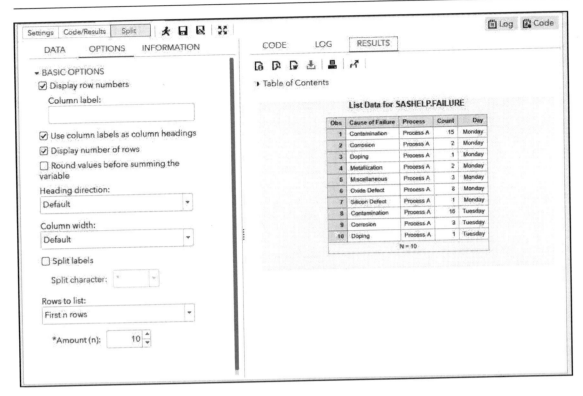

Figure 5.5: SAS Studio List Data task results

SAS Studio **Tasks** and **Snippets** for graphs both use the same underlying ODS-related procedures; however, snippets provide pre-written code with data and statements that a user can submit and get a resulting report on. **Tasks** provide the user with a template to fill in all the necessary values, such as a data table name, and to assign roles to columns in order to produce specific graphs on the data of their choice. In the following exercise, the reader will first use a graph snippet and view the result, and then use a graph task to produce the same result. This will show the user that if they are manually producing the same report on a regular basis, for example weekly or monthly, which they originally created using a built-in SAS Studio task, they can save time by taking the code generated by the task and saving it as a user-created snippet.

On the left side of SAS Studio, select the **Snippets** section and then expand **Snippets**, followed by **Graph**, and double-click on the **VBox Plot** snippet:

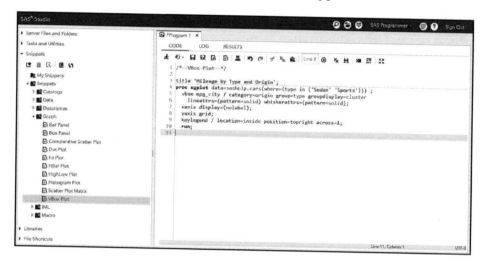

Figure 5.6: SAS Studio VBox Plot snippet

Submit this code by selecting the running man icon, which will produce the following result:

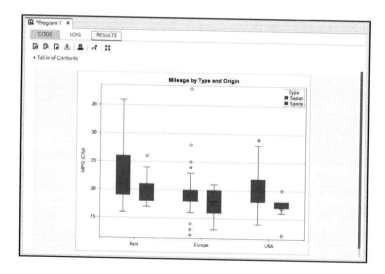

Figure 5.7: SAS Studio VBox Plot result

The reader will now be tasked, pun intended, with reproducing the same results using the SAS Studio **Box Plot** graph task. On the left-hand side of SAS Studio, select the **Tasks and Utilities** section and expand **Tasks**, followed by **Graph**, and double-click the **Box Plot** task. In the **DATA** drop-down box, select SASHELP.CARS:

Figure 5.8: SAS Studio Box Plot task

Notice that no code has been generated in the **CODE** section. Now do the following:

1. Select the + icon associated with the **Analysis variable: (1 item),** choose **MPG_City,** and select **OK.**
2. Select the + icon associated with the **Category variable: (1 item)** and choose **Origin,** and select **OK.**
3. Select the + icon associated with the **Group variable: (1 item)** and choose **Type,** and select **OK.**
4. Expand the **WHERE CLAUSE FILTER**, check the **Apply where clause** checkbox, and type in the following: type in ('Sedan','Sports').
5. Set the title to Mileage by Type and Origin.

6. Finally, select the **OPTIONS** tab, expand **LEGEND DETAILS,** and assign the **Legend location** to **Inside**:

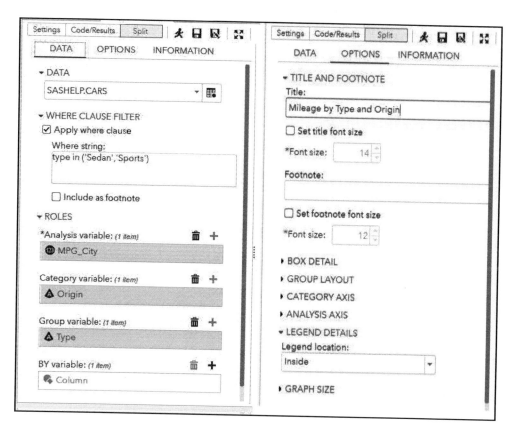

Figure 5.9: Box Plot data and OPTIONS settings

Submit this by selecting the running man icon and it will produce the same plot as the **VBox Plot** snippet did, as shown in *Figure 5.7*.

# BASE procedures designed for reporting

The chart and plot BASE procedures produce very basic results using ASCII character sets, which allow a user to produce charts and plots on a system that does not support graphics. The print procedure prints the columns and rows of a data table in basic table forms and has been used in some of the prior examples in this book. To produce more complex and customized tables that can include descriptive statistics for some or all of the data used in the report, a programmer can use the TABULATE procedure.

## TABULATE procedure examples

To produce a table that shows the revenues associated with four different electrical consumers, commercial, industrial, other, and residential, across multiple years, type the following code in a SAS Studio program section and submit it:

```
proc tabulate data=sashelp.electric;
    class customer year;
    var revenue;
    table year, revenue*customer;
quit;
```

| Year | Revenue ($B) Sum Customer | | | |
|---|---|---|---|---|
| | Commercial | Industrial | Other | Residential |
| 1994 | 63.40 | 48.07 | 6.69 | 84.55 |
| 1995 | 66.37 | 47.18 | 6.57 | 87.61 |
| 1996 | 67.83 | 47.54 | 6.74 | 90.50 |
| 1997 | 70.50 | 47.02 | 7.11 | 90.70 |
| 1998 | 72.58 | 47.05 | 6.86 | 93.36 |
| 1999 | 72.77 | 46.85 | 6.80 | 93.48 |
| 2000 | 78.41 | 49.37 | 7.18 | 98.21 |
| 2001 | 85.74 | 50.29 | 8.15 | 103.16 |
| 2002 | 87.12 | 48.34 | 7.12 | 106.83 |
| 2003 | 96.26 | 51.74 | 0.51 | 111.25 |
| 2004 | 100.55 | 53.48 | 0.52 | 115.58 |
| 2005 | 110.52 | 58.45 | 0.64 | 128.39 |

Figure 5.10: Proc TABULATE example 1 result

While this table looks fine, let's use some other statements with the TABULATE procedure to make a more complex table that also looks better. Type the following code in a SAS Studio program section and submit it:

```
proc tabulate data=sashelp.electric;
   class customer year;
   var revenue;
   table year all='Total for all years',
         revenue*(customer all='Total Revenue for
year'*[style=[background=yellow]])*f=dollar12.2;
quit;
```

| | Revenue ($B) | | | | |
| | Sum | | | | |
| | Customer | | | | Total Revenue for year |
| | Commercial | Industrial | Other | Residential | |
| Year | | | | | |
| 1994 | $63.40 | $48.07 | $6.69 | $84.55 | $202.71 |
| 1995 | $66.37 | $47.18 | $6.57 | $87.61 | $207.72 |
| 1996 | $67.83 | $47.54 | $6.74 | $90.50 | $212.61 |
| 1997 | $70.50 | $47.02 | $7.11 | $90.70 | $215.33 |
| 1998 | $72.58 | $47.05 | $6.86 | $93.36 | $219.85 |
| 1999 | $72.77 | $46.85 | $6.80 | $93.48 | $219.90 |
| 2000 | $78.41 | $49.37 | $7.18 | $98.21 | $233.16 |
| 2001 | $85.74 | $50.29 | $8.15 | $103.16 | $247.34 |
| 2002 | $87.12 | $48.34 | $7.12 | $106.83 | $249.41 |
| 2003 | $96.26 | $51.74 | $0.51 | $111.25 | $259.77 |
| 2004 | $100.55 | $53.48 | $0.52 | $115.58 | $270.12 |
| 2005 | $110.52 | $58.45 | $0.64 | $128.39 | $298.00 |
| Total for all years | $972.03 | $595.36 | $64.90 | $1,203.63 | $2,835.92 |

Figure 5.11: Proc TABULATE example 2 result

Notice how we didn't have to change the underlying data table to change the look and feel of the report, since the formatting and style statements only take effect during the generation of the report.

# REPORT procedure example

As described in the *SAS® 9.4 Programming Documentation / Base SAS Procedures Guide - Report Procedure Overview: REPORT procedure* (http://documentation.sas.com/?cdcId=pgmsascdc cdcVersion=9.4_3.2docsetId=procdocsetTarget=p1q3wfvkgh3br6n1b5jcho2njs3n.htm locale=en), *The REPORT procedure combines features of the PRINT, MEANS, and TABULATE procedures with features of the DATA step in a single report-writing tool that can produce a variety of reports.*

The most basic report generated by the REPORT procedure is a table listing report, just like the one produced by using the PRINT procedure. However, the REPORT procedure can produce detailed reports in which each row represents one observation per row, or it can produce summary reports in which each row can represent a summary or aggregation of more than one observation. In addition, summary lines can be added to both detail and summary reports. Summary lines summarize numeric data based on a set of detailed rows or all of the detailed rows.

Type the following code in a SAS Studio program section and submit it:

```
/* Define a user defined format in order to control the background color of
*/
/* the computed column difference within proc report code that follows.
*/
proc format;
    value predfmt low-<0='red'
    0-high='green';
run;

proc report data=sashelp.prdsal2;

    title 'Sales vs Predicted Sales by Year';
    column year country prodtype product actual predict difference;
    define year / group;
    define country / group;
    define prodtype / group;
    define product / group;
    define actual / analysis sum format=dollar14.2;
    define predict / analysis sum format=dollar14.2;
    define difference / 'Difference' computed format=dollar14.2
                        style(column)=[BACKGROUNDCOLOR=predfmt.];
    break after year / summarize page;
    compute Difference;
        Difference=actual.sum - predict.sum;
    endcomp;
    compute after year / style=[BACKGROUNDCOLOR=yellow];
        length text $ 40;
```

```
        if Difference < 0 then text='Overall sales were less than
    predicted.';
        else text='Overall sales beat the prediction!';
        line text $40.;
    endcomp;
run;
```

Notice how controlling the output as well as customizing the look makes it much easier to derive insights from the information than if the tables were in a more basic-looking output.

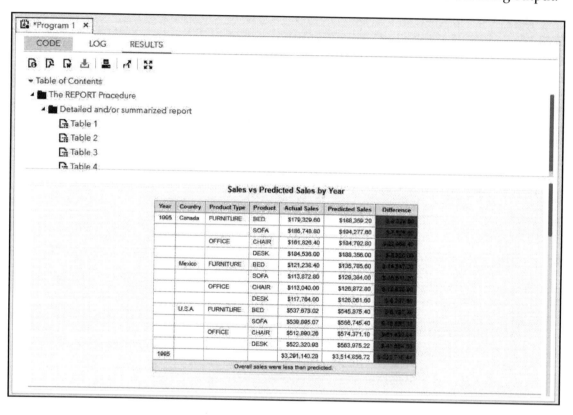

Figure 5.12: PROC REPORT example result

In this case, there is either a real problem with our ability to sell our products, or the process we use for predicting sales needs to be revised. There are only two instances, over all these years, for one product, in the United States that exceeded the predicted sales, which, due to the customization in the code, makes it very easy to see those highlighted green items, each of which was the **SOFA**, on table two and four of the output.

# The Output Delivery System

As described in the *SAS® 9.4 Programming Documentation / Getting Started with the SAS Output Delivery System: What is the Output Delivery System?* (`http://documentation.sas.com/?cdcId=pgmsascdccdcVersion=9.4_3.2docsetId=odsgsdocsetTarget=n17cfayv9ukj7kn10100lwysw5dm.htmllocale=en`) *The Output Delivery System (ODS) enables you to customize the content of your output, choose how your output is formatted, and customize the appearance of your output.* The ODS provides templates that define the structure of output for both SAS data step code and SAS procedures. Programmers can make use of these templates as is, or customize them and/or create new templates for their own use/reuse. The ODS also provides style templates that can be used as is, or once again be customized and/or create new style templates for their own use/reuse. When new ODS formats are added by SAS or by users, they become available for use with any pre-existing reports. The ODS saves users time and effort because it allows you to produce the same report in multiple formats during one execution of the code, so it's possible to produce a web-based, HTML-based version of a report while at the same time writing a PDF version that may be stored in an archive and in a PowerPoint format for a presentation. The ODS needs two components—the data component and the table template. These two components then make up what is known as the as the output object. The output object is what supports writing the output into all the other supported output formats, such as HTML, PDF, RTF, and so on.

By default, the ODS will write output into the user's current working directory; however, a programmer can write output to specific operating system directories/locations easily by specifying a path and filename when opening an ODS destination, for example:

```
ODS HTML file='somename.html';
```

Now, the next output SAS generates will be in HTML format and stored in the user's working directory, in a file named `somename.html`. If you wanted to store this output in `/dept/documents/projectx/somename.html`, then the programmer would use the following ODS statement:

```
ODS HTML file='/dept/documents/projectx/somename.html';
```

# ODS Tagsets

SAS supported output formats make use of tagsets, which are shipped with SAS. In addition, pre-production tagsets are sometimes available on `http://support.sas.com` to allow users access to formats being considered for official support in an upcoming release. One of the most popular tagsets is `EXCELXP`, which generates output in XML that can then be opened in Microsoft Excel 2002 and later, as well as with the **Calc spreadsheet** program from `http://OpenOffice.org`.

Here is a simple example of using the ODS and the `EXCELXP` tagset to create an XML file from the `SASHELP.CLASS` dataset. Type the following code into a SAS Studio program section and submit it:

```
ods tagsets.excelxp file="/folders/myfolders/sasuser.v94/class.xls"
style=statistical;

proc print data=sashelp.class;
run;

ods tagsets.excelxp close;
```

This will print an HTML result in SAS Studio and write out a `class.xls` file into your `sasuser.v94` directory. After submitting this code, expand the **Server Files and Folders** on the left side of SAS Studio, then expand **My Folders** and `sasuser.v94`. The `class.xls` file should be under this folder with the appropriate icon showing that it is a spreadsheet:

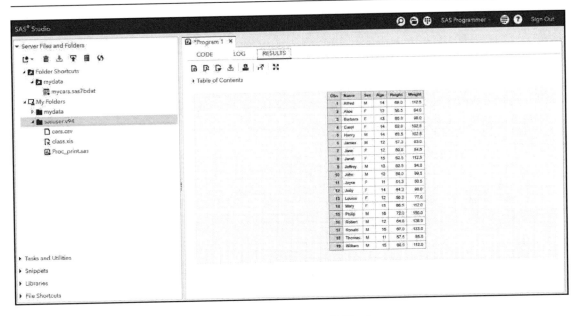

Figure 5.13: ODS with TAGSET EXCELXP result

# ODS trace

A programmer can use the ODS trace statement to see the number of objects a procedure or data step code produces as part of its default output. Type the following code in a SAS Studio program section and submit it:

```
ods trace on / label;
proc univariate data=sashelp.class;
quit;
ods trace off;
```

The univariate procedure produces five objects per variable it analyzes, which correspond to five tables in the outputs `Moments`, `BasicMeasures`, `TestForLocation`, `Quantiles`, and `ExtremeObs`.

The `output/log/results` from SAS Studio can be maximized within SAS Studio or opened in its own window by clicking on the icon associated with maximizing the view which will open the section as a new tab within the web browser.

Click on the **LOG** tab from the last code that was submitted and then click on the **Open in a new web browser icon**, which allows the reader to see all five ODS table objects associated with the Age variable from SASHELP.CLASS:

```
Output Added:
-------------
Name:       Moments
Label:      Moments
Template:   base.univariate.Moments
Path:       Univariate.Age.Moments
Label Path: 'The Univariate Procedure'.'Age'.'Moments'
-------------

Output Added:
-------------
Name:       BasicMeasures
Label:      Basic Measures of Location and Variability
Template:   base.univariate.Measures
Path:       Univariate.Age.BasicMeasures
Label Path: 'The Univariate Procedure'.'Age'.'Basic Measures of Location and Variability'
-------------

Output Added:
-------------
Name:       TestsForLocation
Label:      Tests For Location
Template:   base.univariate.Location
Path:       Univariate.Age.TestsForLocation
Label Path: 'The Univariate Procedure'.'Age'.'Tests For Location'
-------------

Output Added:
-------------
Name:       Quantiles
Label:      Quantiles
Template:   base.univariate.Quantiles
Path:       Univariate.Age.Quantiles
Label Path: 'The Univariate Procedure'.'Age'.'Quantiles'
-------------

Output Added:
-------------
Name:       ExtremeObs
Label:      Extreme Observations
Template:   base.univariate.ExtObs
Path:       Univariate.Age.ExtremeObs
Label Path: 'The Univariate Procedure'.'Age'.'Extreme Observations'
-------------
```

Figure 5.14: ODS trace for UNIVARIATE procedure

# ODS document and the DOCUMENT procedure

Using a combination of the ODS  document statement and the DOCUMENT procedure allows a
programmer to store objects that make up a report that has been produced by a procedure
or data step program. Then, a programmer can either modify the report objects to produce a
different version of them, or produce the same report in a different format without having
to rerun the original code that produced the report. Type the following code in a SAS Studio
program section and submit it:

```
ODS document name=work.mydoc;

proc print data=sashelp.class;
quit;

ODS document close;

ODS RTF file="/folders/myfolders/sasuser.v94/mydoc.rtf";
ODS PDF file="/folders/myfolders/sasuser.v94/mydoc.pdf";

proc document name=work.mydoc;
    replay / dest=(rtf pdf);
quit;

ODS RTF close;
ODS PDF close;
```

After submitting this code, expand the **Server Files and Folders** section on the left side of SAS Studio, and then expand **My Folders** and `sasuser.v94` to see the `mydoc.rtf` and `mydoc.pdf` files.

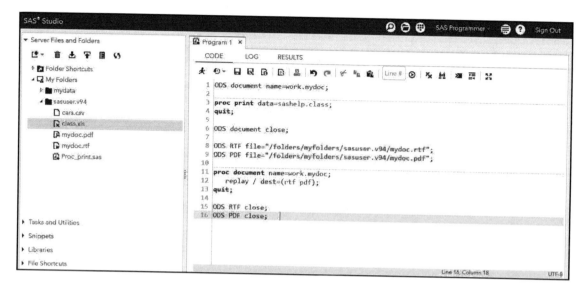

Figure 5.15: ODS document example

By double-clicking on either or both of these files, they will download in your web browser and can then be viewed by opening the file like any other web browser download.

# ODS Graphics

SAS/GRAPH is not included in the SAS® University Edition; however, as the reader has already seen, there are plenty of graphics and plots that can be produced using SAS Studio **Tasks** and **Snippets** because these rely on the five ODS Graphics procedures, which are sometimes referred to as **ODS Statistical Graphics** procedures. As described in *SAS® 9.4 Programming Documentation / SAS ODS Graphics: Procedures Guide*(http://documentation. sas.com/?cdcId=pgmsascdccdcVersion=9.4_3.2docsetId=grstatprocdocsetTarget= n1e0ztxxbnqjgnn182s1te817t3i.htmlocale=en) *There are five ODS Graphics procedures. Each has a specific purpose:*

- *SGPLOT creates single-cell plots with a variety of plot and chart types, and overlays.*

- *SGPANEL creates classification panels for one or more classification variables. Each graph cell in the panel can contain either a simple plot or multiple overlaid plots.*

*Note that the SGPLOT and SGPANEL procedures largely support the same types of plots and charts. For this reason, the two procedures have an almost identical syntax. The main distinction between the two procedures is that the SGPANEL procedure produces a panel of graphs, one for each level of a classification variable.*

- *SGSCATTER creates scatter plot panels and scatter plot matrices with optional fits and ellipses.*
- *SGRENDER produces graphs from graph templates that are written in the Graph Template Language (GTL). You can also render a graph from a SAS ODS Graphics Editor (SGE) file.*
- *SGDESIGN creates graphical output based on a graph file that has been created by using the ODS Graphics Designer application.*

The SAS® University Edition SAS Studio does not include the ODS Graphics Designer application; however, if you are using a fully licensed version of SAS Studio, this interactive application can be started by selecting the **More applications options** icon in the upper-right-hand corner, and then **Tools**.

*The ODS Graphics procedures enable you to create complex statistical graphs that use the principles of effective graphics (for more information about the principles of effective graphics, see Cleveland (1993) and Robbins (2005)) to accurately communicate the results of your analysis to your consumers. The minimal coding required enables you to focus on your statistical analysis instead of the visual appearance of your graphs.*

Expand the **Tasks and Utilities** section on the left side of SAS Studio and then expand **Tasks** and **Graph**. Right-click on the **Bar Chart** graph task and select **Properties** to see which ODS Graphics procedure, the SGPLOT procedure, is used with this task:

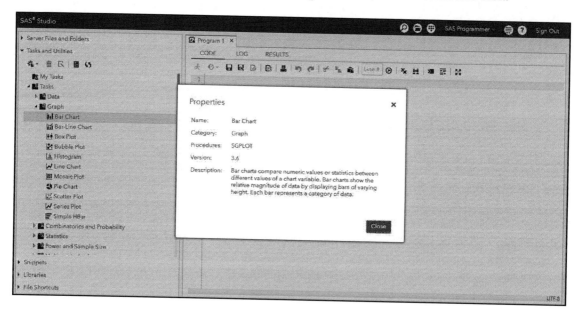

Figure 5.16: SAS Studio Bar Chart graph task uses the SGPLOT ODS Graphics procedure

Likewise, the reader can view the properties on all the graph tasks and the graph snippets to see which of the ODS Graphics procedures are used with each task or snippet. One way the reader can learn more about these ODS Graphics procedures is to work with the SAS Studio tasks and snippets, since they generate the code that can then be copied and modified as needed.

Select the **Snippets** section on the left-hand side of SAS Studio, and then expand **Snippets** and then **Graph**, and double-click on **Dot Plot**:

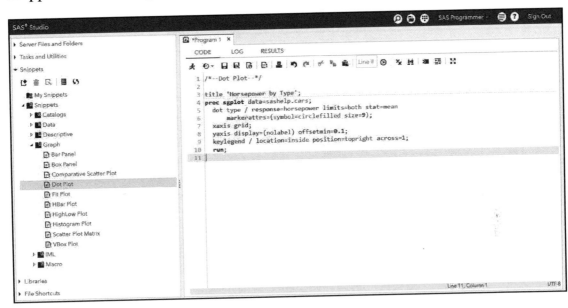

Figure 5.17: SAS Studio Dot Plot snippet

Notice that the ODS Graphics procedure used by this snippet is the SGPLOT procedure. Submit this code by selecting the running man icon:

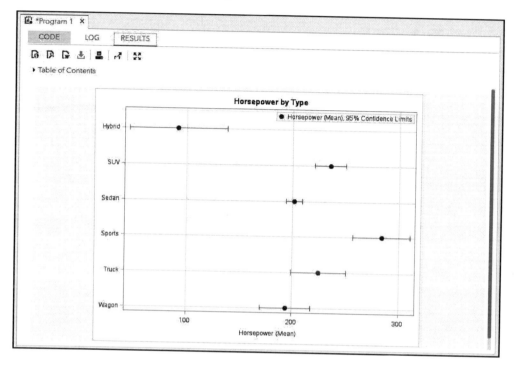

Figure 5.18: SAS Studio Dot Plot example 1 results

Now return to the **CODE** tab and update the code with the following changes:

- Change Horsepower by Type to Height by Gender
- Change data=sashelp.cars to data=sashelp.classfit
- Change dot type / response=horsepower to dot sex / response=height

The code should now look as follows:

```
/*--Dot Plot--*/

title 'Height by Gender';
proc sgplot data=sashelp.classfit;
   dot sex / response=height limits=both stat=mean
       markerattrs=(symbol=circlefilled size=9);
   xaxis grid;
   yaxis display=(nolabel) offsetmin=0.1;
   keylegend / location=inside position=topright across=1;
   run;
```

Submit the code by selecting the running man icon:

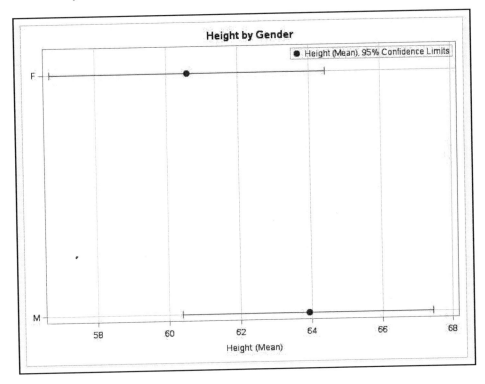

Figure 5.19: SAS Studio snippet Dot Plot example 2 results

# How to make a user-defined snippet

A snippet can be any code a programmer wants to save as a snippet that can be rerun whenever needed. To make a user-defined snippet based on this updated **Dot Plot** code, right-click on **My Snippets** on the left side of SAS Studio and select **New code snippet**. This will bring up another program window on the right side of SAS Studio named **Snippet1**. Copy and paste the code from the **CODE** tab in the other program window into the **CODE** tab of **Snippet1**, which should change its name to **\*Snippet1**. Select the save icon, which is the third icon from the left and looks like a *3 1/2* inch hard disk. This will bring up the **Add to My Snippets** window, which allows the programmer to name their snippet. Name it MyDotPlot and select **Save**:

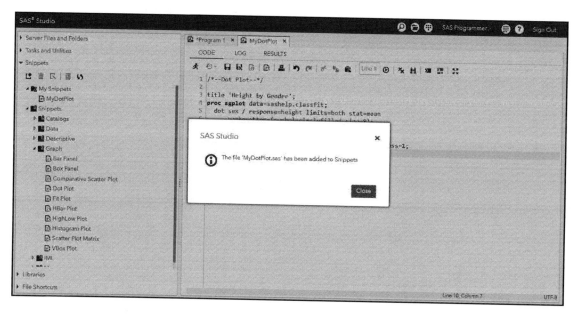

Figure 5.20: Save My Snippet named MyDotPlot

Notice that the new snippet is now saved under **My Snippets** on the left side of SAS Studio, as seen in *Figure 5.20*. Select the **Close** button in the information window that informed the programmer that the file MyDotPlot.sas has been added to the Snippets section.

# Summary

We learned about SAS Studio **Tasks** and **Snippets**, how they are both used to produce reports, and how to use PROC TABULATE and PROC REPORT BASE procedures to make more complex table-based reports than with using PROC PRINT.

We also walked through the ODS and how it enables the production of output in a variety of different output formats, such as HTML, PDF, and RTF. We were introduced to the five ODS Graphics procedures.

Finally, we learned how we can make our own snippets, which are saved under **My Snippets** in SAS Studio.

In the next chapter, the reader will learn about the DS2 language, which is another programming language included in BASE SAS.

# 6

# Other Programming Languages in BASE SAS® Software

When processing big data where it is stored, the data does not have to be copied or moved across the network. The DS2 language, which is another proprietary SAS programming language included in BASE SAS, plays an important and vital role in the processing of data where it is stored. This is especially true in cases where SAS data step logic can be transformed into DS2, which allows that logic to run in environments where DS2 is supported and the SAS data step is not. The processing environments that are most important with respect to supporting DS2 in the big data analytics space are SAS® Viya™ and the **Cloud Analytics Server (CAS)**, the **SAS Embedded Process**, and the **SAS Event Stream Processing (ESP)** engine. All of these will be discussed in more detail in Chapter 7, *SAS® Software Engineers the Processing Environment for You*. In addition, similar to DS2, the Federated SQL or FedSQL language was added to BASE SAS, and it plays a role in processing big data and big data analytics.

In this chapter, we will cover the following topics:

- The DS2 programming language
- The FedSQL programming language

# The DS2 programming language

As described in *SAS® 9.4 Programming Documentation / DS2 Reference - What is DS2*(http://
documentation.sas.com/?cdcId=pgmsascdccdcVersion=9.4_3.2docsetId=ds2ref
docsetTarget=p0qrslgyjx5ti6n), *The DS2 language shares core features with the DATA step.
However, DS2's capabilities extend far beyond those of the DATA step. DS2 is a procedural
language that has variables, scope, methods, packages, control flow statements, table I/O statements,
and parallel programming statements. Methods and packages give DS2 modularity and data
encapsulation. DS2 enables you to insert SQL directly into the SET statement, thus blending the
power of two powerful data manipulation languages.*

DS2 intersects with the SAS data step; however, it supports much more than character and
numeric datatypes. DS2 supports the following datatypes: BIGINT, BINARY(n), CHAR(n),
DATE, DECIMAL|NUMERIC(p,s), DOUBLE, FLOAT, INTEGER, NCHAR(n), NVARCHAR(n),
REAL, SMALLINT, TIME(p), TIMESTAMP(p), TINYINT, VARBINARY(n), and VARCHAR(n).

DS2 can access many different types of data sources, and at the time of writing this book,
they include—Aster, DB2 on Unix and Windows operating systems, Greenplum, Hadoop
(Hive and HDMD), **Memory Data Store (MDS)**, MySQL, Netezza, ODBC-compliant
databases (such as Microsoft SQL Server), Oracle, PostgreSQL, SAP (read-only), SAP
HANA, SASHDAT files (only when used with PROC HPDS2), SAS datasets, SAS **Scalable
Performance Data (SPD)** engine datasets, SAS SPD server tables in Unix and Windows
operating environments, SAP IQ, and Teradata for Unix and Windows.

 Not all datatypes are available for table storage on each data store.

# When to use DS2

As described in *SAS® 9.4 Programming Documentation / DS2 Reference - Introduction to the DS2
Language: When to use DS2* (http://documentation.sas.com/?cdcId=pgmsascdc
cdcVersion=9.4_3.2docsetId=ds2pgdocsetTarget=p1shb3eskw9xh9n1orhpgt608it7.htm
locale=en), *it is not necessary to convert all data step programs into DS2.
Typically, DS2 programs are written for applications that carry out the
following actions:*

- *Require the precision that results from using the new supported datatypes*
- *Benefit from using the new expressions or write methods or packages available in the DS2
  syntax*

- *Need to execute SAS FedSQL from within the DS2 program*
- *Execute outside a SAS session, for example, in-database processing on Hadoop or Teradata, in SAS Viya, or the SAS Federation Server*
- *Take advantage of threaded processing in products such as the SAS In-Database Code Accelerator and SAS Enterprise Miner*

SAS Scoring Accelerator offerings run DS2-based programs that have been automatically generated from SAS Enterprise Miner or SAS Model Manager. SAS Scoring Accelerator offerings are a unique deployment mechanism for SAS that convert the end result of a predictive modeling process, the score code, into a native method or function call within a data storage system like an MPP database, Hadoop, or SAP HANA. This means you don't have to move data out of where it is stored to score it, which saves a tremendous about of time and allows you to extend the functionality of the underlying data storage system from simply storing data, to deriving new predictive insights from data as soon as it enters the storage system.

In addition, DS2 can be deployed to execute within the SAS ESP engine, which moves analytics out of systems and puts it on the edge or embeds them with devices that make up the **Internet of Things (IoT)**.

# How is DS2 similar to the data step?

DS2 shares many of the same elements as data step and those elements behave the same way. These elements include SAS formats, SAS functions, many SAS statements, and the data step list of keywords are in the list of keywords for DS2. Furthermore, many of the tasks performed in data step can be performed in DS2, such as processing arrays and hash tables, converting between datatypes, and calculating date and time values.

# How are DS2 and DATA step different?

DS2 differs from data step in many ways, some of which are as follows:

| DS2 | DATA step |
|---|---|
| Variables have scope | All variables are global |
| Variables must be declared before they are used | Variables don't have to be explicitly declared before they are used |
| Keywords are reserved words | There are no reserved words |
| Single and double quotes follow ANSI standard usage | Single and double quotes can both be used to define a character constant |

| | |
|---|---|
| Variable attributes can be defined with a single declare statement with a having clause | Multiple statements must be used to set variable attributes |
| Many ANSI variable types are supported | Only numeric and character types are supported |
| Missing and null values are supported | Only missing values are supported and there is no concept of a null value |
| To overwrite a table the overwrite option must be explicitly used | Existing tables can be overwritten in place without using special options |
| Same table cannot be read and written in one step. Instead, a temporary table must first be created, then the target table dropped, and finally, the temporary table is renamed to the target table. | A table can be read and written over all in one step |

For more information and details about the differences between DS2 and DATA Step, see *SAS® 9.4 Programming Documentation / DS2 Reference - Differences between DS2 and the DATA Step* (http://documentation.sas.com/?docsetId=ds2refdocsetTarget= n0yp3l3ohcnz3kn1wuy8p5sl4r7d.htmdocsetVersion=9.4locale=ja).

# Programming in DS2

Programming blocks are defined as sections of a DS2 program that encapsulate variables and code. There are five types of programming blocks in DS2:

- The data program block with delimiters: DATA...ENDDATA
- The program block with delimiters: PACKAGE...ENDPACKAGE
- The method block with delimiters: METHOD...ENDMETHOD
- The thread program block with delimiters: THREAD...ENDTHREAD
- The DO loop block with delimiters: DO...END

A typical DS2 program is made up of a list of declarations, followed by a list of method statements.

# DS2 methods

There are two types of method statements in DS2, **system methods** and **user-defined methods**.

DS2 methods are similar to functions in the C programming language and methods in the Java programming language.

Because executable code can only reside within a method, the method is the fundamental building block in the DS2 language.

## DS2 system methods

Each DS2 program always contains implicitly or explicitly these three main system methods: `init()`, `run()`, and `term()`. If a programmer fails to explicitly define any one of these system methods, the compiler will add an empty version of the method on the fly. Methods provide the concept of variable scope, so any parameters that are passed in or any variables declared within a method have local scope, meaning they are only known within the bounds of that method.

Parameters and return values are not allowed to be defined or used in system methods. If a programmer defines a parameter in a system method, it will cause an **ERROR** to occur. There is one other system method, `setparams()`, which executes once when called from a data program to initialize the parameters of a parameterized thread.

When a DS2 program executes, the `init()` method will always execute once at the beginning of the program, followed by the execution of the `run()` method. The `term()` method executes once prior to the program ending without explicitly being called. All other methods need to be explicitly called in order for the code within them to execute as part of the program.

## DS2 user-defined methods

User-defined methods are similar to user-defined functions or subroutines in other programming languages, meaning they are methods that a programmer develops and is meant for reuse by them or by other programmers. Unlike system methods, which execute automatically and don't take parameters or return values, user-defined methods must be called, can take parameters, and can return values. In addition, just like other languages, user-defined methods can be overloaded. This means two or more of them can exist with the same name, within the same scope of a program, as long as their parameter signature is unique.

A parameter signature refers to the number and types of parameters passed to a user-defined method.

# DS2 packages

DS2 allows for the bundling together of variables and methods into named objects called packages, which can be saved and reused by DS2 programs. The DS2 package is very similar to a class in an **object-oriented programming** (**oop**) language, and its main benefit is its ability to be reused. A DS2 package is not a program, but a template for instantiating an object that can be used within a program. Similar to DS2 methods, there are two types of packages, predefined packages shipped by SAS as part of the DS2 language, and user-defined packages written by one programmer that can be shared with others.

## DS2 predefined packages

As described in *SAS® 9.4 and SAS Viya 3.2 Programming Documentation / DS2 Reference - DS2 Programmer's Guide - DS2 Concepts - DS2 Packages - Predefined DS2 Packages- Predefined DS2 Packages: Overview of Predefined DS2 packages, SAS provides the following predefined packages for use in the DS2 language:*

- FCMP: *Supports calls to* FCMP *functions and subroutines from within the DS2 language.*

- Hash *and* hash *iterator: Enables you to quickly and efficiently store, search, and retrieve data based on unique lookup keys. The* hash *package keys and data are variables. Key and data values can be directly assigned constant values or values from a table, or values can be computed in an expression.*

- HTTP: *Constructs an HTTP client to access HTTP web services.*

- JSON: *Enables you to create and parse JSON text.*

- Logger: *Provides a basic interface (open, write, and level query) to the SAS logging facility.*

- Matrix: *Provides a powerful and flexible matrix programming capability. It provides a DS2-level implementation of SAS/IML functionality.*

- PCRXFIND *and* PCRXREPLACE: *Provides a way to find a substring within a given string or replace a substring. The* PCRXFIND *and* PCRXREPLACE *packages are not supported on the CAS server.*

- SQLSTMT: *Provides a way to pass FedSQL statements to a DBMS for execution, and to access the result set returned by the DBMS.*

- TZ: *Provides a way to process local and international time and date values.*

For more information and details of these predefined packages, refer to *SAS® 9.4 and SAS Viya 3.2 Programming Documentation / DS2 Reference - DS2 Packages: Predefined DS2 Packages* (`http://documentation.sas.com/?cdcId=pgmsascdc&cdcVersion=9.4_3.2&docsetId=ds2p g&docsetTarget=n1vcyhfhq2l0p4n1x3ggi7i6g0aa.htm&locale=en`)

## DS2 user-defined packages

A SAS programmer can develop their own user-defined packages. In essence, a programmer can bundle a set of methods together and save them in a package, which they can then instantiate within another DS2 program using the `declare package` statement or the `_NEW_` operator.

 A user cannot hide a predefined package by attempting to save a package with the same name as the existing predefined package. When instantiated in a program, the predefined package would be used in this case, regardless of a user-defined package with the same name.

# Running DS2 programs

DS2 programs can be submitted to run several different ways. Within BASE SAS, DS2 programs are submitted by using the DS2 procedure through programming in a SAS Windows environment, a code node within SAS Enterprise Guide, or SAS Studio. Since this book uses the SAS® University Edition, SAS Studio and the DS2 procedure will be used to execute DS2 programs because the only requirement is BASE SAS.

 The DS2 procedure can be used not only to submit and execute DS2 programs in BASE SAS, but can also be used to submit DS2 programs to SAS Viya or on the CAS. If you have access to an SAS Viya environment, then SAS Studio can be used to submit DS2 programs two ways—using the DS2 procedure basically the same way a programmer would to BASE SAS, or by using the run DS2 action in conjunction with the CAS procedure to run the DS2 code on the CAS server. As noted in *SAS 9.4 and SAS Viya 3.2 Programming Documentation / DS2 Programmer's Guide - Introduction - Introduction to the DS2 Language: Running DS2 Programs*, NOTE: *Unless you are using Python or Lua, it is recommended to use PROD DS2 to submit DS2 code to the CAS server.*

The ability to learn and to execute DS2 programs with only BASE SAS as a requirement is another way in which the SAS platform allows a programmer to continue to leverage their skills learned on smaller sized data, and transfer those skills directly into performing big data analytics with SAS, leveraging SAS Viya and the CAS parts of the overall SAS platform offering.

All the other methods of executing DS2 programs require licensing of additional SAS® software offerings that are part of the overall SAS platform processing environment. To submit DS2 programs directly to a data source like an RDBMS, the appropriate SAS/ACCESS engine for that data source and the SAS Code Accelerator for that data source needs to be licensed. To submit DS2 programs to run within a SAS Federation Server, the SAS Federation Server needs to be licensed. Finally, to submit DS2 code to execute either in a single machine running multiple threads or to a distributed computing environment, at least one of the SAS high performance offerings such as SAS High Performance Statistics, which comes with the HPDS2 procedure, must be licensed. The HPDS2 procedure allows the DS2 code to be submitted in the SAS client environment, but actually executes in the location specified by the programmer. This is how the DS2 programmer can take advantage of the multiple threads and/or the distributed computing environment. Examples of a distributed computing environment includes supported MPP databases or supported distributions of Hadoop.

## The DS2 procedure

In order to write DS2 programs to execute within BASE SAS, a programmer makes use of the DS2 procedure and writes the DS2 code between PROC ds2; and a run; statement. In other words, we use this type of code block:

```
proc ds2 /* <options> */;
   /* DS2 code including methods and packages */
run;
quit;
```

The reader can use this code block to check whether they have access to run DS2 programs in BASE SAS. Type this code in a SAS Studio program section and submit it. If an **ERROR:** appears in the **LOG** section, the reader will need to work with their SAS administer to determine whether they are properly licensed to make use of DS2 or to determine a fix for their environment:

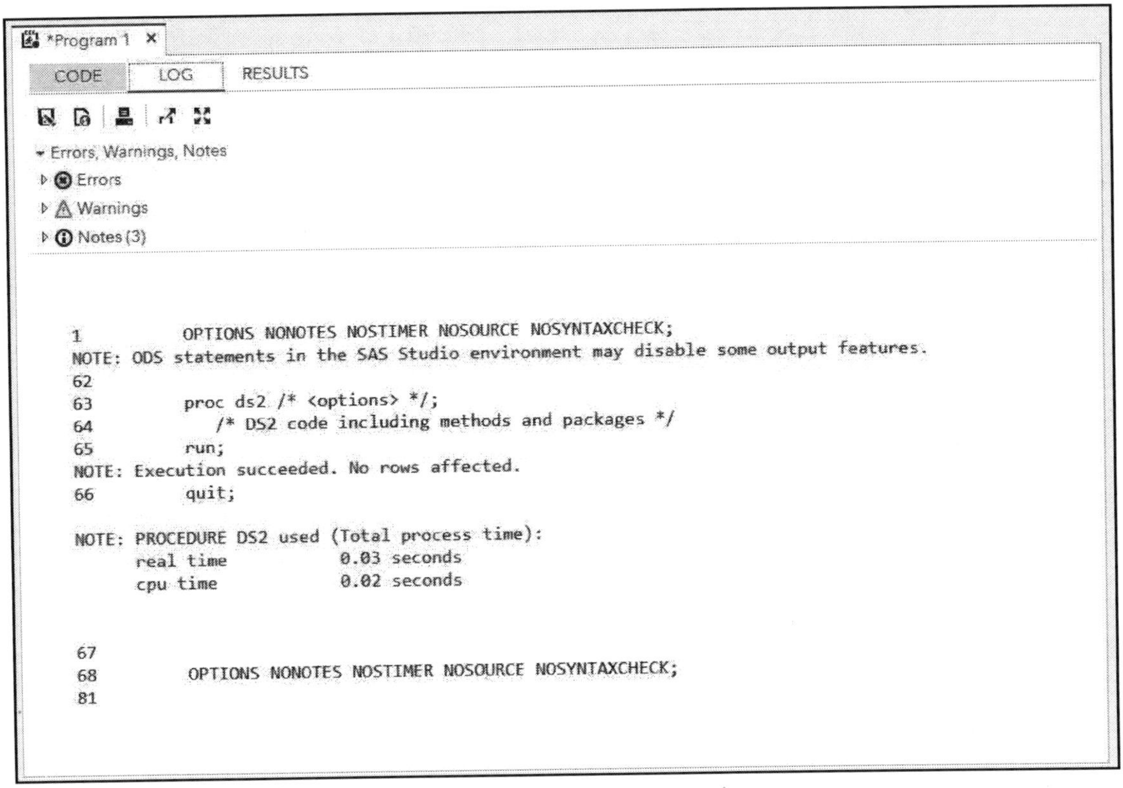

Figure 6.1: SAS Studio LOG verifying that DS2 is available

## DS2 Hello World program – example 1

As is the programming tradition, the first program example for DS2 will make use of writing `Hello World`. By default, if the libraries or `libs` DS2 procedure is not specified, then a data connection will be opened to all SAS libraries within that particular user's SAS session; therefore, in the code example that follows, the `libs=work` option limits the `ds2` procedure to only open one data connection to the `work` library. Type the following code in a SAS Studio program section and submit it:

```
proc ds2 libs=work;
    data _null_;
        method init();
        end;
        method run();
            declare varchar(20) msgtext;
            msgtext = 'Hello World';
            put msgtext;
```

```
            end;
        method term();
            end;
        enddata;
    run;
```

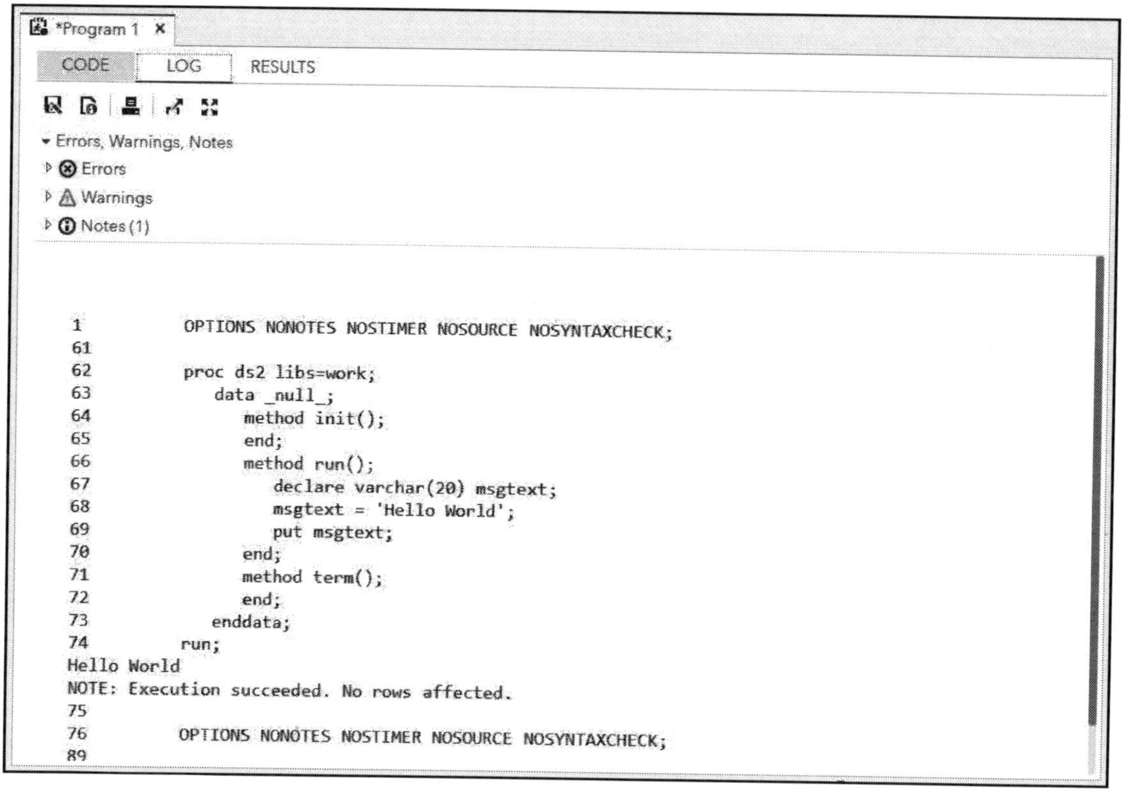

Figure 6.2: DS2 program using the run() method

As mentioned previously, it is not necessary to always explicitly define the `init()`, `run()`, and `term()` methods; however, this is good coding practice in case someone else who may not be as familiar with DS2 programming needs to support the code in the future. In this simple type of program, the programmer could have easily put the three lines of code used in the `run()` method in any of the system methods, and the same result of `Hello World` would be printed to **LOG** because all the system methods execute once without having to be called explicitly.

# DS2 Hello World program – example 2

Let's modify this code by adding a user-defined method called `main()`, and move the executable code from `run()` into this new `main()` method:

```
proc ds2 libs=work;
   data _null_;
      method init();
      end;
      method main();
         declare varchar(20) msgtext;
         msgtext = 'Hello World';
         put msgtext;
      end;
      method run();
      end;
      method term();
      end;
   enddata;
run;
```

What happens when you submit this code? It appears as though nothing happens, meaning `Hello World` is not written to the **LOG** section and no **ERROR** is generated. Since `main()` is a user-defined method, it must be explicitly called for the code to execute as part of the program. To make this new version of the code work, put the `main();` method call in any of the three system methods, for example, in the `term()` method as the following code shows. This will ensure the code within `main()` executes and writes the **Hello World** message to the **LOG**:

```
proc ds2 libs=work;
   data _null_;
      method init();
      end;
      method main();
         declare varchar(20) msgtext;
         msgtext = 'Hello World';
         put msgtext;
      end;
      method run();
      end;
      method term();
         main();
      end;
   enddata;
run;
```

`Hello World` will be written to **LOG** as seen in *Figure 6.2*.

## DS2 Hello World program – example 3

Now, rewrite this DS2 program so that it uses a user-defined method with a parameter to produce the same result. Type the following code in the SAS Studio program section and submit it:

```
proc ds2 libs=work;
    data _null_;
        declare varchar(20) msgtext;
        method init();
        end;
        method pmethod(varchar(20) msg);
            put msg;
        end;
        method run();
            msgtext = 'Hello World';
            pmethod(msgtext);
        end;
        method term();
        end;
    enddata;
run;
```

Once again, the output will be `Hello World` written to the **LOG** as seen in *Figure 6.2*. The `declare` statement makes `msgtext` a global variable within the scope of this entire DS2 program. This allows the `run()` method to assign the value of `Hello World` to `msgtext` and then that gets passed into the user-defined `pmethod()` method. The `msg` variable within `pmethod` is defined as `varchar(20)` and only has local scope within the `pmethod()` method, which means `msg` cannot be referred to outside the boundaries of the `pmethod()` method. To verify this, change the code by adding the statement `put msg;` in the `term()` method, as shown in the following code block, and submit it:

```
proc ds2 libs=work;
    data _null_;
        declare varchar(20) msgtext;
        method init();
        end;
        method pmethod(varchar(20) msg);
            put msg;
        end;
        method run();
            msgtext = 'Hello World';
            pmethod(msgtext);
        end;
        method term();
            put msg;
        end;
```

```
            enddata;
        run;
```

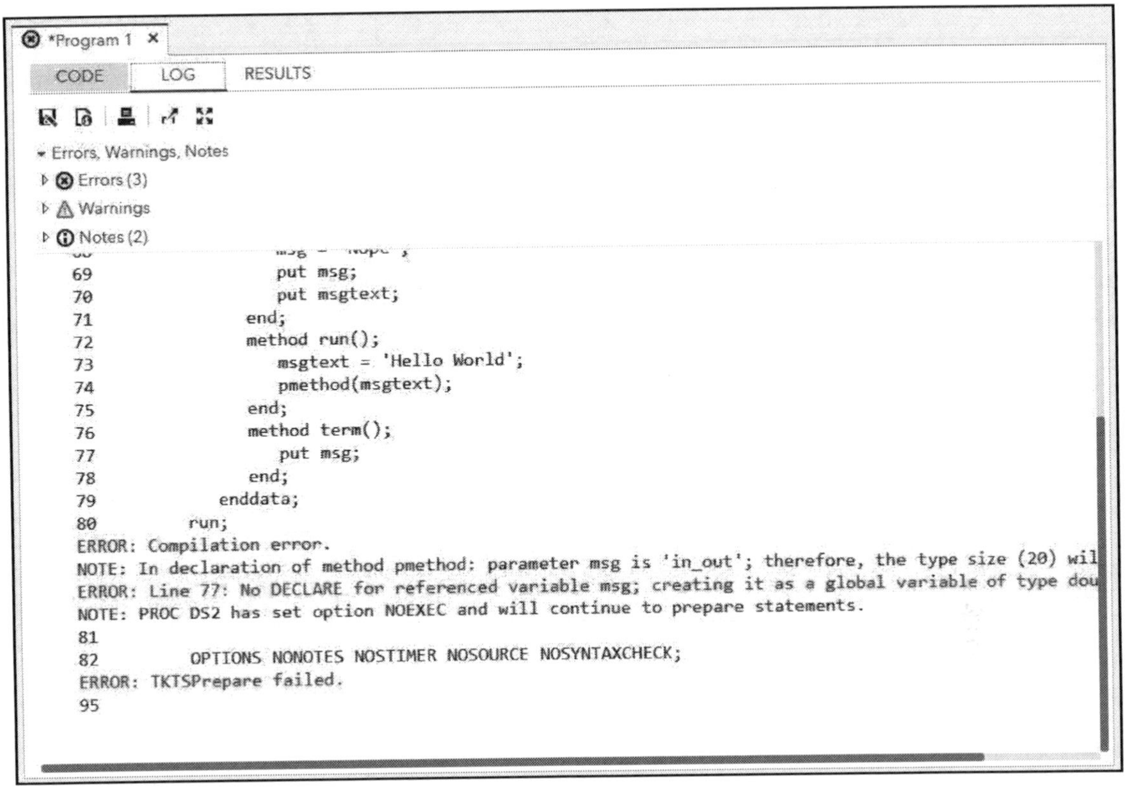

```
enddata;
run;
```

Content inside the program window:

```
69                  put msg;
70                  put msgtext;
71              end;
72          method run();
73                  msgtext = 'Hello World';
74                  pmethod(msgtext);
75          end;
76          method term();
77                  put msg;
78          end;
79          enddata;
80      run;
ERROR: Compilation error.
NOTE: In declaration of method pmethod: parameter msg is 'in_out'; therefore, the type size (20) wil
ERROR: Line 77: No DECLARE for referenced variable msg; creating it as a global variable of type dou
NOTE: PROC DS2 has set option NOEXEC and will continue to prepare statements.
81
82          OPTIONS NONOTES NOSTIMER NOSOURCE NOSYNTAXCHECK;
ERROR: TKTSPrepare failed.
95
```

Figure 6.3: DS2 error due to referring to a variable out of scope

## DS2 Hello World program – example 4

In order to help explain the concept of variable scope, change the code again by removing the put msg; statement from the term() method in order to avoid that **ERROR**. Make the following changes to the pmethod() and run() methods, and then submit the code:

```
proc ds2 libs=work;
    data _null_;
        declare varchar(20) msgtext;
        method init();
        end;
        method pmethod(varchar(20) msg);
            msg = 'Nope';
            put 'In pmethod: ' msg;
```

```
        end;
      method run();
          msgtext = 'Hello World';
          pmethod(msgtext);
          put 'In run: ' msgtext;
      end;
      method term();
      end;
    enddata;
  run;
```

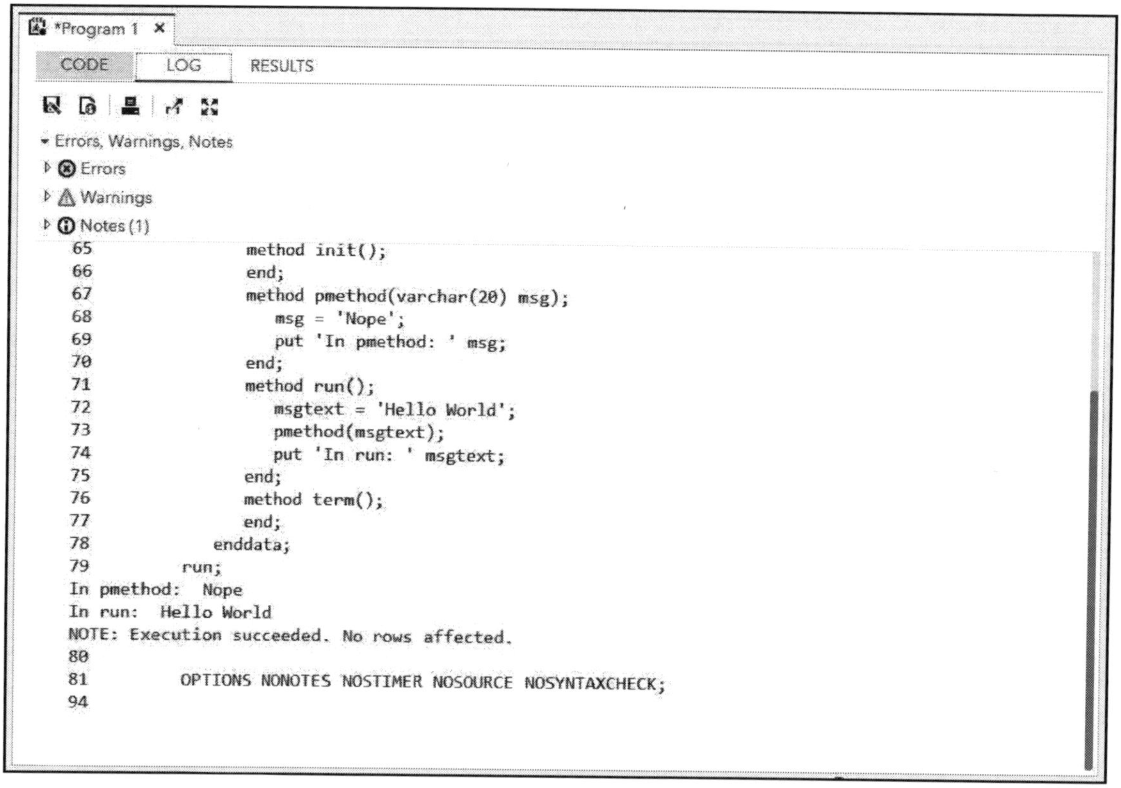

Figure 6.4: DS2 variable scope example 1

Even though the global variable `msgtext` is passed in as a parameter to the `pmethod()` method, its value of `Hello World` is copied into the local variable `msg`. The first executable line of the `pmethod()` method then assigns a new value of `"Nope"` to `msg`, and this is why the resulting output to the **LOG** is `In pmethod: Nope`. However, once the execution returns to the `run()` method, `msgtext` has not been altered, so `In run: Hello World` is written to **LOG**.

# DS2 Hello World program – example 5

DS2 provides a way for programmers to have methods to actually change the value of the variable being passed into a method using the IN_OUT parameter option. Change the previous code simply by adding the IN_OUT option to the pmethod parameter msg as seen in the following code block, and submit it:

```
proc ds2 libs=work;
    data _null_;
        declare varchar(20) msgtext;
        method init();
        end;
        method pmethod(IN_OUT varchar(20) msg);
            msg = 'Nope';
            put 'In pmethod: ' msg;
        end;
        method run();
            msgtext = 'Hello World';
            pmethod(msgtext);
            put 'In run: ' msgtext;
        end;
        method term();
        end;
    enddata;
run;
```

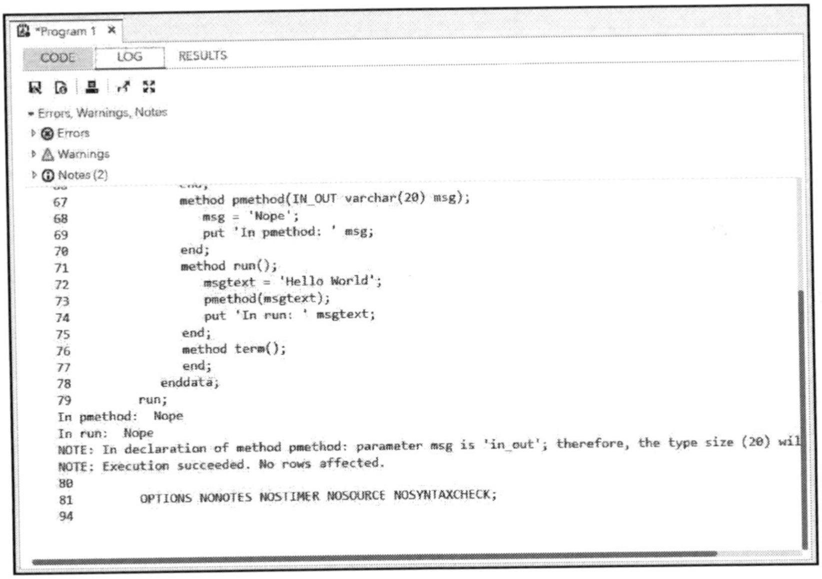

Figure 6.5: DS2 variable scope example 2

The IN_OUT method parameter options make it so easy! Instead of a copy of the value of the parameter being passed, the parameter uses the actual value of the variable passed. So, any changes made to the local variable actually get stored in the variable space assigned to the variable being passed in as the parameter. This is just one way in which variables can be passed in and out of a method in order to execute some code and provide a result.

## DS2 program with a method that returns a value

Methods can also be set up so that they return a value that is used in assigning another variable a value. Here is a simple example of a method that returns an integer value, which gets assigned to an integer within the scope of the calling method. Type the following code in a SAS Studio program section and submit it:

```
proc ds2 libs=work;
   data _null_;
      method init();
      end;
      method myadd(int x, int y) returns int;
          return x + y;
      end;
      method run();
         declare int a;
         declare int b;
         declare int add_result;
         a=10;
         b=5;
         add_result=myadd(a,b);
         put 'a plus b is equal to: ' add_result;
      end;
      method term();
      end;
   enddata;
run;
```

In this example, there are no global variables declared.

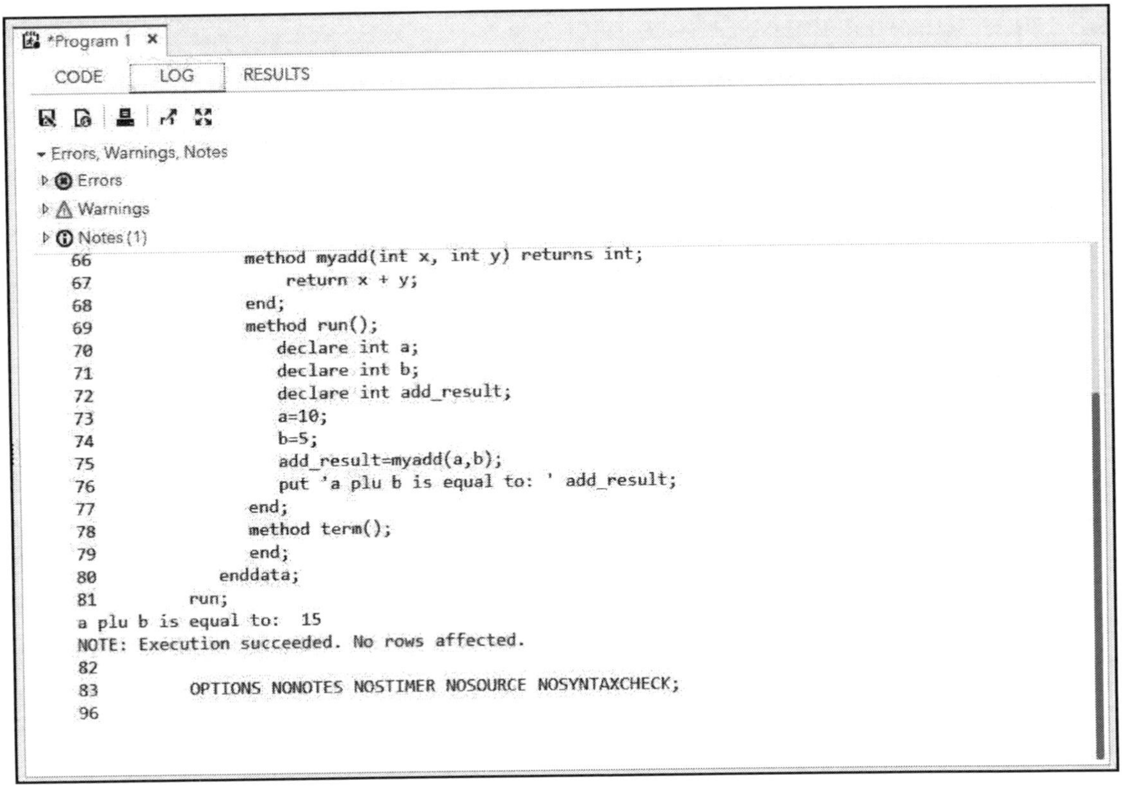

```
 *Program 1   ✕

   CODE     LOG     RESULTS

 ▣ ▣ ▣ ⚐ ⟨⟩
 ▾ Errors, Warnings, Notes
 ▷ ⊗ Errors
 ▷ ⚠ Warnings
 ▷ ⓘ Notes (1)
    66              method myadd(int x, int y) returns int;
    67                   return x + y;
    68              end;
    69              method run();
    70                  declare int a;
    71                  declare int b;
    72                  declare int add_result;
    73                  a=10;
    74                  b=5;
    75                  add_result=myadd(a,b);
    76                  put 'a plu b is equal to: ' add_result;
    77              end;
    78              method term();
    79              end;
    80          enddata;
    81      run;
 a plu b is equal to:   15
 NOTE: Execution succeeded. No rows affected.
    82
    83          OPTIONS NONOTES NOSTIMER NOSOURCE NOSYNTAXCHECK;
    96
```

Figure 6.6: DS2 method return example

Instead, variables a, b, and add_result are local integers within the run() method, and variables x and y are local integers within the myadd() method. The myadd() method returns an integer value, and as such, the add_result variable is assigned the integer returned by the myadd() method call.

## DS2 program with a user-defined package

In this example, the reader will change the code from the previous example so that a user-defined package contains the `myadd()` method, which is then instantiated and used in the second part of this DS2 program. Type the following code in a SAS Studio program section and submit it:

```
proc ds2 libs=work;
    package myexample;
        declare int x y;
        method myadd(int x, int y) returns int;
            put 'In package myexample';
            return x + y;
        end;
    endpackage;
run;

    data _null_;
        declare package myexample add();

        method init();
        end;

        method run();
            declare int a;
            declare int b;
            declare int add_result;
            a=10;
            b=5;
            add_result= add.myadd(a,b);
            put 'a plus b is equal to: ' add_result;
        end;
        method term();
        end;
    enddata;
run;
```

Notice the use of the `run;` statement to separate the two executable DS2 programs defined in this code. The first part is bound by `package/endpackage`, which gets saved as a compiled object of the `myexample` package in the `work` library named `myexample`. The second part is bound by `data/enddata`, which makes use of the package by the `declare package` statement:

```
*Program 1  ✕

  CODE      LOG      RESULTS

  ▣ ▣ ▤ ✗ ✕

  ▾ Errors, Warnings, Notes
  ▷ ⊙ Errors
  ▷ ⚠ Warnings
  ▷ ⓘ Notes (3)
   77              end;
   78
   79          method run();
   80              declare int a;
   81              declare int b;
   82              declare int add_result;
   83              a=10;
   84              b=5;
   85              add_result= add.myadd(a,b);
   86              put 'a plus b is equal to: ' add_result;
   87          end;
   88          method term();
   89          end;
   90        enddata;
   91      run;
  In package myexample
  a plus b is equal to:  15
  NOTE: Execution succeeded. No rows affected.
   92
   93        OPTIONS NONOTES NOSTIMER NOSOURCE NOSYNTAXCHECK;
  106
```

Figure 6.7: DS2 user-defined package example

The print statement in the myexample package was added simply to show the reader that the package was where the addition occurred after passing in variables a and b from the data/enddata program.

> In a production environment, user-defined packages should be saved to a permanent library that is accessible by all programmers so that the packages and methods defined within the packages can be leveraged by all DS2 programmers, without having to write their own independent methods that do the same actions.

If the reader attempts to submit the preceding code again instead of executing correctly, an **ERROR** will be generated because the package `myexample` already exists and DS2 does not allow overwriting an in-place package. If a programmer needs to develop and test packages before saving them to be used in production, all that needs to be added is the appropriate `drop package` statement prior to defining the package. See the following code block for what needs to be added to the previous code:

```
proc ds2 libs=work;
    drop package work.myexample;
run;

    package myexample;
        declare int x y;
        method myadd(int x, int y) returns int;
            put 'In package myexample';
            return x + y;
        end;
    endpackage;
run;

    data _null_;
        declare package myexample add();

        method init();
        end;

        method run();
            declare int a;
            declare int b;
            declare int add_result;
            a=10;
            b=5;
            add_result= add.myadd(a,b);
            put 'a plus b is equal to: ' add_result;
        end;
        method term();
        end;
    enddata;
run;
```

Now that you have learned some things about the DS2 programming language, we will introduce the SAS FedSQL language.

# The FedSQL programming language

As described in *SAS® 9.4 and SAS Viya 3.2 Programming Documentation / FedSQL Reference - Introduction to the FedSQL Language* (`http://documentation.sas.com/?cdcId=pgmsascdc cdcVersion=9.4_3.2docsetId=fedsqlrefdocsetTarget=titlepage.htmlocale=en`):

*SAS FedSQL is a SAS proprietary implementation of ANSI SQL: 1999 core standard. It provides support for new data types and other ANSI 1999 core compliance features and proprietary extensions. FedSQL provides a scalable, threaded, high-performance way to access, manage, and share relational data in multiple data sources. When possible, FedSQL queries are optimized with multi-threaded algorithms in order to resolve large-scale operations.*

*For applications, FedSQL provides a common SQL syntax across all data sources. That is, FedSQL is a vendor-neutral SQL dialect that accesses data from various data sources without having to submit queries in the SQL dialect that is specific to the data source. In addition, a single FedSQL query can target data in several data sources and return a single result table.*

*The FedSQL language is available now for Base SAS users as well as for users of SAS Federation Server.*

The benefits of using the `FEDSQL` procedure instead of the `SQL` procedure, which has been part of BASE SAS for many years, are very similar to the ones listed in the *When to use DS2* section; it focuses on situations where more data types need to be supported and/or more precision is needed when processing data from outside data sources. For more details about the benefits of using the `FEDSQL` procedure instead of the `SQL` procedure, see the following SAS documentation, *SAS 9.4® and SAS Viya 3.2 Programming Documentation / Base SAS Procedures Guide - Procedures - FEDSQL Procedure - Concepts: FEDSQL Procedure - Benefits of FedSQL* (`http://documentation.sas.com/?cdcId=pgmsascdccdcVersion=9.4_3.2 docsetId=procdocsetTarget=n00g8bz9ootfssn17qb0olsr5vmq.htmlocale= en#n0xmd2cjyk1mmhn1v083n9zo6kss`)

# How to run FedSQL programs

As described in the SAS documentation *SAS® 9.4 and SAS Viya 3.2 Programming Documentation / FedSQL Reference - FedSQL Language Reference - FedSQL Language Concepts: Running FedSQL Programs* (http://documentation.sas.com/?cdcId=pgmsascdc cdcVersion=9.4_3.2docsetId=fedsqlrefdocsetTarget=n041mwqsfionp4n16qdhpo3svmuv. htmlocale=en), there are several ways to run FedSQL programs:

- *Through the SAS windowing environment or SAS Studio by using the FEDSQL procedure. The FedSQL procedure can be used to submit FedSQL statements in Base SAS, SAS Viya, and on the SAS Cloud Analytic Services (CAS) server.*
- *Through the FedSQL.execDirect action to the CAS server. The FedSQL execDirect action can be called from a SAS Studio session or from a Python, Lua, or R program. In SAS Studio, the FedSQL.execDirect action is used with the CAS procedure.*
- *From a JDBC, ODBC, or OLE DB client by using SAS Federation Server.*
- *Directly to the SAS Federation Server using the SAS LIBNAME engine for SAS Federation Server. You can specify FedSQL statements in the PROC SQL EXECUTE statement in the same way that you execute DBMS-specific SQL statements.*
- *From a DS2 program.*

You can not only execute FedSQL from DS2 programs, but also invoke the DS2 package method expression as a function in a FedSQL SELECT statement. For more details on how to use FedSQL and DS2 together, see the following SAS documentation *SAS® 9.4 and SAS Viya 3.2 Programming Documentation / DS2 Programmer's Guide - DS2 Concepts - DS2 Packages - Using DS2 and FedSQL: Dynamically Executing FedSQL from DS2.*

For the purposes of this book, examples will be provided using the FEDSQL procedure from SAS Studio and using FedSQL with DS2.

## FedSQL program using the FEDSQL procedure

In this example, the reader will create a new WORK dataset from an existing dataset associated with the library Fedtemp. This uses the v9 engine to assign the library, which is then used within the FEDSQL procedure code. Bring up a new program section within SAS Studio and type the following code:

```
libname Fedtemp v9 "/opt/sasinside/SASHome/SASFoundation/9.4/sashelp";

proc fedsql;
```

```
    create table work.mycars as
    select * from Fedtemp.cars;
quit;
```

On the left-hand side of the SAS Studio session, select **Libraries** and example **My Libraries** so that you can see the WORK library.

Now, submit the code by selecting the running man icon:

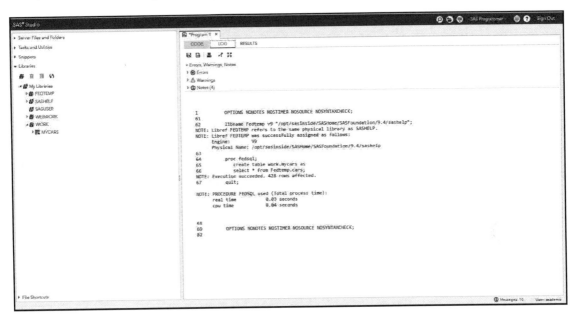

Figure 6.8: FEDSQL procedure example results

There should not be any **ERRORS** in the **LOG** section and the user should now see the WORK.MYCARSdataset under the WORK library in the left section of SAS Studio. Return to the **CODE** section and execute the code again by selecting the running man icon. Are you surprised to see the ERROR generated this time?

**ERROR: Base table or view already exists MYCARS**

If you are used to working with databases, this will not surprise to you since databases require a table to be dropped before it can be recreated. If you were already a SAS programmer, this would come as a surprise because typical SAS programming allows one to write over SAS data sources on the fly, without having to drop or delete them.

This feature of allowing SAS to write over an existing dataset does not apply if the SAS session is using a library that points to tables stored in a database, regardless of whether you're using the SQL procedure or the FEDSQL procedure. This is because, at that point, the database system has control over how the table processing is allowed to occur.

Since this is a SAS source, simply change the code from using the FEDSQL procedure to using the SQL procedure, as follows. You will see how the SQL procedure executes with no **ERROR** and overwrites the existing WORK.MYCARS dataset:

```
libname Fedtemp v9 "/opt/sasinside/SASHome/SASFoundation/9.4/sashelp";

proc sql;
    create table work.mycars as
    select * from Fedtemp.cars;
quit;
```

Run this code by selecting the running man icon. Not only does this SQL code not throw an **ERROR** to the **LOG** as expected, but also it pops up the resulting output table in the **OUTPUT DATA** section to the right of the SAS Studio session:

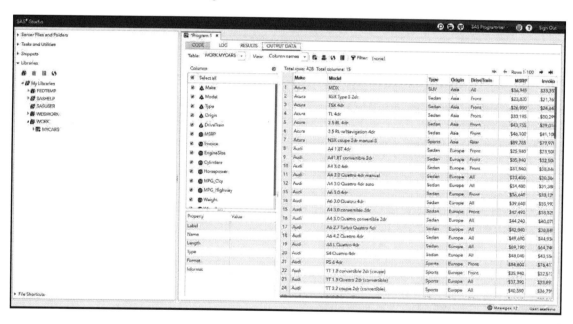

Figure 6.9 SQL procedure result instead of FEDSQL

This difference highlights the fact that FEDSQL was designed to follow the processing guidelines associated with the ANSI standard it was based on, in order to make sure it interacts in a compliant manner when pushing its Federated SQL into a variety of SQL-compliant data sources. Clear out the **CODE** section of your program and continue with the next example.

# Using FedSQL with DS

Type the following code, which combines FedSQL with DS2 by executing a call to a DS2 method as part of the select statement, used by the FEDSQL procedure:

```
data work.fedds2;
   do i=1 to 3;
      do j=1 to 3;
         x=i;
         y=j;
         output;
      end;
   end;
run;

proc ds2;
   package myfedds2;
      method myadd(double x, double y) returns double;
         return x + y;
      end;
   endpackage;
quit;

proc fedsql;
   select * from work.fedds2 where myfedds2.myadd(x,y) in (2,4,6);
quit;
```

Execute this code by selecting the running man icon:

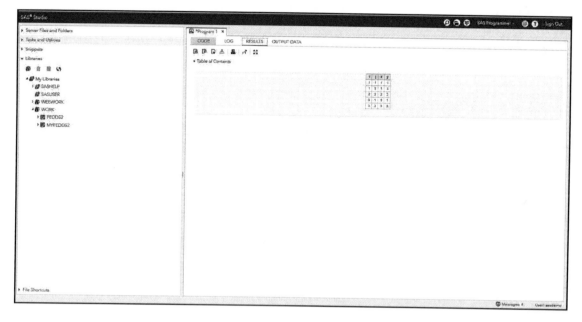

Figure 6.10: FedSQL with DS2 example results

# Summary

You were introduced to two additional programming languages included in BASE SAS, the DS2 language and the FedSQL language.

You learned how DS2 is similar and different from the data step and learned that the DS2 language is an oop language. In addition, you were given an overview of DS2 methods and packages.

We covered variable scope as it pertains to an oop language such as DS2. You learned how to use the DS2 procedure and executed several hands-on exercises to learn some of the basics of writing DS2 programs.

Furthermore, you learned through example how to use the FEDSQL procedure to execute FedSQL programs from SAS Studio as well as FedSQL with DS2.

In the next chapter, you will be exposed to the different types of architectures that are part of the SAS platform and will find out how the platform is engineered to enable users to perform big data analytics with SAS.

# 7

# SAS® Software Engineers the Processing Environment for You

In this chapter, we will cover the following topics:

- The SAS platform
- **Service-Oriented Architecture (SOA)** and microservices
- SAS server versus SAS grid
- In-database processing
- In-memory processing
- Open platform and open source
- Running SAS processing outside the SAS platform
- SAS® Viya™, the newest part of the SAS platform

## Architecture

While working with small data such as the size of data that fits on a desktop or laptop, processing speed is impacted by several factors, such as the speed of the processor or processors, the amount of memory, and the size of the usable disk space. While it is important to optimize the resources at the desktop level to ensure the best response times and the amount of work that can be done, it becomes vital in working with big data to have the proper analytic processing environment setup using the proper configurations and options.

This will ensure a team of architects, data scientists, and business analysts can prepare, analyze, and most importantly, actually put the results of analytics into production as fast as necessary to gain value or provide a competitive advantage.

It is the overall enterprise architecture that allows for big data analytics to process efficiently and to succeed in providing value, or else it becomes a bottleneck that needs to fixed. Analytical insights have to be delivered in a timely manner to enable organizations to continue to grow and thrive. Without the proper analytic processing environment, decision makers will not have access to the best data driven information. This is why the SAS platform is designed by software engineers to enable SAS processing to take advantage of the underlying hardware technologies. This frees SAS programmers and data scientists to focus more on the business value of their work, instead of taking the time and effort required to learn how to allocate memory, write, and validate their own versions of well known and documented algorithms. It also lessens the need to learn in depth about several different programming languages with different syntax, configurations, and options necessary to run those languages effectively, especially on data at scale.

# The SAS platform

While SAS is powerful on a desktop, when big data analytics is part of your objective or goal, the environment being used should at least be a server or be deployed on a SAS grid, in order to have the necessary hardware and processing power to run analytics in a timely manner. Data has grown so large that even servers and a SAS grid won't necessarily be able to handle the volume, velocity, and variety of big data. As a result, SAS developers in R&D have continued to innovate and respond to their customer's needs by developing new techniques and solutions that involve in-database and in-memory processing capabilities. In-database processing moves SAS processing into the data storage system so that the data doesn't have to be copied to the SAS server for processing, and allows the underlying data storage system to run the analysis. Likewise, in-memory technology reduces disk-to-disk data movement across networks. It allows SAS (using patented technology) to load data into an in-memory analytic engine and run the analysis on all of the data using all the CPUs, and by treating the separate independent caches of memory as if they were a single, large shared pool.

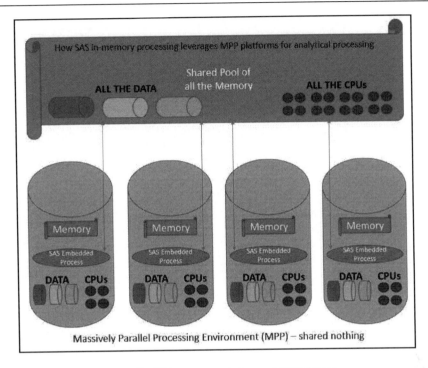

Figure 7.1: How SAS in-memory processing leverages an MPP environment

Originally, SAS was developed in the 1970s to run on mainframes, but early in the 1980s, the SAS leadership made a decision to completely rewrite the SAS system, as it was called back then, in the C programming language. This turned the SAS language into the first version of the SAS platform. This made SAS a portable analytic processing environment that could run across a wide variety of operating systems such as Unix, Windows, MVS, CMS, and VMS. At this point, roughly 95% of the code was able to be used on any of these operating systems with dedicated SAS R&D host developers, who worked on optimizing the execution of SAS on their particular host operating system. The reader needs to understand that at this time, which predates the Java programming language, there were no other programming languages available in which one could develop code on one operating system such as Unix, and deploy it into production on a variety of other operating systems. This shows one way in which SAS has always recognized that the real value of analytics is achieved only when the results can be put to use or deployed into a production system, regardless of what type of operating system or systems are involved. This vital lesson has continued to be the main focus of the SAS platform and the offerings that SAS develops based on customer-focused feedback. This still helps drive innovation and ongoing changes to the software today.

# Service-Oriented Architecture and microservices

During the 1990s, the second version of the SAS platform came into being as SAS became the only metadata-based platform designed to support the entire end-to-end analytics life cycle. This was described earlier in `Chapter 1`, *Setting Up the SAS® Software Environment*, under the *History of the SAS analytics platform* section. It included data management, analytical data management and preparation, analytic discovery, insight development, and deploying analytical insights into production. This second version of the SAS platform was designed to be SOA compliant and as such, takes a **monolithic** approach in how it gets deployed, configured, and maintained. What all this really means is that if any part of this SOA part of the SAS environment needs to be updated or changed, the entire system needs to be taken offline for some time in order for additions or updates to be made.

 This does not apply only to the SAS platform, but to all SOA enterprise type solutions.

More recently, microservices-based platforms (of which many are big data platforms, including cloud platforms, as well as newly developed offerings for the SAS platform) have been embraced. Microservices take a different approach than SOA in that services provide specific functionalities that are small in scope, but bundled together with other services to provide an enterprise-level platform of functionality. Microservices allow systems to continue to function without the need for interruption when doing additions or updates because they are independent of each other, and therefore can be stopped and started quickly without affecting the entire system. In addition to this benefit, microservices provide an environment with more resiliency. This allows the system to recover more quickly from disruptions because more than one instance of a particular service can be running, so it will still function properly if one of these instances happens to stop running for any reason.

# Differences between SOA and microservices

Even though SOA and microservices have some common features, such as allowing different pieces of functionality to be developed by different teams of developers, with SOA, the developers must all understand the common communication mechanism shared across the platform. With microservices, there isn't a common communication mechanism because the services communicate with each other through sets of language-agnostic APIs. Within an SOA-based application, a single function that has a problem such as a memory leak can become a bottleneck, and a single point of failure for the entire environment.

However, with microservices, one instance of a service that may develop a memory leak does not affect the other instances performing the same function, and as such it will not become a single point of failure. In SOA, all services share a common data storage system, while in microservices, each service may contain its own independent data storage. A service within an SOA environment may contain microservices; however, a microservice does not contain an SOA service.

 Regardless of which architecture is chosen, developers must deal with the complexities of that particular architecture and with working in distributed environments.

# SAS server versus a SAS grid

The SAS platform can be run on a single server environment based on **Symmetrical Mutliprocessing (SMP)**, which means programs are processed using multiple CPUs that share a common operating system and memory. This is referred to as a **share everything environment**. The SAS platform has been designed to make the most of this multiprocessing environment with different SAS options and configuration settings. In addition, over the years, certain SAS procedures have been rewritten to take full advantage of multiple cores and multiple threads associated with the advancements made in CPU development. SAS programmers didn't have to learn new syntax for these procedures, though they might have needed to add new options to their existing programs, or have their server administrator set a new configuration option in order to take advantage of the this improved performance enabled by these types of changes. Even if they didn't change their programs to take advantage of new performance enhancements, their programs would still run as they had previously. Running on a single server means that to improve overall performance or add more users to the environment without impacting the existing response times, it will need to be scaled up.

This means, if possible, adding more CPUs, memory, and/or storage to the existing server or upgrading to a completely new server with more CPUs, more memory, and more storage:

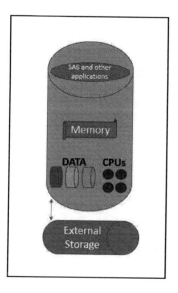

Figure 7.2: Simple SMP server with optional externally attached storage

While single-server environments are still very common today, and in some cases make the most sense when it comes to big data analytics, this type of environment is not feasible due to the effort and expense it would take to try and scale up continuously to meet the ever-growing needs associated with more data and more users needing access to this data.

This is why organizations working with big data--particularly big data analytics--prefer a distributed type of processing environment, which is provided using the MPP type of design. This is also why SAS developed what can be considered the third version of the SAS platform in the 2000s called the **SAS Grid Manager**, which will be referred to as simply as the SAS grid for the rest of this book:

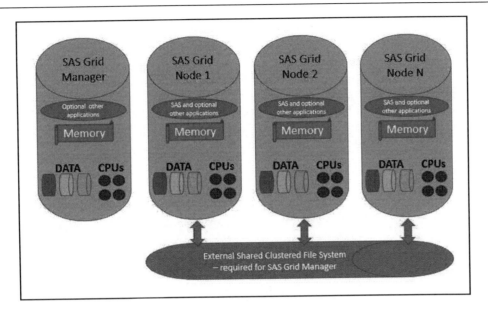

Figure 7.3: SAS grid runs distributed across multiple servers

This distributed processing environment makes scaling out possible instead of scaling up. Scaling out means additional servers can be added as new nodes within the SAS grid, without changing any of the existing hardware in place. This makes it possible to use less expensive commodity hardware servers, such as those referred to as blades. You can also start out with a two-node SAS grid and grow it over time in order to meet performance needs, increase in data processing size, and/or the addition of more users requiring access to the system.

SAS allows the environment to combine both scaling up and scaling out at the same time if the business needs require it. Attaining consistent and reliable performance for big data analytics requires the right choice of scalable hardware and the proper software designed specifically to make the most of that underlying hardware.

Over the years, the size of data that the SAS platform needed to process effectively within faster and faster response times demanded by customers continued to grow. SAS responded with new and different offerings. One of those offerings was a specialized SAS storage option called the **SAS Scalable Performance Data Server (SPDS)**, which was discussed briefly in `Chapter 1`, *Setting Up the SAS® Software Environment*. SPDS was designed as an MPP system that broke up large data files into smaller subsets, and stored these subsets across a distributed server environment.

The development and deployment/use by customers of the SPDS predates the public availability of Hadoop by many years. The architectures of both systems are similar because they both make use of the MPP design. This should not be interpreted to imply that SPDS was or is the same type of MPP big data compute platform, but this does show that SAS customers were enabled to process big data and that SAS developers were designing the SAS platform to work efficiently with big data well before the term big data was coined and defined by the three V's—volume, variety, and velocity.

Prior to Hadoop being made available through the open source Apache project, many SAS customers had been combining the processing power of a SAS grid with a SAS SPDS in order to effectively process what at that time was considered huge data for other systems, especially when it came to being able to apply advanced analytical processing on that size of data. Everyone who works with technology knows that things change, and technology advancements come along quite often that impact or disrupt the entire software and hardware industries. Hadoop was one of those changes that SAS and every other vendor had to figure out how best to leverage and/or what needed to be redesigned or redeveloped in order to best process analytics in conjunction with this big data compute environment.

Hadoop is now one of the biggest MPP-based computing environments widely accepted and in use today. But prior to its introduction and adoption, several new database vendors such as Teradata and Greenplum entered the database market, offering MPP designed databases to challenge the existing SMP-based database vendors. In additon, following the introduction of these new MPP database offerings, many of the SMP-based database vendors transitioned their offerings from SMP to MPP design as well, such as Oracle and DB2. One of the unique strengths of the SAS platform has always been the fact that SAS is database agnostic, which allows it to work with data from any source. When these MPP databases entered the market, SAS had been working with the vendors to develop SAS/ACCESS engines to specifically work with their databases, whether they were SMP or MPP. It was at this time that SAS developed their first in-database processing technology and offerings.

# In-database processing

SAS in-database processing technology is when SAS processing gets pushed down into a database or data storage system, such as Hadoop or SAP HANA. This technology was originally co-developed with MPP database vendors, for example, Teradata and Greenplum. By pushing certain SAS processing down into the database, much time was saved since the data was processed by the database initially and sent back a result set to SAS for further processing, instead of simply pulling all the data out of the database and then doing all the processing within the SAS environment.

# In-database procedures

Initially, there were only six BASE SAS procedures that could take advantage of in-database processing FREQ, RANK, SORT, REPORT, SUMMARY/MEANS, and TABULATE. In addition, formats can also be created and then pushed or published into a database or storage system to further allow more SAS processing to take place within the database. All of these in-database procedures are supported in the following systems: Aster, DB2, Greenplum, Hadoop, HAWQ, Impala, Microsoft SQL Server, Netezza, Oracle, PostgreSQL, Redshift, SAP HANA, and Vertica.

> The only additional software besides BASE SAS that is required to take advantage of these six procedures running in-database is the licensing of the specific SAS/ACCESSS interface associated with that particular data source.

There are several other procedures across a few other SAS offerings, co-developed to have in-database processing capabilities within Teradata. In addition to the six BASE procedures listed previously, the following procedures can run in-database within Teradata CORR, CANCORR, DMDB, DMINE, DMREG, FACTOR, PRIMCOMP, REG, SCORE, TIMESERIES, and TRANSPOSE.

> The TRANSPOSE procedure has also been enhanced to run in-database within Hadoop; however, it requires the licensing of additional software beyond just BASE and the SAS/ACCESS interface for Hadoop.

In the case of in-database processing, the parts that run within the data storage system run under the rules and constraints that have been set up by the administrators of that particular database or big data platform:

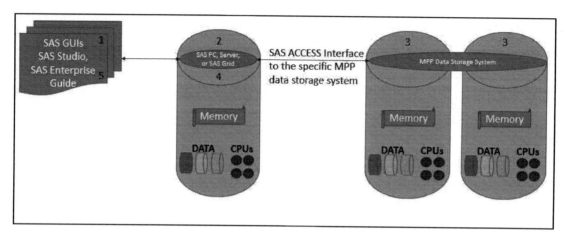

Figure 7.4: In-database processing

SAS code is submitted by a SAS client or GUI in step 1 of *Figure 7.4* to the SAS environment, whether it is a **SAS PC, Server, or SAS Grid** (step 2 in *Figure 7.4*). The SAS environment then executes the code and passes along any of the in-database processing steps via the appropriate **SAS ACCESS Interface to the specific MPP data storage system** for processing within the data storage system (step 3 in *Figure 7.4*). The **MPP Data Storage System** then returns a result set from the in-database processing to the SAS environment for any additional processing needed (step 4). Then, the execution results are sent back to the SAS client (step 5).

For complete details about in-database processing associated with BASE procedures and the use of the proper SAS ACCESS interface see, *Part 6: In-Database Procedures and the system options that affect in-database processing* and *Part 7: System Options Reference of the SAS documentation: SAS® 9.4 and SAS Viya 3.2 Programming Documentation / In-Database Products: User's Guide - SAS® 9.4 In-Database Products: User's Guide, Seventh Edition* (http://documentation.sas.com/?cdcId=pgmsascdccdcVersion=9.4_3.2 docsetId=indbugdocsetTarget=titlepage.htmlocale=en)

# Additonal in-database processing SAS offerings

In addition to the in-database processing capabilities that come with the use of a SAS ACCESS interface to a supported data storage system, there are other SAS offerings available that enable even more SAS processing to run in-database on the supported systems. These other offerings rely on the **SAS Embedded Process (SASEP)** to be installed across the data storage system. The SASEP is a portable, lightweight execution container for SAS code that makes SAS portable and deployable on a variety of platforms. In the case of these SAS in-database offerings, the SAS Scoring Accelerator, the SAS Analytics Accelerator, and the SAS Code Accelerator, the SASEP serves to extend the functionality of the data storage system beyond its normal capabilities:

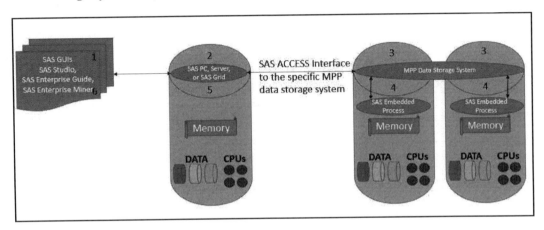

Figure 7.5: In-database processing with SASEP

The difference between *Figure 7.4* and *Figure 7.5* is that, in this case, the code that runs within the MPP data storage system actually processes the data using the SASEP to run SAS logic within the data storage system.

## SAS Scoring Accelerator

The SAS Scoring Accelerator is an add-on for customers that have licensed SAS/STAT or SAS Enterprise Miner on a server or SAS grid. The SAS Scoring Accelerator enables a user to automatically publish the logic from the supported SAS/STAT procedures or nodes within SAS Enterprise Miner that produces scoring logic into a native function within the supported data storage system.

This automated process developed by SAS developers takes the SAS code that is generated for scoring and converts it into a DS2 program on the fly. It is this DS2 program that is then published into the data storage system and executes within the SASEP when called.

Once this logic has been published as a native call within the data storage system, the SAS scoring logic can be utilized or called within that system like any other of its native functions. This means that all of the execution of the scoring logic happens within the data storage system without any execution or processing to be done by the SAS environment that published the scoring logic. This saves a tremendous amount of time to value because there is no need to move data outside where it is stored to be scored.

Scoring data is the true value generated by a predictive model, because it provides the user with a number between *0* and *1* or the percentage of likelihood of an event to take place before it actually does. The higher the value, the greater the confidence that the event will happen. For more details about the SAS Scoring Accelerator, see *Part 2: SAS Scoring Accelerator* of *SAS documentation: SAS® 9.4 and SAS Viya 3.2 Programming Documentation / In-Database Products: User's Guide - SAS® 9.4 In-Database Products: User's Guide, Seventh Edition* (http://documentation.sas.com/? cdcId=pgmsascdccdcVersion=9.4_3.2docsetId=indbugdocsetTarget= p1qb084tkpqjvvn1reip5mnx21sl.htmlocale=en).

## SAS Code Accelerator

The SAS Code Accelerator allows more than the scoring logic from a predictive model to be moved into and executed within the supported data storage systems. The SAS Code Accelerator allows users to publish a DS2 thread program into the data storage system to have it executed in parallel within the data storage system. At the time of writing this book, this functionality was supported in Hadoop, Teradata, and Greenplum.

The SAS Code Accelerator for Hadoop and the SAS Code Accelerator for Teradata also allows users to publish and execute DS2 data programs within the data storage system. For more details about the SAS Code Accelerator, see *Part 3: SAS In-Database Code Accelerator of the SAS documentation: SAS® 9.4 and SAS Viya 3.2 Programming Documentation / In-Database Products: User's Guide - SAS® 9.4 In-Database Products: User's Guide, Seventh Edition* (http://documentation.sas.com/?cdcId= pgmsascdccdcVersion=9.4_3.2docsetId=indbugdocsetTarget= titlepage.htmlocale=en).

While in-database processing is great for continuing to use the data storage system as usual and to reduce the movement of data across the network, there are times when analytic processing needs more resources, such as all the CPUs and all the system memory, to process some types of analytics. In these cases, the database rules and resource management systems will not allow this to happen, because it would impact all the other applications that are sharing all the same resources used by the data storage system. This is why SAS developers continued to innovate and lead them to develop at the requests of our customers in-memory processing technology.

# In-memory processing

In-memory processing technology developed by SAS moves beyond the bounds associated with the database or big data platform, and allows the SAS processing to access as much of the system resources necessary to execute successfully. This may require the use of all the CPUs and all the memory in order to deliver the required answer in time to assist decision makers. The ability to analytically process all the data and return results in seconds or minutes which normally took days or weeks provides users with what is called the ability to fail fast.

> Failing fast is a good capability since it enables a single data scientist to test out multiple theories or approaches in a fraction of the time that they were used to having to run only one theory to address a complex business question or situation.

SAS developers initially developed two types of in-memory processing techniques to address two different use cases that had been gathered from our customers.

## SAS High-Performance Analytics Server

One use case was aimed at providing individual users the ability to use very large data to develop predictive models through the typical iterative approach data scientists have traditionally done in performing their data mining related work. In this type of work, each user that ran analytics on a set of data was allocated enough memory to copy all the data into their own set of memory, run their analytics on the data held in memory, and then drop the data from memory. This enabled a single user that had access to the proper environment to run a specific set of SAS analytics in a fraction of the time required in their old processing environment.

This specific set of SAS analytics was a set of newly developed SAS high-performance procedures or HP PROCs that were developed to make use of this technology. All of these HP PROCs were initially available in a single offering known as the SAS High-Performance Analytics Server. For more details on the SAS High-Performance Analytics Server, see the following SAS documentation: https://support.sas.com/documentation/onlinedoc/hp-analytics-server/index.html

Instead of having all these HP PROCs only available in one large bundle, the capabilities are bundled as high performance procedures and included within the standard offerings associated with the types of analysis performed by these high performance procedures: within SAS/STAT the SAS® High-Performance Statistics procedures are included, within SAS/ETS the SAS® High-Performance Econometrics procedures are included, within SAS/OR the SAS® High-Performance Optimization procedures are included, within SAS Forecast Server the SAS® High-Performance Forecasting procedures are included, within SAS Enterprise Miner the SAS® High-Performance Data Mining nodes and procedures are included, and with SAS Text Mining the SAS® High-Performance Text Mining procedures are included.

One of the challenges with these HP PROCs is that each job that runs an HP PROC grabs its own individual chunk of memory. So if three jobs are submitted that use a table that is 1 GB in size, the system they run on has to have at least 3 GB of free memory for all three jobs to run concurrently. Then each copy of the data is dropped out of memory as each job's execution finishes:

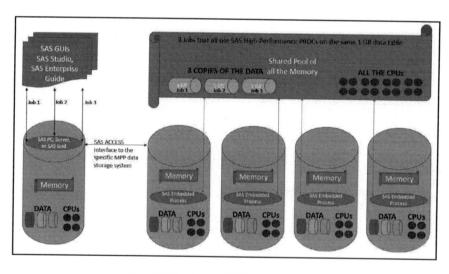

Figure 7.6: High-performance PROCs in-memory processing

# SAS LASR Analytics Server

The second use case was designed to lift one copy of data into one instance of the necessary memory to hold it while many users are given access to it and allowed to perform analysis and reporting. This data remains in this allocated memory until a user or administrator with the proper permission removes it from memory. This second case led to the development of SAS's first version of an in-memory analytics server called the **SAS LASR Server**. Customers cannot license the SAS LASR Server by itself, instead, SAS developed solutions which made use of this SAS LASR Server for the back end for holding data in-memory and performing actions many of which are analytic actions, upon this data. The advantage of this design is that only one copy of the data is needed to be held in memory and can be used by multiple users at the same time. SAS® Visual Analytics (VA) and SAS® Visual Statistics (VS) were the first solutions developed to make use of the SAS LASR Server which could be installed and used either on a single server environment or on a distributed server environment. The distributed server environment allows these solutions to easily scale out using inexpensive commodity blade hardware, and is only limited in the size of data they can process by the amount of memory available within their environment:

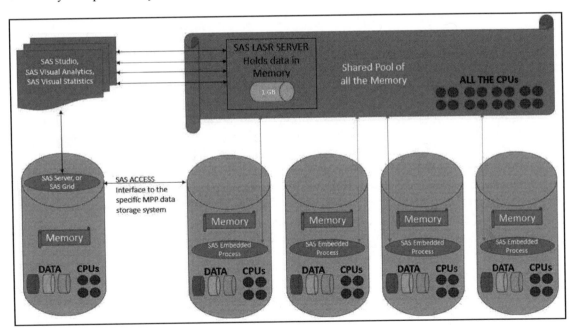

Figure 7.7: SAS LASR Server in-memory processing

For more details about the SAS LASR Analytics Server, see the SAS documentation available here: https://support.sas.com/documentation/onlinedoc/lasrserver/index.html.

# SAS Cloud Analytics Server

SAS continued to improve and innovate as has been it's history, and developed what many consider it's 3rd generation in-memory technology, know as the SAS® Cloud Analytics Server (CAS). This third generation in-memory technology combined the best features of the first two while improving on the overall resiliency and fail over capabilities, along with being designed to run more seamlessly with cloud platforms. Running SAS in the cloud will be discussed further in this chapter under the *SAS running in a Cloud* section. Like the SAS LASR Server, the CAS is not available as a standalone solution, but instead, CAS serves as the key in-memory analytics server within the SAS Viya architecture, where SAS Viya is the microservices based architecture of the overall SAS platform. CAS will be discussed further in this chapter under the *SAS running in a Cloud* section. For details on CAS, specifically see this part of the *SAS Viya related documentation: SAS Viya 3.2 Administration / CAS Fundamentals* (http://documentation.sas.com/?cdcId=pgmsascdccdcVersion=9.4_3.2 docsetId=casfundocsetTarget=titlepage.htmlocale=en).

SAS customers drove the development of these new in-memory offerings and were excited with how much data they could process and the magnitudes of improvement in the time it takes to successful run their analytics. When Hadoop was being adopted as a big data platform, SAS in-memory offerings allowed customers to leverage this for big data analytics. In this type of MPP environment, the SASEP would be installed on all the nodes of the Hadoop cluster and as such your SAS analytics could now be co-located and run where your big data was stored. Have you figured out a potential downside in co-location? SAS's customers did, once they got over the excitement of the speed at which analytics could be implied to all their data at once. By enhancing this big data storage and compute platform to perform analytics, one is changing the fundamental use of what Hadoop was originally designed to do, which is to serve as a big data storage and compute platform, not an analytics compute platform. The reason this is a problem is that when certain analytic workloads run within this MPP environment, they use all the memory and all the processing resources to complete their task; and when this happens, all the other processes and systems that share the data within this platform either slow down or simply stop working. You may ask yourself, *What about the resource management features of Hadoop such as Yarn? Can't they resolve this contention for resources issue?* Well, yes it can, and SAS processing can be controlled by Yarn, but when this happens, your analytics processing time is impacted in much the same way as when they run in-database. How does one resolve this issue? With dedicated hardware for performing in-memory analytics:

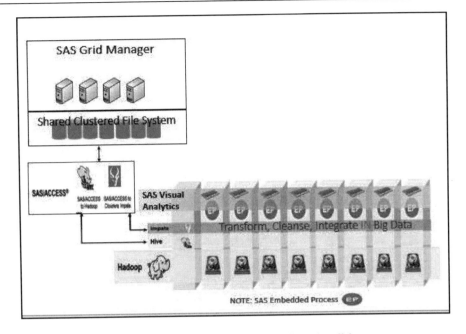

Figure 7.8: SAS Grid Manager with in-memory co-located processing on Hadoop

# Dedicated hardware for in-memory processing

SAS listened to their customers and developed the capability to run the SAS processing from data that resides in a large Hadoop cluster in-memory on hardware that is dedicated for use for SAS processing running, alongside the regular big data storage and compute platform. The SASEP is still the key that allows this alongside dedicated in-memory analytics processing of data that resides in a separate Hadoop big data storage and compute platform without impacting the processing of the entire Hadoop system. In this case, the SASEP is still installed across each node in the Hadoop cluster, but the SASEP is also installed across the nodes in the dedicated alongside environment as well. With this architecture, the data is still lifted in a massively parallel way into memory within the Hadoop cluster, but then the SASEPs serve as a lighting fast memory to memory data transfer from the Hadoop cluster into the dedicated analytics environment.

This prevents the need for a disk to disk copy or duplication of the big data stored in Hadoop and allows for the alongside system resources to be 100% dedicated to doing SAS analytical processing without impacting the performance of the original Hadoop environment:

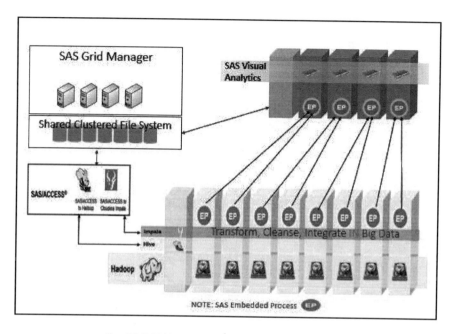

Figure 7.9: SAS Grid Manager with in-memory processing alongside Hadoop

# Open platform and open source

SAS has always been an open platform, which means it has been developed to integrate and work with other systems through commonly accepted standards and communication protocols. Whether it's through SOA based web services, data access, APIs or through microservices based services, data access, or APIs SAS continues to embrace working with other systems and protocols. SAS is committed to ensure it's technology works well with open source. For example, SAS is a **Gold member of Cloud Foundry**, which is the world's largest leading open source platform for cloud applications. SAS is also a member of the **Open Data Platform Initiative (ODPi)** and a founding member of Hortonwork's **Data Governance Initiative (DGI)**, which is a joint engineering initiative aimed at addressing the enterprise requirements for comprehensive data governance.

For more information on Cloud Foundry, go to the organization's web page www.cloudfoundry.org. For more information on ODPi, go to its organization's web page https://www.odpi.org/.

The SAS platform has Python, Lua, and REST APIs and has developed different ways to integrate with R, for example, through SAS/IML (Interactive Matrix Language) or the open source node within SAS Enterprise Miner as well as having an R API which are discussed a bit more later in this chapter under the *SAS Viya the newest part of the SAS platform* section. The SAS platform and its solutions are not meant to replace open source, but instead SAS has been designed to integrate, complement, and work with open source technologies to enable the development of an enterprise analytics platform. There are two main ways in which SAS and open source integrate and enhance each other—SAS running within open source environments such as Hadoop or OpenStack, and running open source within SAS.

# Running SAS from an iPython Jupyter Notebook

The SAS® University Edition allows a user to not only make use of the SAS Studio GUI for programming in SAS, but also start a Jupyter Notebook to be used as the interface to work with SAS as well. Make sure you have your SAS® University Edition virtual machine running, and type the following in your browser's URL: http://localhost:10080.

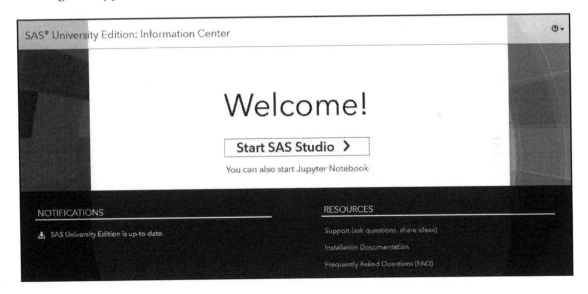

Figure 7.10: Opening Window for SAS® University Edition virtual machine

To start the Jupyter Notebook, simply click on the **start Jupyter Notebook** link:

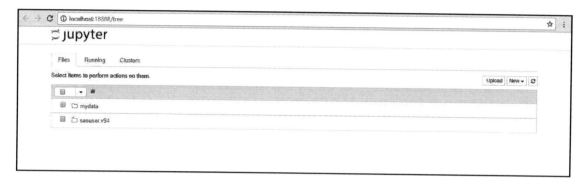

Figure 7.11: Starting a Jupyter Notebook within SAS® University Edition

In the upper right-hand corner of the Jupyter Notebook, select **New** | **SAS**:

Figure 7.11: Jupyter Notebook new SAS

Now, type the following SAS code in the Jupyter Notebook In [ ]: section:

```
data work.temp;
    x=1;
run;

proc print data=work.temp;
run;
```

The Jupyter Notebook should now look like the following.

Figure 7.12: Jupyter Notebook SAS kernel with SAS code

Select **Cell** | **Run Cells** and select **Below**, which will submit the SAS code and return the results of the PROC `print` to the Jupyter Notebook:

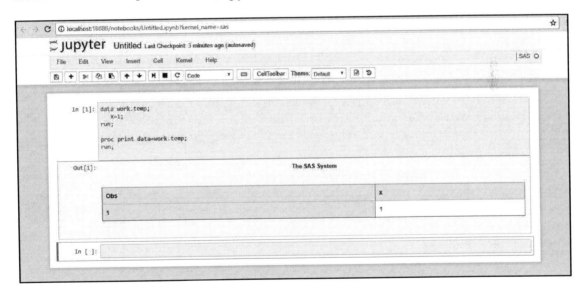

Figure 7.12: SAS results return and displayed in the Jupyter Notebook

What about the SAS **LOG**? This is available as well, by selecting the icon to the right of the **Theme** dropdown box:

```
←  →  C   ⓘ about:blank

11   ods listing close;ods html5 file=stdout options(bitmap_mode='inline') device=png; ods graphics on / outputfmt=png;
NOTE: Writing HTML5 Body file: STDOUT
12
13   data work.temp;
14       x=1;
15   run;
NOTE: The data set WORK.TEMP has 1 observations and 1 variables.
NOTE: DATA statement used (Total process time):
      real time           0.00 seconds
      cpu time            0.00 seconds

16
17   proc print data=work.temp;
18   run;
NOTE: There were 1 observations read from the data set WORK.TEMP.
NOTE: PROCEDURE PRINT used (Total process time):
      real time           0.01 seconds
      cpu time            0.01 seconds

19
20   ods html5 close;ods listing;

21
```

Figure 7.13: SAS LOG from within the Jupyter Notebook

This **sas_kernel** for the Jupyter Notebook is available to anyone worldwide through the well- known online code development and sharing platform GitHub©. For this **sas_kernel** and other open source contributions from SAS developers, visit the SAS® software repositories located at `https://github.com/sassoftware`:

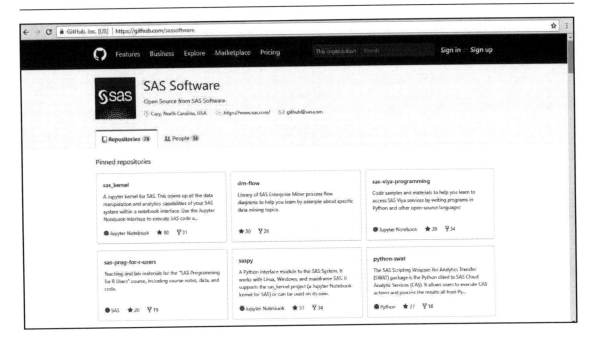

Figure 7.13: SAS® software GitHub repositories

The reader can take any of the previous code examples within this book and run them using the Jupyter Notebook as their interface instead of SAS Studio. Let's run one of the previous examples from Chapter 5, *Reporting with SAS® Software*, which generated some graphical output instead of just a table. Bring up a new SAS program within the Jupyter Notebook and type the following code, or read the tip after it:

```
/*--VBox Plot--*/

title 'Mileage by Type and Origin';
proc sgplot data=sashelp.cars(where=(type in ('Sedan' 'Sports'))) ;
  vbox mpg_city / category=origin group=type groupdisplay=cluster
    lineattrs=(pattern=solid) whiskerattrs=(pattern=solid);
  xaxis display=(nolabel);
  yaxis grid;
  keylegend / location=inside position=topright across=1;
  run;
```

This is the code generated from one of the snippets within SAS Studio; see *Figure 5.6* from `Chapter 5`, *Reporting with SAS® Software* . Instead of typing this code, the reader can save some time. Bring up a SAS Studio instance in one web page, and on the left, select the **Snippets** section. Then expand **Snippets**, followed by **Graph**, and double-click on the **VBox Plot** snippet. Now, open another tab in the web browser and type `https://localhost:10080`. Select **start Jupyter Notebook** to have both interfaces open at once. Instead of typing the preceding code in the Jupyter Notebook, the reader can now copy and paste the code from the SAS Studio program section into the Jupyter Notebook SAS program.

Either way, you should end up with a Jupyter Notebook SAS program that looks like the following:

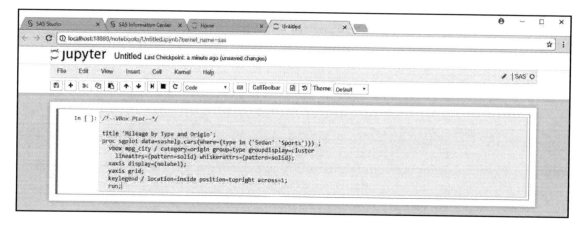

Figure 7.14: Jupyter Notebook with SAS code from SAS Studio Snippets

Now, select **Cell | Run Cells** and Select **Below** to submit the SAS code.

When the code is submitted, there may be a bit of time lag between submitting and returning the results to the Jupyter Notebook. If so, the reader will see another Jupyter Notebook input cell pop up immediately before the Jupyter Notebook Output cell that contains the graph in *Figure 7.15*.

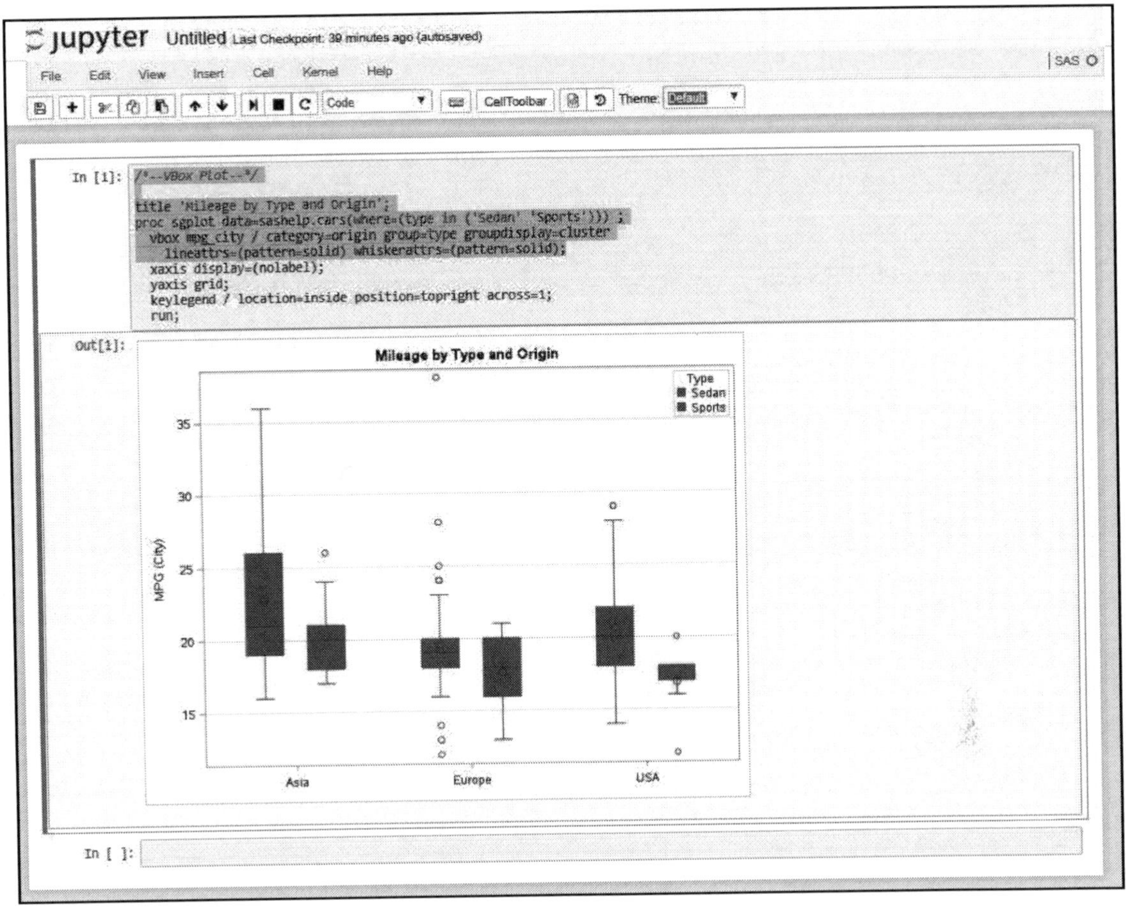

Figure 7.15: SAS Studio VBox Plot snippet code results within Jupyter Notebook

This graph output is the same as was generated in *Figure 5.7* however, this output is now savable outside the SAS environment as it can be saved inside this Jupyter Notebook as a `named.ipjnb` file. This is just one way in which SAS inter-operates with open source technology.

Now, let's try submitting a DS2 code example through the Jupyter Notebook interface. Type the following code into a new SAS code Jupyter Notebook input cell:

This is the same DS2 code program that was used at the end of Chapter 6, *Other Programming Languages in BASE SAS® Software*, of this book.

```
proc ds2 libs=work;
   package myexample;
      declare int x y;
      method myadd(int x, int y) returns int;
          put 'In package myexample';
          return x + y;
      end;
   endpackage;
run;

   data _null_;
      declare package myexample add();

      method init();
      end;

      method run();
         declare int a;
         declare int b;
         declare int add_result;
         a=10;
         b=5;
         add_result= add.myadd(a,b);
         put 'a plus b is equal to: ' add_result;
      end;
      method term();
      end;
   enddata;
run;
```

Once again, select **Cell | Run Cells** and Select **Below** to submit the SAS code, which should produce the following output:

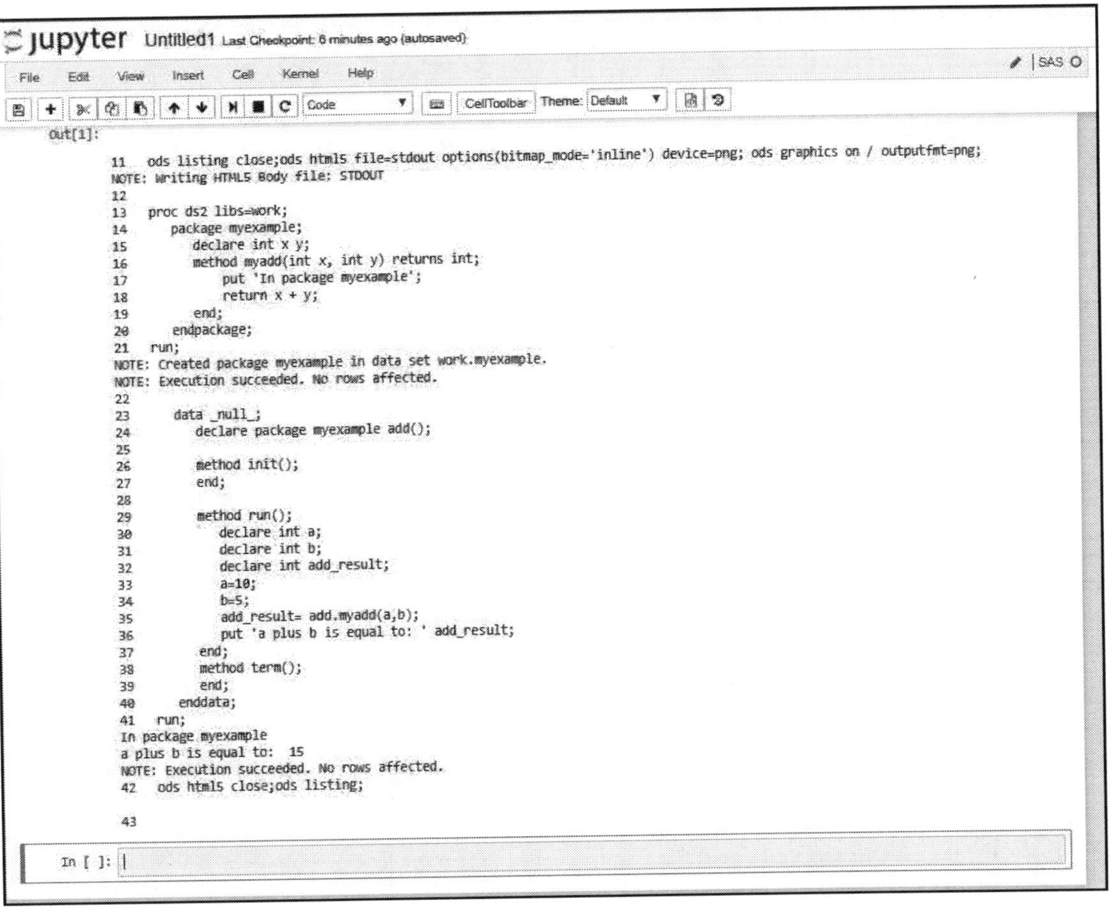

Figure 7.16: DS2 Program results within Jupyter Notebook

# SAS running in a cloud

One cannot talk about big data or big data analytics without also talking about running in a cloud. What is a cloud? According to the **National Institute of Standards and Technology (NIST)**, cloud computing is defined as follows:

> *"Cloud computing is a model for enabling convenient, on-demand network access to a shared pool of configurable computing resources (e.g., networks, servers, storage, applications, and services) that can be rapidly provisioned and released with minimal management effort or service provider interaction."*

The reader can just think of the cloud as a large computer server farm or data center meant to reduce the overall cost of running and administering the IT infrastructure, by allowing clients to rent, compute, application, and data storage services without having to buy, install, configure, and administer all these on their own hardware.

There are four main cloud deployment models:

- Public cloud
- Private cloud
- Community cloud
- Hybrid cloud

From a technical perspective, the SAS platform and its solutions can all be deployed and run in any of the cloud environments. However, from a support and business perspective, SAS supports running in public, private, and hybrid environments; the hybrid environment in this case must be made up of public and private clouds that work together.

For more details on cloud computing, be sure to review the NNIST cloud computing program at https://www.nist.gov/programs-projects/nist-cloud-computing-program-nccp.

## A public cloud

A public cloud is hosted by a cloud provider, so technically, public simply means it is available to any person or organization in the general public who pays the cloud provider for the use of their private space within the cloud providers vast server farm. Each client then runs their own application with their own data within their own secure environment, which makes use of a subset of the overall underlying computing resources of the server farm or cloud.

Public clouds are physically located off-premises from all their respective clients. The main providers or host companies for public clouds used by individuals or organizations are:

- **Amazon Web Services (AWS)**
- Google Cloud Platform
- IBM SoftLayer
- Microsoft Azure

## A private cloud

A private cloud is very much like the public cloud described previously; however, in this case, the cloud happens to be located on-premise at the client's location. On-premise cloud providers are:

- OpenStack
- Microsoft Azure Stack

Functionality wise, these private clouds work the same way as the public cloud, but the server farm in this case resides within the client's own data-center. Therefore, the client's applications and data remain under their full control, because the cloud hardware is physically located in their own premises.

## A hybrid cloud

As described previously, a hybrid cloud is an environment in which a combination of other cloud environments work together in some manner to achieve a particular client's needs. SAS supports this hybrid model when it involves the use of private and public clouds. A typical use case that may involve this type of hybrid environment would be allowing for more cloud elasticity than is available in whichever is the smaller overall environment. The vast majority of these situations will involve a smaller private cloud and the use of extra compute resources from the public cloud when needed. The term **cloud bursting** falls within this type of use case, and usually means that during a particular time within a week, month, quarter, or year, additional computing power is needed in order to complete a task on a larger set of data than at any other time. This saves time and money because the client isn't paying for the extra hardware or storage that isn't normally needed on a day-to-day basis, but rents the additional resources when they are needed to meet these higher processing times.

# Running SAS processing outside the SAS platform

In order to save time and resources, and to solve problems as quickly as possible, analytics must be implemented outside traditional data storage systems or analytical processing environments.

## The SAS Embedded Process

This is what led SAS to develop in-database and in-memory processing technologies, which were discussed earlier in this chapter. The SASEP is the underlying technology that enables in-database processing, and plays a key role in supporting in-memory solutions by prepping, transforming, and lifting data into memory. As the SASEP is more of an enabling technology, programmers make use of it once it has been installed and configured by an administrator or technical architecture. For more details of all the solutions that rely on the SASEP, see the following *SAS documentation: SAS® 9.4 and SAS Viya 3.2 Programming Documentation / In-Database Products: Administrator's Guide - SAS® 9.4 In-Database Products: Administrator's Guide, Eighth Edition* (http://documentation.sas.com/?cdcId=pgmsascdc cdcVersion=9.4_3.2docsetId=indbagdocsetTarget=titlepage.htmlocale=en).

In order to continue pushing SAS and analytical processing outside the normal bounds of not only the SAS platform, but also the confines of data storage systems, SAS developed the SAS® Event Stream Processing engine.

## The SAS Event Stream Processing engine

Event stream processing falls under the complex event streaming domain, and the SAS Event Stream Processing engine allows SAS processing and analytics to occur on data in stream. It can be installed not only within the internal networks running in companies, manufacturing plants, utilities, and so on, but also outside this network where the Internet or an electric grid or equipment exists. By having an event stream processing engine processing data in stream decisions or actions on what to do with this data or actions that should take place because of this data can now be processed in real-time.

This engine is not just a one-way path, so additional rules and updated analytics can be pushed into it when needed, and as such, changes to actions and decisions can be done in place without having to physically change out hardware. This is the key technology that enables proactive preventive maintenance on all sorts of equipment, such as those used on a manufacturing line, as part of the electrical grid, within a refinery, oil or gas rigs, locomotives, planes, vehicles, or even appliances.

This technology does not replace the traditional offline analysis of data, but adds to the ability to make use of analytics-driven insights in the collection of data, as well as applying both rules and analytics wherever it makes the most sense to improve processes or to resolve issues.

# SAS Viya the newest part of the SAS platform

SAS Viya is the newest part of the SAS platform and is based on microservices. As mentioned previously in this chapter the core of this SAS Viya architecture is the CAS. SAS developers have not only rewritten procedures to take advantage of this new architecture but also continued to develop new and improved procedures. SAS Viya has been designed to be cloud ready, meaning it integrates and operates within a variety of the cloud platforms available in the market today. SAS has been rolling out new offerings on SAS Viya, and this microservices-based architecture allows three different deployment options:

- **Full deployment** (both programming and visual interfaces): This is the default option
- **Programming-only deployment**: This excludes general services and visual interfaces
- **Visual-only deployment**: This excludes SAS Studio and most SAS programming functionality

To further integrate SAS with other systems and programming languages, SAS Viya supports APIs aimed at developers for SAS, REST, Python, Java, Lua, Python, and R. BASE SAS containing PROC CAS, which allows SAS solutions not based on SAS Viya to connect and run CAS actions in a SAS CAS. SAS has launched a new web portal specifically for developers and data scientists at https://developer.sas.com/home.html to guide users on how best to make use of these APIs for developing applications:

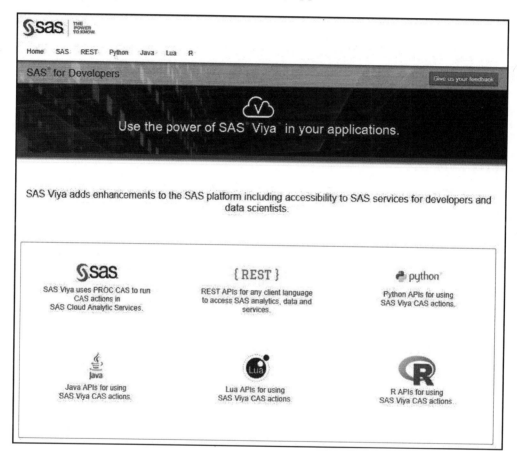

Figure 7.17: SAS for developers web page

# SAS Viya programming

There are different options that allow for users and programmers to interact with solutions that run on the SAS Viya part of the SAS platform. You will already familiar with one way, because it's using SAS Studio in very much the same way which has already learned through the examples in this book. When SAS Studio connects to an environment in which SAS Viya in included, new features within SAS Studio that run CAS actions become available to the user.

There are three main ways in which a user or programmer can interact with the core component of SAS Viya, which is the CAS:

- Through a GUI as part of the SAS Viya-based solution
- Through a programming interface, such as SAS Studio using SAS procedures
- Through direct invocations of CAS actions (through PROC CAS from a SAS or through one of the supported APIs for REST, Python, Java, Lua, or R)

From a user or developer's standpoint about the amount of control/flexibility or access to options that impact CAS actions running within CAS, the most constraints are through the solution GUIs. This is because they are designed to be the easiest to use, followed by SAS procedures to make it easier to use existing SAS programming skills to take advantage of CAS. These SAS procedures have been redesigned to call CAS actions behind the scenes, followed by the most flexible way to integrate with CAS, which is through CAS actions.

For more details on programming with SAS Viya and CAS, see the following SAS documentation *SAS® 9.4 and SAS Viya 3.2 Programming Documentation / Introduction to SAS Viya Programming* (`http://documentation.sas.com/?cdcId=pgmsascdccdcVersion=9.4_3.2docsetId=indbugdocsetTarget=titlepage.htmllocale=en`).

# SAS Viya-based solutions

Here is a quick list of the some of the solutions that have been made available recently on the SAS Viya architecture:

- **Versions 8.x of SAS VA**: Prior versions of SAS VA ran on LASR versus CAS
- **Versions 8.x of SAS VS**: Prior versions of SAS VS ran on LASR versus CAS
- **SAS® Visual Data Mining and Machine Learning**
- **SAS® Visual Forecasting**
- **SAS® Visual Investigator**

- **SAS® Econometrics**
- **SAS® Optimization**

 For more information on any of these SAS Viya products, please refer to the following web page `https://www.sas.com/en_th/software/viya.html`.

# Summary

You now have a deeper overview of the SAS platform and learned that SAS programming skills can easily be applied to doing big data analytics, because the coding stays relatively the same when using SAS on any size of data. However, when working on big data, it's the SAS environment that must be set up and configured properly in order for the processing to return results in a timely manner.

You saw how SAS enables processing on a server, on a SAS grid, in a database, and in memory as a way to reduce data movement or duplication, as well as enable the capability to do analytics on big data.

In addition, you learned how the SAS platform is open and how SAS integrates and works with open source technologies. You gained some hands-on experience using SAS with the open-source-based iPython Jupyter Notebook.

You learned about the different cloud environments and deployments in which SAS technologies are designed to integrate with open source in order to provide an enterprise analytics platform. You were introduced to the technologies that allow SAS processing, business rules, and analytics, to run not only outside the SAS platform but also outside data storage systems. Even to run on the edge and beyond in order to support the needs of customers, as both companies and people figure out the best way to interact with the IoT.

You were given more details about the microservices-based architecture of the SAS platform, SAS Viya, and the current list of SAS Viya products that have been made available at the time of publishing this book.

In the next and final chapter of this book, you will learn why SAS programmers love SAS. In addition, you will be introduced to some of the benefits associated with building an **Analytics Center of Excellence (ACE)**. There will be an overview of the different roles for the members of a successful ACE team, as well as the skills associated with each role.

# 8

# Why SAS Programmers Love SAS

I hope the reader is well on their way to considering themselves a SAS programmer, and as such already understands why SAS programmers love SAS. In this final chapter, the reader will learn:

- Reasons why SAS programmers love SAS
- Benefits from the development of an **Analytics Center of Excellence (ACE)**
- The roles for those who make up an ACE and the skills associated with each role
- How SAS participates in and promotes Data4Good

## Why SAS programmers love SAS

SAS programmers love SAS for many reasons, which sometimes are hard to quantify. For example, a colleague of mine, Lisa Dodson, explains one reason this way. "Many SAS users will talk about how much they like SAS because it makes it easy for them to work with any data. What does that really mean? Well, if you dive a bit deeper into this statement, it points to SAS' data access capabilities, which free the end user from having to know what data types from different data sources are". In other words SAS' access layer auto-magically takes care of translating data types to and from the SAS environment.

This is just one example of the power of SAS' data management capabilities that makes SAS programmers love SAS. The TRANSPOSE procedure, along with the FIRST. and LAST. dataset capabilities, which were covered in Chapter 3, *Data Preparation Using SAS Data Step and SAS Procedures,* are other examples of the data management capabilities built into SAS that make it easier for SAS programmers to do their jobs. Now, let's explore a couple of other examples.

# Examples of why SAS programmers love SAS

The following examples makes use of visuals in helping to explain reasons why SAS programmers love SAS, in particular when it comes to the amount of code one has to write to achieve a result using SAS versus the equivalent in another programming language to achieve the same result.

 In this first example, the other programming language is SQL.

A SAS programmer would write the following four lines of SAS code and most likely not even think about how much time SAS is saving them, because they are simply used to this being the way they work using SAS. Behind the scenes, the SAS platform is using a combination of its **SAS ACCESS** technologies, in this case connecting to data stored in a DB2 database, and some of its in-database processing technology built into the BASE SAS RANK procedure, which was discussed in Chapter 7, *SAS® Software Engineers the Processing Environment for You:*

```
proc rank data=indb2.db2_order_item out=work.order descending ties=low;
    var quantity product_id;
    ranks QuantityRank ProductRank;
run;
```

Here is just a part of the SQL code that gets automatically generated for the SAS user and passed down into the database for processing. Why did I only include a part of the SQL code? Because there is quite a lot more and seeing just this part of the equivalent SQL is enough to make the point and explain it to others:

```
WITH "subquery0" ( "COSTPRICE_PER_UNIT", "DISCOUNT", "ORDER_ID",
"ORDER_ITEM_NUM","PRODUCT_ID", "QUANTITY", "TOTAL_RETAIL_PRICE" ) AS (
SELECT "COSTPRICE_PER_UNIT", "DISCOUNT", "ORDER_ID", "ORDER_ITEM_NUM",
"PRODUCT_ID", "QUANTITY", "TOTAL_RETAIL_PRICE" FROM "DB2_ORDER_ITEM" )
SELECT "table0"."ORDER_ID", "table0"."ORDER_ITEM_NUM",
"table0"."PRODUCT_ID", "table0"."QUANTITY", "table0"."TOTAL_RETAIL_PRICE",
"table0"."COSTPRICE_PER_UNIT", "table0"."DISCOUNT", "table2"."rankalias1"
AS "QUANTITYRANK", "table1"."rankalias0" AS "PRODUCTRANK" FROM "subquery0"
AS "table0" LEFT JOIN ( SELECT DISTINCT "PRODUCT_ID", "tempcol0" AS
"rankalias0" FROM ( SELECT "PRODUCT_ID", MIN( "tempcol1" ) OVER (PARTITION
BY "PRODUCT_ID" ) AS "tempcol0" FROM ( SELECT "PRODUCT_ID", CAST(
ROW_NUMBER() OVER (ORDER BY "PRODUCT_ID" DESC ) AS DOUBLE PRECISION ) AS
"tempcol1" FROM "subquery0" WHERE ( ("PRODUCT_ID" IS NOT NULL ) ) ) AS
"subquery2" ) AS "subquery1" ) AS "table1" ON ( ("table0"."PRODUCT_ID" =
"table1"."PRODUCT_ID" ) ) LEFT JOIN ( SELECT DISTINCT "QUANTITY",
"tempcol2" AS "rankalias1" FROM ( SELECT "QUANTITY", MIN( "tempcol3" ) OVER
( PARTITION BY "QUANTITY" ) AS "tempcol2" FROM ( SELECT "QUANTITY", CAST(
ROW_NUMBER() OVER ( ORDER BY "QUANTITY" DESC ) AS DOUBLE PRECISION ) AS
"tempcol3" FROM "subquery0" WHERE ( ( "QUANTITY" IS NOT NULL ) ) ) AS
"subquery4" ) AS "subquery3" ) AS "table2" ON ( ( "table0"."QUANTITY" =
"table2"."QUANTITY" ) )
```

I would also like to ask you this question: which piece of code would you like to maintain, especially if something changes? Because, as we all know, something always does change.

Similarly, a colleague of mine, Adam Pilz, uses the following two visuals when he talks about the power of SAS versus the amount of code and time that would be needed to achieve the same data and text mining results. The following is a process flow diagram which Adam built using the drag-and-drop interface of SAS Enterprise Miner.

Next to the diagram are the 5000 lines of code that were autogenerated based on the work done in the diagram:

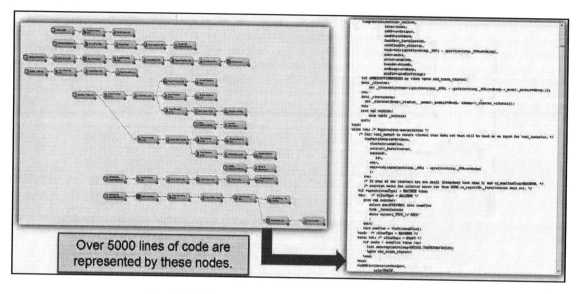

Figure 8.1: One SAS enterprise flow that generates 5000 lines of production-ready code

It took Adam about two hours to build out this complex data mining flow which contains 55 nodes and performs all the necessary steps of the analytics life cycle, from data import to running multiple predictive models such as regressions and decision trees, along with performing text mining, and results in the autogeneration of the necessary 5000 lines of code which are ready to be put into operation.

 All the green checks on the nodes in the diagram mean the code ran successfully without any errors. The code in the right-hand box in *Figure 8.1* is only a very small part of the 5000 lines of code which were generated for the user based on the work done in the drag-and drop interface seen on the left side of *Figure 8.1*.

As Adam typically asks when presenting this information, *who could write 5000 lines of complex data and text mining code in two hours in any language, let alone be assured it was tested and validated, and then prepare the necessary score code to put into production?*

Adam also happens to be a Python programmer as well and uses Python when it makes sense, along with SAS, to solve problems, especially in cases where using both enables the issue to be solved in the most efficient way possible, or where the problem would not be able to solved using just one or the other in isolation. For example, here is a situation where the two lines of code in the **Edit Rules** tab are shown in the middle window in *Figure 8.2*, an example of a complex language-based rule that is autogenerated by a SAS interface. This particular complex language-based text parsing rule, which SAS autogenerated for the user, would be extremely difficult or next to impossible to achieve in any other language, especially in just two lines of code:

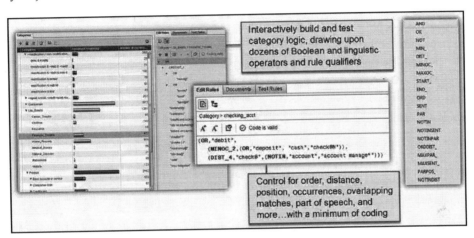

Figure 8.2: Example of a complex language-based rule that is autogenerated by a SAS interface

# Additional coding examples

The reader has only just begun the scratch the surface of The Power to Know® and the depth and breadth of SAS programming capabilities. Here are several other useful SAS procedures and examples to continue your introduction to SAS programming.

## The COMPARE procedure

The COMPARE procedure is a BASE SAS procedure which is quite useful in helping to identify potential data quality issues in similar data sources, or when a user wants to see the changes they have made to a source table prior to replacing the source table with a new or updated version. Bring up a new SAS Studio program and type the following code:

```
proc compare base=sashelp.class compare=sashelp.classfit printall;
run;
```

The `printall` option with the COMPARE procedure will produce a complete report of the differences in the two datasets.

Submit the code by selecting the running man icon. Notice that the even though no errors were generated and the **RESULTS** section pops up, the yellow triangle icon is in the tab for the program section. This means warnings were generated, so change to the **LOG** section:

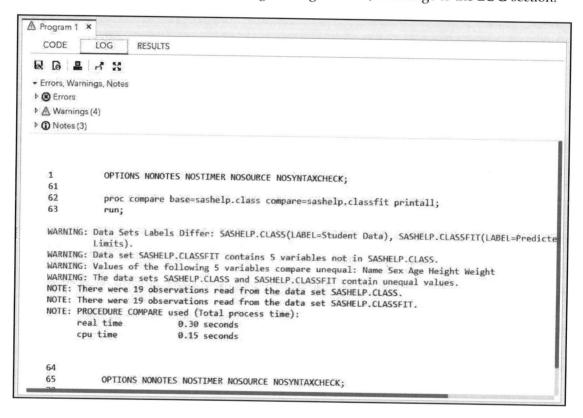

Figure 8.3: Warning generated in LOG by PROC COMPARE

This warning provides some insight into the differences between the two tables being compared. Now change back to the **RESULTS** section. The following screenshot shows the first part of the report generated by the COMPARE procedure:

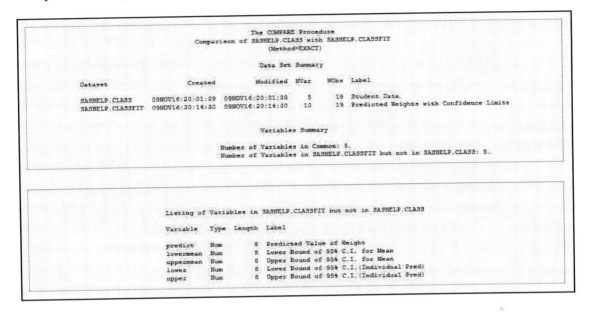

Figure 8.4: Top part of difference report generated by PROC Compare

Scroll down to the next two tables of output to see more information:

```
                        Observation Summary

                   Observation     Base  Compare

                   First Obs          1        1
                   First Unequal      1        1
                   Last  Unequal     19       19
                   Last  Obs         19       19

Number of Observations in Common: 19.
Total Number of Observations Read from SASHELP.CLASS: 19.
Total Number of Observations Read from SASHELP.CLASSFIT: 19.

Number of Observations with Some Compared Variables Unequal: 14.
Number of Observations with All Compared Variables Equal: 5.

                    Values Comparison Summary

Number of Variables Compared with All Observations Equal: 0.
Number of Variables Compared with Some Observations Unequal: 5.
Total Number of Values which Compare Unequal: 59.
Maximum Difference: 62.
```

```
                     The COMPARE Procedure
        Comparison of SASHELP.CLASS with SASHELP.CLASSFIT
                        (Method=EXACT)

        All Variables Compared have Unequal Values

        Variable  Type  Len  Ndif   MaxDif

        Name      CHAR    8    14
        Sex       CHAR    1     6
        Age       NUM     8    11    3.000
        Height    NUM     8    14   17.700
        Weight    NUM     8    14   62.000
```

Figure 8.5: Second set of tables in difference report generated by PROC compare

Scroll down to the next set of tables to see more detailed information about the differences in the variables that matched from the first table and the second table. The procedure will show the differences, based on observation one from table one compared to observation one in table two. This first table shows a list of the differences by observation number in the value stored in the character variables Name and Sex:

Value Comparison Results for Variables

| Obs | | Base Value Name | Compare Value Name | | Base Value Sex | Compare Value Sex |
|-----|--|------------|---------------|--|------|------|
| 1 | \|\| | Alfred | Joyce | \|\| | M | F |
| 2 | \|\| | Alice | Louise | \|\| | F | F |
| 3 | \|\| | Barbara | Alice | \|\| | F | F |
| 4 | \|\| | Carol | James | \|\| | F | M |
| 5 | \|\| | Henry | Thomas | \|\| | M | M |
| 6 | \|\| | James | John | \|\| | M | M |
| 7 | \|\| | Jane | Jane | \|\| | F | F |
| 8 | \|\| | Janet | Janet | \|\| | F | M |
| 9 | \|\| | Jeffrey | Jeffrey | \|\| | M | F |
| 10 | \|\| | John | Carol | \|\| | M | M |
| 11 | \|\| | Joyce | Henry | \|\| | F | M |
| 12 | \|\| | Judy | Judy | \|\| | F | F |
| 13 | \|\| | Louise | Robert | \|\| | F | M |
| 14 | \|\| | Mary | Barbara | \|\| | F | F |
| 15 | \|\| | Philip | Mary | \|\| | M | F |
| 16 | \|\| | Robert | William | \|\| | M | M |
| 17 | \|\| | Ronald | Ronald | \|\| | M | M |
| 18 | \|\| | Thomas | Alfred | \|\| | M | M |
| 19 | \|\| | William | Philip | \|\| | M | M |

Figure 8.6: Detailed differences of observations in base table versus compare table, showing character variables generated by PROC compare

Scroll down to see a similar difference in numeric variables, but as you can see, for numeric variables the actual values are shown along with the difference in the two, as well as the percentage difference in the two values:

```
                              The COMPARE Procedure
                     Comparison of SASHELP.CLASS with SASHELP.CLASSFIT
                                    (Method=EXACT)

                          Value Comparison Results for Variables


          ||   Base   Compare                  ||   Base    Compare
     Obs  ||   Age      Age     Diff.   % Diff  ||  Height   Height   Diff.    % Diff
     ---  ||  ------  -------  -------  -------  ||  ------   ------  -------  -------
          ||
      1   ||  14.0000  11.0000  -3.0000  -21.4286 ||  69.0000  51.3000 -17.7000  -25.6522
      2   ||  13.0000  12.0000  -1.0000   -7.6923 ||  56.5000  56.3000  -0.2000   -0.3540
      3   ||  13.0000  13.0000        0        0  ||  65.3000  56.5000  -8.8000  -13.4763
      4   ||  14.0000  12.0000  -2.0000  -14.2857 ||  62.8000  57.3000  -5.5000   -8.7580
      5   ||  14.0000  11.0000  -3.0000  -21.4286 ||  63.5000  57.5000  -6.0000   -9.4488
      6   ||  12.0000  12.0000        0        0  ||  57.3000  59.0000   1.7000    2.9668
      7   ||  12.0000  12.0000        0        0  ||  59.8000  59.8000        0        0
      8   ||  15.0000  15.0000        0        0  ||  62.5000  62.5000        0        0
      9   ||  13.0000  13.0000        0        0  ||  62.5000  62.5000        0        0
     10   ||  12.0000  14.0000   2.0000   16.6667 ||  59.0000  62.8000   3.8000    6.4407
     11   ||  11.0000  14.0000   3.0000   27.2727 ||  51.3000  63.5000  12.2000   23.7817
     12   ||  14.0000  14.0000        0        0  ||  64.3000  64.3000        0        0
     13   ||  12.0000  12.0000        0        0  ||  56.3000  64.8000   8.5000   15.0977
     14   ||  15.0000  13.0000  -2.0000  -13.3333 ||  66.5000  65.3000  -1.2000   -1.8045
     15   ||  16.0000  15.0000  -1.0000   -6.2500 ||  72.0000  66.5000  -5.5000   -7.6389
     16   ||  12.0000  15.0000   3.0000   25.0000 ||  64.8000  66.5000   1.7000    2.6235
     17   ||  15.0000  15.0000        0        0  ||  67.0000  67.0000        0        0
     18   ||  11.0000  14.0000   3.0000   27.2727 ||  57.5000  69.0000  11.5000   20.0000
     19   ||  15.0000  16.0000   1.0000    6.6667 ||  66.5000  72.0000   5.5000    8.2707
          ||
          ||
     N    ||      19       19       19       19  ||      19       19       19       19
     Mean ||  13.3158  13.3158        0   0.9716 ||  62.3368  62.3368        0   0.6341
     Std  ||   1.4927   1.4927   1.8257  14.5580 ||   5.1271   5.1271   7.0416  11.4959
     Max  ||  16.0000  16.0000   3.0000  27.2727 ||  72.0000  72.0000  12.2000  23.7817
     Min  ||  11.0000  11.0000  -3.0000 -21.4286 ||  51.3000  51.3000 -17.7000 -25.6522
     StdErr||   0.3424   0.3424   0.4189   3.3401 ||   1.1762   1.1762   1.6155   2.6373
     t    ||  38.8847  38.8847   0.0000   0.2909 ||  52.9971  52.9971   0.0000   0.2404
     Prob>|t| ||  <.0001   <.0001   1.0000   0.7745 ||  <.0001   <.0001   1.0000   0.8127
          ||
     Ndif ||      11  57.895%                     ||      14  73.684%
     DifMeans ||  0.000%   0.000%        0        ||  0.000%   0.000%        0
     r, rsq ||   0.252    0.063                   ||   0.057    0.003
```

Figure 8.7: Detailed differences of observations in base table versus compare table, showing numeric variables generated by PROC compare

Imagine the amount of code a programmer would need to write in other languages to not only make these comparisons between data tables, but also to generate these reports in easy to understand formats.

## The OPTIONS procedure

The `OPTIONS` procedure is very helpful in determining what SAS system options are in place for your particular SAS environment. Type the following code in a new SAS Studio program section:

```
proc options; run;
```

Submit the code by selecting the running man icon, and when the **LOG** section pops up, scroll the **LOG** output to the top using the scroll bar on the right-hand side of the **LOG** section:

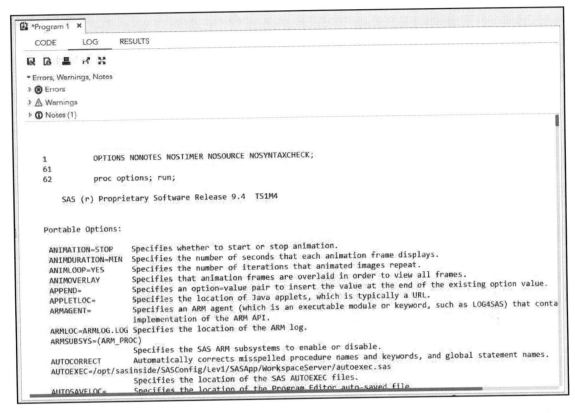

Figure 8.8: Partial output from PROC OPTIONS

This listing of system options and their values can be very useful; for example, the location of the SAS environment's `autoexec` file is important since any SAS code added to this file will be executed whenever the environment is started. As can be seen in this partial output, the `autoexec.sas` file for the SAS® University Edition is located at `/opt/sasinside/SASConfig/Lev1/SASApp/WorkspaceServer/autoexec.sas`.

As one can see from the number of portable system options, along with the list of host-specific options, SAS provides programmers and the SAS administrator of the environment a lot of flexibility in how the environment is meant to operate within the host operating system that SAS is installed in.

Other options of interest are `CPUCOUNT`, which gives you the number of processors that thread-enabled applications can expect to be available for concurrent processing, and under host options, `MEMSIZE`, which specifies the limit of virtual memory that can be used by a SAS session. In some cases, when processing complex analytics and/or large amounts of data, `MEMSIZE` is something that may need to be adjusted in order to reduce the overall time for specific jobs to run.

# Analytics is a great career

This book's primary focus has been to provide the reader with an introduction to becoming a SAS programmer who will be able to do big data analytics with SAS. However, it is just as important for the reader to understand that to be truly successful at performing big data analytics, it will take more than one individual to achieve big results. It can start with just one programmer, but it will require a team of people with different skill sets that complement each other to change an organization's culture to use analytics. It will benefit you, your team, and your organization to take up this challenge because some of the benefits that can be achieved by implementing analytics help organizations to do the following:

- Derive a competitive advantage
- Solve problems that have never successfully been solved previously
- Help derive new questions that drive innovation throughout an organization

As such, it is important to understand how one can champion analytics and help advocate for the creation of a group and processes within an organization whose focus is in providing analytic value within a group, department, and eventually the entire enterprise. This group is oftentimes called an ACE.

# Analytics Center of Excellence

There are several books and whitepapers on the topic of centers of excellence, and a few of those have been written to specifically describe ACE. Several of Tom Davenport's books address this issue, as well as *Business Transformation: A Roadmap for Maximizing Organizational Insights* written by a SAS colleague of mine, Aiman Zeid. Over the course of my career, I have not only personally helped many SAS customers develop plans on how to develop an ACE for their own organizations, but have also served in different roles within ACEs within my own company.

As a result, I will describe some of the people that should be involved in not only making the ACE, but in supporting and nurturing it to ensure it thrives and provides its members with satisfying careers and their organizations with the great benefits that come from becoming an analytical data-driven organization.

Quick question—what is the definition of the best analytic model? If someone answers this question from a technical/statistical perspective and references the best p-value or R-squared value, they are thinking too much about the math instead of about the business value. This is an indication that while this person may be valuable within an ACE, they are most likely not the best choice to fill the leader role. The best answer to this question is the model that is actually used in production because this is the one that improves the overall results achieved by the organization.

## The executive sponsor

In order to have a truly successful ACE that serves the entire organization, an executive sponsor who believes in the power of analytics to drive better decision making must be identified, as without executive support, it becomes difficult to fund the staffing and make the proper investments that will be needed to get analytics off the ground. Because analytics tend to challenge existing processes or the standard way business has already been done, this executive needs to be a visionary who can convince their peers of the value analytics will provide their respective groups, as well as the overall value they will bring to the company.

Analytics can provide value to an individual or a group, but without an executive to champion the work done by this type of group, the work will typically continue to operate in isolation instead of growing to impact the larger organization as a whole.

## The data scientist

It should come as no surprise that one of the key members of an ACE would be someone with the title data scientist. As a matter of fact, their tends to be the need to have more than one data scientist; these creative types tend to work better in groups, since they like to share ideas with each other, which tends to lead to more creative solutions to the complex problems that can be addressed by the ACE. While many people may want the title of data scientist, this role is best filled by someone who is skilled in one or more of the three branches of statistics that fall under the umbrella term of advanced analytics. These three areas tend to be defined as data mining, forecasting, and optimization. While it is possible to find individuals who are proficient in all three areas, it is more usual to find someone really good in one or two of the three.

It is also most common to find individuals who have mastered one area and will therefore try to approach solving problems by making use of their particular domain, instead of approaching the problem with the analytics or combination of analytics that might be a better solution. This is why I would recommend having several data scientists on the team with domain knowledge in one or two analytic areas, so that they can learn and challenge one another, and develop answers to problems as a group that they may not have been able to develop as individuals working in isolation.

While it is common to recruit data scientists based on them having some type of statistical degree, I would argue not to limit your search to such a narrow area. Broaden your search to include mathematical degrees, engineering degrees, computer science degrees, as well as social sciences, which tend to focus on human behavior. The best data scientists are not necessarily those with the most advanced degrees within their fields, but those people who tend to be lifelong learners and curious about solving problems.

# The data manager

This role is just as important as the data scientist because, as anyone who works with data can attest, 80% of the work is related to collecting the data and making sure it's in the right format and environment that allows for the efficient processing of it to take place. This role is also key in taking the analytic insights derived by the data scientists and helping to deploy them into production systems to ensure the value of these insights actually improve the business. This role may sometimes go by other terms, such as an analytical database administrator or maybe a data steward. Not only is the person skilled in data management and data preparation, but also in system administration as well, because they are responsible for making sure the analytical environment of the platform is running smoothly and interacts with the other enterprise systems.

This role is someone who doesn't need to know how to do the analytics, but understands the value of making sure the data gets prepared efficiently for the others within the ACE to work with it. This member is usually recruited from computer science or computer engineering degree programs, and understands setting up enterprise systems and data storage systems in ways to ensure efficient processing of analytical workloads. Typically, there are two of these members to ensure at least one is always available to make sure the analytics platform is up and running for the rest of the group.

# The business analyst

Similar to the data scientist role, there will be multiple business analysts working within an ACE either full-time or potentially located in other departments loosely associated with the ACE. These business analysts are the ones who make use of the analytics developed in collaboration with the ACE team members to better serve their respective business groups with more informative, proactive, data-driven business processes and reports. The business analyst role can sometimes morph into a citizen data scientist type of role depending on the attitude and skills of the analyst. A citizen data scientist is someone who learns to develop their own analytic skills, but not to the depth or breadth of someone who is on the data science team. Once again, depending on the individual citizen data scientist, they may be able to grow into a data scientist role over time, thereby providing another potential career path for these particular employees. This role tends to be highly skilled in doing ad hoc reports and in building out production level dashboards and reports for their respective organizations.

Business analysts can be recruited from a wide range of different backgrounds.

# The ACE leader

This group will also need a good leader, not just a manager. While the ACE lead will need good management skills, it is more important to have very good or great leadership skills. While this leader may be able to delegate management of the group to other members, it will be their responsibility to make sure they lead the group to success. This person will serve as the main communications champion for the ACE to the rest of the organization, as well as being the member of the ACE team to work most closely with the executive sponsor. This person will need to be able to talk about the business value of analytics, not the math, and continuously advocate and sell the value provided by analytics across the organization. This person will need to be able to talk with confidence to executives about the business value of analytics without being too technical, with data scientists about analytics, and with the data manager and others more on the IT side of the organization about hardware.

# Where should an ACE be located?

Where should your ACE sit within your organization? Some will argue that an ACE should be formed within IT, while others will champion it to be part of the business. Either form will work, but the core team should be brought together and given a mission or charter to support issues within all the business units or departments that the ACE is tasked with supporting.

For more information about how to develop and staff an ACE, the whitepaper *Getting the Right People on the Big Data Bus*, written by Tamara Dull and Anne Buff, is recommended.

# Analytics across industries

Analytics are used to improve all types of organizations and improve efficiency in many industries.

# Analytics improving healthcare

Analytics has driven improvements in healthcare by helping to reduce patient re-admittance after undergoing surgery. Another incredible example of analytics helping to improve health outcomes is the optimization done by SAS working in collaboration with the Duke **Neonatal Intensive Care Unit (NICU)**. This study showed the cost per patient and cost per week at the best NICUs were lower and the average lengths of stays were longer.

# Analytics improving government services

Other examples of analytics helping society can be seen across many areas of local, state, and federal governments across the world. Analytics are used to improve child welfare systems and in the United States uncover fraud in medicare and medicaid claims. Analytics help governments around the world improve on tax compliance, improve safety by working with law enforcement agencies, and improve everyday living, working with smart city initiatives. For more details on how SAS and analytics can help society and people, read the SAS whitepaper *Doing good with government data*:

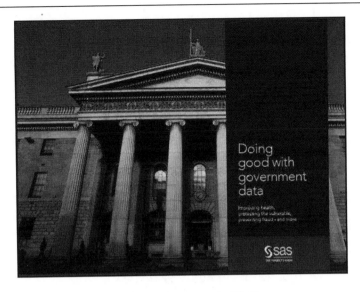

Figure 8.9: Doing good with government data SAS whitepaper

At the time of writing, the paper was available at this web page: ;https://www.sas.com/content/dam/SAS/en_us/doc/whitepaper1/doing-good-with-government-data-109009.pdf

# Analytics in financial services

It should not come as a surprise to anyone to find out that analytics has been leveraged successfully and continues to be used heavily in the financial services industries. These are some of the industries that push analytics and big data analytics to their limits because they have already seen the value they provide in reducing risk and increasing revenue, whether this is in figuring out whether a person or client is an acceptable risk for a loan, or what insurance policies should be priced at in order to make them a profitable product. Financial services is one of the leading industries when it comes to investing in technology, and big data analytics is just one example in which financial service companies have been leading the way for other industries.

# Analytics in energy

While both the oil and gas and utilities industries have been using analytics to one degree or another for years, both of these industries are currently in a huge shift in how they are using analytics to improve their overall operations and services to their customers.

In the past, analytics may have been used in a couple of departments, but they were not necessarily discussed in the annual reports. With the combination of big data, advancements in technology, and the large number of experienced employees either retiring or near retirement, these industries are seeking to take advantage of big data analytics to help them to operate successfully in the age of the digital oil field and the smart grid.

# Analytics in manufacturing

Manufacturing is yet another industry that is transforming itself in the age of the **Internet of Things (IoT)** and actually has been working at using data and analytics to improve their results for some years. They coined their own term, known as the **Industrial Internet of Things (IIoT)**. Whether you are talking about hi-tech manufacturers or auto manufacturers, the rise of sensors and equipment that provides data on every aspect of the manufacturing process, or how a car is operating, manufacturers are on the front lines of how big data analytics will integrate with everyone's normal life activities.

# Analytics are great for society

Analytics can also be used in industries whose goals are in line with doing good not only for the organization itself, but for those individuals that interact with the industry and ultimately for the betterment of society at large. There are many examples of the use of analytics to achieve goals that are in line with the betterment of society overall. Did you know that statistics and mathematics were used to help the Allies turn the tide and win World War II? Alan Turing was able to use mathematics to code-break the German Enigma machine being used by German U-boats, and the top secret, at the time, **Statistical Research Group (SRG)** used statistics to, among other notable achievements, advise the U.S. Air Force which areas of planes to reinforce with armor to improve the odds of the planes returning from missions instead of being shot down.

# Project Data Sphere®

As described on their website at (`https://www.projectdatasphere.org/projectdatasphere/html/about`), Project Data Sphere®, **LLC**, an independent, not-for-profit initiative of the CEO Roundtable on Cancer's **Life Sciences Consortium (LSC)**, operates the Project Data Sphere® platform, a free digital library-laboratory that provides one place where the research community can broadly share, integrate, and analyze historical patient-level data from academic and industry phase III cancer clinical trials.

The Project Data Sphere® platform is available to researchers affiliated with life science companies, hospitals, and institutions, as well as independent researchers. Anyone interested in cancer research can apply to become an authorized user.

The technology platform; was built by SAS, who will continue to host the online service, provide analytics software, and give technical domain expertise for this initiative. For more information on Project Data Sphere®, visit their website at `http://www.` `projectdatasphere.org`.

# SAS and Data4Good

Companies and programmers today are still working together on very meaningful endeavors that have incredible impact on all of our daily lives, whether it's applying analytics as part of their businesses, organizations, or jobs, or using analytics for non-profit and totally altruistic endeavors such as Data4Good:

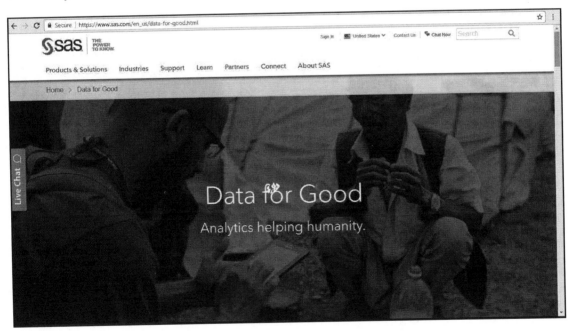

Figure 8.10: SAS and Data4Good

# GatherIQ™ – get involved in crowdsourcing to solve social issues

Join the crowd and make a difference in the world. This app brings together the power of SAS® software and people from around the world to work toward solving some of the world's most pressing social problems.

Figure 8.11: GatherIQ™ at gatheriq.analytics

# References

There are many websites, blogs, and groups where you can learn more about SAS, ask questions, and receive help from other users. This is a list of several links that I personally use and find very helpful:

- `http://support.sas.com`: Official SAS documentation, SAS communities, SAS Technical Support, free SAS Training, SAS Certification, and SAS books. Two of the subsections I find quite useful are `http://support.sas.com/rnd/index.html` and `http://support.sas.com/training/tutorial/index.html`.
- `http://blogs.sas.com`: The official directory of blogs written by SAS employees.

- `http://www.lexjansen.com`: Type in any key word(s) and this site searches over 29,000 user-written papers from SAS user conferences from all over the world. This site is great at helping you find specific examples of how other SAS users conquered similar or the same type of problem you are looking to solve.
- `http://robslink.com/SAS/Home.htm`: Provides hundreds of examples of producing all sorts of graphs to display information, and typically provides you with the code and the data used to produce the end result.
- `https://github.com/sassoftware`: Open source code from the SAS software. Two of the best contributions IMO are `Jupyter kernel for SAS` and `SAS Scripting Wrapper for Analytics Transfer (SWAT)`.
- `https://www.youtube.com/user/SASsoftware`: All sorts of videos about SAS, SAS events, teaching the basics of SAS programming and analytics, highlighting SAS customer stories, and more...
- The SAS-L listserv is still going strong after all these years: `http://listserv.uga.edu/archives/sas-l.html`. What's nice about this source is that several decades of archives are searchable.

# Summary

The reader learned some reasons SAS programmers love SAS and was given visual examples to make it easier to explain these reasons to others. Then the reader was given a few additional coding examples to highlight more SAS programming capabilities.

The reader was introduced to several benefits that organizations achieve when they develop an ACE. Then, the reader was given an overview of the roles that make up successful ACEs, along with the skill sets associated with each role.

The reader was given examples of how analytics are used across a variety of industries and are used to help improve society at large. The reader learned about how SAS as a company promotes and participates in Data4Good, and finally, the reader was shown how they themselves can get involved and assist in helping solve difficult social issues by joining in and making use of the GatherIQ™ mobile application.

# Index